BEST of the BEST
from
ALABAMA

Selected Recipes from Alabama's
FAVORITE COOKBOOKS

BEST
of the BEST
from
ALABAMA

Selected Recipes from Alabama's
FAVORITE COOKBOOKS

EDITED BY
Gwen McKee
AND
Barbara Moseley

Illustrated by Tupper England

QUAIL RIDGE PRESS

THE ALABAMA HERITAGE COOKBOOK© 1984 Heritage Publications; AUBURN ENTERTAINS© 1983, 1986 Auburn Entertains; BIRDIES IN THE OVEN/ACES IN THE KITCHEN© 1986 Patricia Y. Leverett; BRAVO! APPLAUDABLE RECIPES© 1977 Mobile Opera Guild; CALLING ALL COOKS© 1982 Telephone Pioneers of America Alabama Chapter No. 34; COOKBOOK© 1981 The Women of the Church, First Presbyterian Church; COOKS AND COMPANY© 1988 Muscle Shoals District Service League; COTTON COUNTRY COOKING© 1972 The Decatur Junior Service League, Inc.; DELECTABLE DISHES FROM TERMITE HALL© 1982 Eugene Walter; DINING UNDER THE MAGNOLIA© 1984 Scott Wilson; DOWN HOME IN HIGH STYLE© 1985 Down Home in High Style, Inc.; EUFAULA'S FAVORITE RECIPES© 1985 The Eufaula Tribune; FAMILY SECRETS© 1985 The William Henry Thomas Family; GAZEBO I CHRISTMAS COOKBOOK© 1984 Rex Barrington; GAZEBO I COOKBOOK© 1982 Rex Barrington; THE GREAT COOKBOOK© 1986 Altrusa Club of Greater Gadsden, Inc.; HEIRLOOMS FROM THE KITCHEN© 1985 Joan Hutson; HUNTSVILLE ENTERTAINS© 1983 Historic Huntsville Foundation; HUNTSVILLE HERITAGE COOKBOOK© 1967 The Junior League of Huntsville Inc.; KITCHEN SAMPLER© 1985 The Bessemer Junior Service League; LOAVES AND FISHES FROM THE EASTERN SHORE© 1984 The Episcopal Churchwomen, St. Paul's Episcopal Church; MAGIC© 1982 The Junior League of Birmingham; OLD MOBILE RECIPES© 1956 St. Paul's Episcopal Church; ONCE UPON A STOVE© 1986 Birmingham Children's Theatre; ONE OF A KIND© 1981 Junior League of Mobile, Inc.; RECIPE JUBILEE!© 1964 The Junior League of Mobile, Inc.; SECONDS PLEASE©1978 Nan Dessert, Sara Engelhardt and Betsy Plummer; A SOUTHERN LADY COOKS WITH A GREEK ACCENT© 1980 Sophia Clikas; TREASURED ALABAMA RECIPES© 1967 Kathryn Tucker Windham; TREASURED TASTES© 1986 Mobile College; TREATS FOR MY SWEETS© 1981 Gail C. Jaye; TRY ME© 1984 Arthritis Volunteer Action Committee; TWICKENHAM TABLES© 1988 The Twickenham Historic Preservation District Association, Inc.; WHEN DINNERBELLS RING© 1978 Talladega Junior Welfare League; WHEN YOU CAN'T COOK....OR DON'T WANT TO© 1987 Rex Barrington.

ISBN 0-937552-28-3
First printing, October 1989 • Second, May 1993 • Third, January 1996
Fourth, May 1998 • Fifth, January 2000 • Sixth, March 2001
Seventh, June 2003 • Eighth, November 2004

Library of Congress Catalog Card Number: 89-60781

Cover photo: Bellingrath Gardens and Home, courtesy of Mobile Convention and Visitors Corporation.
Chapter opening photos courtesy of Alabama Bureau of Tourism & Travel.

Manufactured in the United States of America.

QUAIL RIDGE PRESS
P. O. Box 123 • Brandon, MS 39043 • 1-800-343-1583
info@quailridge.com • www.quailridge.com

CONTENTS

Visiting golfers on the Choccolocco Golf Course experience a treat when they encounter the old Choccolocco Schoolhouse between fairways.

PREFACE

Alabama has long been known as the Heart of Dixie, but lately is being called the State of Surprises. And indeed it is! From the mountain lakes of north Alabama to the lovely gulf shore beaches, from the touch-of-the-past Shakespeare Festival to Huntsville's Space and Rocket Center, and from the time-proven Corn Spoon Bread to new and delicious Sliced Strawberries in Lingonberry Caramel Cream, there are surprises from border to border. The land, the people, the events, and the history behind it all, make Alabama a unique place where it is fun to discover it's many surprises.

The forty-five contributing cookbooks in this volume have lent us not only their favorite recipes, but their enthusiasm and excitement as well. We are indeed grateful to the authors, editors, and publishers for their cooperation in making this book possible. Each contributing cookbook has its own special features—recipes, pictures, artwork, anecdotes, history, cooking hints, etc.—and we have attempted to retain their flavors by reproducing the recipes as they appear in each book, changing only typeset style for uniformity. The complete catalog showing and describing each book, along with ordering information begins on page 269. Cooks and collectors interested in more deeply exploring the tastes and styles of Alabama will want to delve into the individual books included in this collection. We do beg forgiveness for any books that might have been included that we inadvertently overlooked.

The tremendous amount of work that goes into compiling this book could not be done without help from so many. Our sincere thanks go to all the food editors from newspapers across the state who recommended cookbooks for inclusion, the book and gift store managers who thoughtfully lent their knowledge of popular books in their area, and the friendly folks who chatted with us about their favorite foods and recipes and cookbooks wherever we traveled—we met no strangers in Alabama. We are grateful in particular to Tommye Miller, Pat Scofield, and Eugene Walter for their help in research, and to Tupper England for her lovely and always appropriate artwork.

We are so pleased to present these Alabama recipes. It is our hope that we have captured some of the tasteful traditions, sumptuous style, and comfortable southern cooking that blend to comprise the cuisine of Alabama.

Gwen McKee and Barbara Moseley

CONTRIBUTING COOKBOOKS

Alabama Heritage Cookbook
Anniversary Collection of Delectable Dishes
Auburn Entertains
Birdies in the Oven/Aces in the Kitchen
Bravo! Applaudable Recipes
Calling All Cooks
Cookbook
Cooks and Company
Cotton Country Cooking
Delectable Dishes from Termite Hall
Dining Under the Magnolia
Dinner on the Ground
Down Home in High Style
Eufaula's Favorite Recipes
Family Secrets
Florence Cook Book
Gazebo I Christmas Cookbook
Gazebo I Cookbook
The Great Cookbook
Hallmark's Collection of Home Tested Recipes
Hearthside at Christmas
Heavenly Hostess
Heirlooms From the Kitchen

CONTRIBUTING COOKBOOKS

Huntsville Entertains
Huntsville Heritage Cookbook
Kitchen Sampler
Kum' Ona' Granny's Table
Loaves and Fishes
Magic
More Fiddling With Food
Old Mobile Recipes
Once Upon a Stove
One of a Kind
Recipe Jubilee!
A Samford Celebration Cookbook
Seconds Please!
A Southern Lady Cooks with a Greek Accent
Sumpthn' Yummy
Treasured Alabama Recipes
Treats For My Sweets
Treasured Tastes
Try Me
Twickenham Tables
When Dinnerbells Ring
When You Can't Cook

Appetizers

Desoto Falls plummets 110 feet into the bottom of Little River Canyon.
Desoto State Park. Near Fort Payne and Mentone.

Cranberry Spiced Tea

9 cups cranberry juice
9 cups pineapple juice, strained
4 1/2 cups water
1 cup brown sugar

4 sticks cinnamon
4 1/2 teaspoons cloves
1/4 teaspoon salt
1 lemon, sliced

Put juice and water in bottom of large party percolator. Place remaining ingredients in top of percolator and percolate as for coffee. Makes 25 punch cups.

Variation: After tea has percolated, add 4 cups Burgundy wine.

Cookbook

Spiced Hot Tea

6 cups water
6 tea bags (regular size)
1 quart water
3 cinnamon sticks
15 whole cloves
2 cups sugar

1 (3-ounce) package cherry
   gelatin
1 (12-ounce) can frozen orange
   juice - prepared
1 (46-ounce) can pineapple juice
1 (8-ounce) bottle of lemon juice

Boil 6 cups of water, pour over tea bags and steep. Place cinnamon sticks and cloves in 1 quart of water and simmer 20 minutes. Add remaining ingredients. Bring to boil and serve or store in refrigerator in covered jars. Keeps indefinitely.

Cherry gelatin gives this spiced tea a special color and an extra special flavor. For the weight watchers, 8 teaspoons of Sweeta can be substituted for the sugar.

Cotton Country Cooking

Party Punch

2 packages cherry Kool-Aid
1 (16-ounce) can frozen orange
   juice
1 large can pineapple juice

2 cups sugar
1 gallon water
1 (16-ounce) can frozen
   lemonade

Mix all ingredients well. Can be served over ice or may be frozen to a slush consistency. To freeze, put in plastic milk jugs and store in freezer. Shake occasionally until punch is a slush. Shake jugs well and pour in punch bowl to serve. Different flavors of Kool-Aid can be used to change flavor.

Calling All Cooks

Mocha Milkshake
Can be used as an elegant dessert.

1 (2-ounce) jar instant coffee
  granules
1/4 cup hot water
1 (16-ounce) can chocolate syrup

1 cup rum
1 tablespoon vanilla
Vanilla ice cream
Milk

In mixing bowl combine coffee granules and water. Stir until dissolved. Add chocolate syrup, rum, vanilla, and stir. Store mixture in covered container in refrigerator. It keeps for months.

To serve: Use 2 tablespoons of mocha base and 1 scoop ice cream for each serving. Put base and ice cream into blender and blend. Add milk to desired consistency. One blender container of mocha milkshakes makes 6 easy, delicious desserts. Serve in tall bubble wine glasses with a chocolate curl on top. Serves 22.

Magic

Christmas Eggnog

The old fashioned Cabaniss recipe for Christmas eggnog was used by S.D. Cabaniss to celebrate each year. It was served not only to the family, but to all the servants as well, and thus caused a delay in the serving of Christmas dinner.

12 eggs, separated
12 tablespoons whiskey
12 tablespoon sugar

1 1/2 quarts whipping cream
1 tablespoon vanilla

Beat egg yellows, add sugar and liquor gradually. Chill. Whip cream and add flavoring. Add to egg mixture gradually. If mixture is too thick, add milk or half-and-half.

Suggestion: For serving over prolonged period, float a half gallon of vanilla ice cream in the punch bowl.

Twickenham Tables

Cranberry Cup

1 quart cranberry juice   1 pint sliced frozen strawberries
1 cup Burgundy

Combine ingredients early in the day and allow to blend. Chill. Serve in champagne saucers or footed juice glasses with cocktail straws. This is a delicious and pretty prelude to a ladies' luncheon. Makes about 1 1/2 quarts.

Huntsville Heritage Cookbook

Orange Gable

2 ounces Amaretto   3 ounces light rum
2 ounces Coco Lopez   3 ounces pineapple juice
2 ounces orange juice

Mix all ingredients in blender with ice until frozen. Serve garnished with slivered almonds and an orange slice if desired.

Try Me

Southern Champagne Punch

2 fifths champagne	1 (28-ounce) bottle soda water
1 fifth Chablis	1 (12-ounce) can frozen lemonade
1 pint vodka	concentrate, undiluted

Chill all ingredients and mix. A moderately strong punch can be made by using 1/2 pint vodka. Can be served from pitcher garnished with fresh fruits or from a punch bowl with an ice ring. If using an ice ring, do not use lemonade in punch but dilute and make ring, adding fresh or canned fruit for decoration. Yield: 15 servings.

The Alabama Heritage Cookbook

White Dubonnet Cocktail

Pour 2 ounces white Dubonnet over ice in wine glass. Add splash of soda (Club soda or Perrier) and a twist of lemon.

Twickenham Tables

Tomato Ice
(For a first course)

1 large can tomato juice	1/2 cup lemon juice
Salt, basil, Worcestershire sauce,	2 egg whites
wine vinegar, horseradish,	
minced parsley to taste	

Mix all ingredients, except egg whites, and freeze in refrigerator tray until half frozen. Add 2 stiffly beaten egg whites. Continue freezing until serving time, stirring occasionally.

Old Mobile Recipes

 The first icemaking machine was invented in Mobile County.

Daffodil Dip for Vegetables

1/2 cup mayonnaise
1 (8-ounce) package cream cheese
1/2 cup parsley, chopped
1 hard-boiled egg

2 tablespoons chopped onion
1 clove garlic, minced
1 tablespoon anchovy paste
1/8 teaspoon pepper

Combine and beat mayonnaise and cream cheese. Add all remaining ingredients, except boiled egg yolk, and blend well. Mash egg yolk through strainer on top of dip. Refrigerate for several hours, but serve at room temperature so it won't be too stiff. Keeps several days in refrigerator.

Anniversary Collection of Delectable Dishes

Vegetable Dip

1 cup mayonnaise
1 cup sour cream
1 small can water chestnuts, drain and chop
1 medium onion, chopped

1 small package frozen chopped spinach
1 package Knorr Swiss vegetable mix

Mix all ingredients and refrigerate overnight.

Treasured Taste

Green Goddess Dip

1 can flat anchovies, well drained
2 green onions, including tops
1 clove garlic, chopped
1 cup parsley, chopped and packed down

1 cup mayonnaise
1 teaspoon wine vinegar

Mix anchovies, green onions, garlic and parsley in blender or food processor. When finely chopped, add mayonnaise and vinegar and process until smooth. Use as dip for raw vegetables.

Loaves and Fishes

Broccoli Dip

1/2 stick margarine	2 (10-ounce) packages frozen
1 tablespoon onion, chopped	broccoli cooked, chopped
2 cans cream of mushroom soup	and drained
2 (5-ounce) rolls garlic cheese,	1 (3-ounce) can mushrooms, sliced
diced	Rye croutons (optional)

Sauté onion in margarine. Add soup and blend well. Add cheese and stir until melted. Add broccoli and mushrooms and mix well. Pour into baking dish. Garnish with rye croutons and bake at 350° for 25-30 minutes. Serve hot with crackers. May be served as a casserole by using 1 can soup and 1 roll cheese.

When Dinnerbells Ring

Bohemian Rye Party Bowl

Buy a round loaf of Bohemian Rye bread (as round as possible). Cut off 2 inches from the top. Pull out insides of loaf until you have a bowl. Cut insides of loaf into bite-sized pieces. Let the "bowl" stay in the air, but put the pieces into a plastic bag.

DIP FOR BOWL:

1 1/3 cups sour cream	2 teaspoons dill weed
1 1/3 cups mayonnaise	2 teaspoons McCormick's
2 tablespoons parsley flakes	Season-All
2 tablespoons instant minced	1 (4-ounce) can chopped black
onion	olives, drained

Combine all the above ingredients, mixing well. Fill the bread "bowl" with the mixture. To serve, arrange the bite-sized pieces around the "bowl" to use for dippers.

Once Upon a Stove

Alice Jane's Curry Dip

1/2 cup mayonnaise
1 cup sour cream
2 tablespoons fresh lemon juice
Salt and pepper to taste
1 scant teaspoon curry powder
1/2 teaspoon paprika
2 tablespoons minced parsley

1/2 teaspoon crushed dried
  tarragon
2 tablespoons grated onion
2 teaspoons prepared mustard
1 tablespoon minced chives
Dash Tabasco (4 drops)

Mix all ingredients and refrigerate the day before you serve. Stir before serving.

Kitchen Sampler

Shrimp Dip

1 (41/2-ounce) can shrimp
1 (3-ounce) package cream
  cheese, softened
1/4 teaspoon grated onion
1/4 teaspoon Worcestershire sauce

1 teaspoon lemon juice
Dash Tabasco sauce
1/3 cup mayonnaise
1/3 cup milk, if needed

Mix all ingredients together; use milk if mixture is stiff. Serve with chips or crackers.

When Dinnerbells Ring

Belle Fontaine Crab Dip

2 (3-ounce) packages cream cheese
1 very small onion, grated fine
Few dashes Worcestershire sauce
1-2 dashes Louisiana hot sauce

Salt and pepper to taste
4 tablespoons mayonnaise
1 pound crabmeat

Mix all ingredients well. Serve as hors d'oeuvre or in stuffed tomato, or with crackers or vegetables as a dip.

Recipe Jubilee!

Herbed Bleu Cheese Dip

1 (8-ounce) package cream cheese, at room temperature
1 (2-ounce) package bleu cheese, at room temperature
1/4 cup sour cream
1 garlic clove, minced

1 scallion, minced
2 tablespoons parsley flakes
2 teaspoons Worcestershire sauce
1 teaspoon dried dill
1/8 teaspoon cayenne pepper

Combine cream cheese, bleu cheese, and sour cream well--this combines best in a food processor or electric mixer. Add remaining ingredients; chill at least one hour. Serve with fresh vegetables or crackers. Serves 8-10. This dip may be prepared a couple of days ahead and stored in the refrigerator. Let stand at room temperature for 30-45 minutes to soften before serving.

Birdies in the Oven/Aces in the Kitchen

Cheese Dip

1 (11-ounce) can Campbell's Cheddar cheese soup
1/2 can of milk (use soup can to measure)

1 pound box Velveeta cheese
1 (7 1/2-ounce) can Old El Paso jalapeño relish (hot or mild, I use hot)

Mix soup, Velveeta cheese and milk over low heat. Stir until well blended. Remove from heat and mix in the jalapeño relish. Keep covered in the refrigerator. Heat as needed. Serve with corn chips. Enough for a party.

Dinner on the Ground

Cucumber Spread
(Satziki)

1 cucumber, peeled and diced
1 (8-ounce) package cream cheese,
   room temperature
2 tablespoons wine vinegar

1 tablespoon salad or olive oil
2 healthy dashes salt
3 garlic cloves, mashed

Wrap cucumber in paper towels until all liquid is absorbed; set aside. Place the cream cheese, vinegar, oil, salt, and garlic into mixing bowl; cream well. Add more oil and vinegar as needed for taste and consistency. Using a spatula, blend in the cucumber. Refrigerate. Serve with crackers, melba toast or points of toasted bread. This keeps well refrigerated tightly in a jar.

A Southern Lady Cooks with a Greek Accent

Vegetable Spread

This is just like peanuts: you can't stop eating it. And with a food processor it's so easy to make.

1 tablespoon plain gelatin
1/4 cup cold water
1/4 cup boiling water
1 cup Hellman's mayonnaise
1/2 teaspoon salt
1 large tomato, chopped
1/2 cup finely chopped celery

1 small onion, chopped fine
1 large carrot, grated
1/2 cucumber, chopped and
   drained
1/2 bell pepper, chopped and
   drained

Dissolve gelatin in cold water; add hot water and cool. Mix with mayonnaise and salt. Add vegetables. Refrigerate overnight. Makes 4 cups. To double recipe, drain all vegetables on paper towels and still use only one envelope of gelatin, 1/4 cup cold water and 1/4 cup boiling water. Spread on rounds of bread for party sandwiches and garnish with a tiny sprig of parsley or serve as a mold with crackers or stuff in a juicy red summer tomato as a salad.

Cookbook

Crabmeat Spread

1 loaf white bread	1 cup finely chopped celery
1 cup finely chopped onion	3 cups mayonnaise
1 pound white crabmeat, fresh, pick-out shells	

Cut bread into small cubes, discarding crusts. Mix bread cubes with onion. Refrigerate overnight. Add other ingredients the next day--better if kept refrigerated six hours before serving. Spread on crackers, stuff in cocktail tomatoes, serve on lettuce, etc. This recipe really extends the crabmeat without changing the color, flavor or texture. It has gotten rave reviews from everyone. I have also used simulated King Crab meat with excellent results. Serves large group.

Try Me

Flaming Kefalotire Cheese
"Saganaki"

1 pound soft Kasserri or Kefalotire cheese	1/2 lemon
2 tablespoons butter or margarine	2 tablespoons brandy (Metaxa)

Heat your broiler, hot! Cut cheese into 3 wedges and arrange on a buttered pan. Pour melted butter over cheese. Place under broiler 4-6 inches; broil until cheese bubbles and turns light brown. Remove from broiler. Pour brandy over cheese; quickly ignite with match. Squeeze lemon juice over cheese as flame diminishes. Cut into smaller pieces and serve; if preferred, guests may cut their own servings.

A Southern Lady Cooks with a Greek Accent

Cheese Olivettes

1/2 pound grated American cheese
1 stick (1/4-pound) margarine
1 cup flour

10 drops Tabasco sauce
1/2 teaspoon garlic salt
Stuffed olives, well drained

Blend cheese and margarine. Add flour, Tabasco and garlic salt and mix until well combined. Flatten a small ball of dough in palm of hand and roll around olive. Continue until all dough is used. Bake at 375° for 15 minutes. Freeze before baking, if desired. Yield: 3 dozen.

Variation: Use an assortment of ripe olives, cocktail onions, whole almonds, or pecan halves instead of the stuffed olives in the center of the balls.

Bravo! Applaudable Recipes

Date Cheese Tidbits

1/2 pound New York State cheese
  (any sharp cheese will do)
1 stick butter
2 cups sifted flour

1/2 teaspoon salt
1/4 teaspoon red pepper
2 packages pitted dates
Pecan halves for each date

Grate cheese, let cheese and butter soften at room temperature. Put cheese in mixmaster bowl and beat. Add butter and continue beating. Add sifted flour, pepper and salt. Roll dough out on a floured board to about 1/8-inch thickness. Cut with biscuit cutter and fold around a date that has been stuffed with pecan half. Bake on ungreased cookie sheet at 350° for about 20 minutes.

These may be frozen for indefinite period but they also keep well in refirgerator in tin can.

Eufaula's Favorite Recipes

Cashew Cheese Wafers
Not a drop will be left.

1 pound sharp Cheddar cheese,
   grated
1/2 pound butter, softened
Salt to taste
1/4 teaspoon cayenne pepper

2 cups all-purpose flour
2 cups dry roasted cashews or
   mixed nuts, finely chopped
Paprika
Onion powder

Mix cheese until creamy. Add butter. Continue beating. Add salt and pepper, add 3 tablespoons flour. Blend well. Continue flour until mixture becomes soft dough and can be rolled into balls without sticking. Add finely chopped nuts. Form small balls. Dust hand and fork with flour. Flatten with fork on cookie sheet. Bake 325° about 20 or 25 minutes. Sprinkle with paprika while hot, after you remove from oven, or sprinkle with onion powder. Better after the first day. Keep in tin. Yield: approximately 100.

Huntsville Entertains

Cheese Ball

This is the cheese ball that we make most often at Gazebo I. One note: Be sure that the pineapple is drained well.

2 (8-ounce) packages cream cheese,
   softened
1 small can crushed pineapple,
   drained
2 tablespoons finely chopped onion

2 tablespoons chopped green onion
2 teaspoons seasoned salt
1 cup chopped pecans plus more
   to roll in

Mix all ingredients together by hand. Shape. Roll in chopped pecans. (You can dust this with paprika or leave it plain instead of rolling it in the pecans.) Refrigerate, but remove from cooler and bring to room temperature to serve.

When You Can't Cook

Do-Ahead Garlic Cheese Roll

This is a real do-ahead since it really should be made at least three or four days before you want to use it.

2 cups sharp Cheddar cheese, grated	**2 teaspoons garlic salt**
1 (3-ounce) package cream cheese	**1/4 cup mayonnaise**
1 teaspoon red pepper	**Chili powder to coat**

Combine everything except chili powder and shape into a long (rather thin) roll. Coat this roll with chili powder; wrap in wax paper and store in refrigerator until time to use.

Serve on a cheese board with crackers. Have a sharp cheese knife on board so guests can help themselves.

When You Can't Cook

Garlic Cheese Ball

2 (8-ounce) packages cream cheese	**1/3 cup chopped olives**
16 ounces sharp cheese, grated	**1/2 cup chopped nuts**
1 clove garlic, crushed or 1/2 teaspoon garlic salt	**1 (4-ounce) jar pimento, chopped**
1/4 teaspoon red pepper	**1 teaspoon Worcestershire sauce**
	Paprika

Allow cream cheese to soften at room temperature. Blend with sharp cheese, mix well with other ingredients. Form into 2 balls and sprinkle well with paprika. Wrap in waxed paper. Chill. These can be made ahead and frozen. Serves 25-35.

DOWN HOME In High Style

Herbed Boursin

1 (8-ounce) package cream cheese	**1 teaspoon dried dill weed**
1 clove garlic, crushed	**2 teaspoons chives, chopped fine**
1 teaspoon caraway seed	**Lemon pepper**
1 teaspoon basil	

Blend cream cheese with garlic, caraway, basil, dill and chives. Roll into a round flat shape. Roll on all sides in lemon pepper. Serve with assorted crackers.

Heavenly Hostess

Mushroom Tartlets

PASTRY:

1 cup butter, softened
1 (8-ounce) package cream cheese, softened

1/2 teaspoon salt
2 cups flour

Mix butter, cream cheese, salt and flour to form a soft dough. Chill overnight. Reserve until ready to bake.

FILLING:

1/2 pound fresh mushrooms, chopped fine
2 tablespoons butter
1/2 cup chopped onion
1/2 teaspoon salt
Dash pepper
1 teaspoon lemon juice

2 teaspoons flour
1/2 cup sour cream
1 teaspoon dill weed
    or 1/4 teaspoon thyme
1 egg yolk
2 teaspoons milk

Break off a portion of dough (keeping remainder chilled until ready to roll) and roll it very thin on a floured surface. Cut with 2-inch cookie cutter and put 1/2 teaspoon of mushroom filling in center of circle, fold over, and crimp with tines of fork. When ready to cook, brush tops with egg yolk beaten with the milk. Bake at 350° degrees for 15 minutes.

These pastries are also good filled with hot pepper jelly rather than the mushrooms. The uncooked pastries may be frozen on a cookie sheet, then placed in freezer bags for later use.

Being a working woman who loves to entertain, I try to keep my freezer filled with individual sealed bags of little nibbles which I can grab at the last minute and serve in 15 minutes--freezer to oven to guest.

Hint: Put a label on each bag with oven temperature and cooking time.

Loaves and Fishes

Asparagus Crisps

1 pound New York State sharp
   cheese, grated
2 tablespoons mayonnaise
1/4 teaspoon red pepper
Horseradish to taste

1 loaf very fresh bread
1 large bell pepper, minced
1 (10 1/2-ounce) can asparagus
   tips

Blend first four ingredients. Remove crusts from bread and spread with a thin layer of cheese mixture. Sprinkle with pepper. Place asparagus on edge of bread and roll; fasten with toothpick. Brush with melted butter before toasting. Place on broiler pan and toast until brown. Cut in half to serve with cocktails. Leave whole to serve with salad or as luncheon bread. Makes 40 small or 20 large crisps.

When Dinnerbells Ring

Bacon-Asparagus Rollups

1 (8-ounce) package cream cheese,
   softened
6 slices cooked bacon, crumbled
1 tablespoon chives
1 cup mayonnaise

1 loaf white bread,
   crusts removed
(15-ounce) can asparagus spears,
   drained
1 stick butter, melted

Preheat oven to 400°· Combine cream cheese, bacon, chives, and mayonnaise. Beat at medium speed 1 minute. Spread mixture on each slice of bread. Roll 2 asparagus spears in each slice of bread and cut into 3 bite-size rolls. Arrange on greased cookie sheet, putting seam side down and brush with melted butter. Bake for 12 minutes. May be prepared ahead and frozen before baking. Yield: about 60.

Magic

 Professional theater comes to Alabama in the Alabama Shakespeare Festival. Founded in Anniston by Martin Platt in 1972, the festival is now housed in Montgomery's Carolyn Blount Theatre.

Caviar Ring

2 (8-ounce) packages cream cheese
8 hard-cooked eggs, chopped
2 tablespoons green onion tops,
 chopped

1 (8-ounce) carton dairy sour
 cream
Red Romanov lumpfish caviar

Beat cream cheese and add eggs and onion tops; mix until smooth. Spray an (8-inch) ring mold with Pam and spoon in cheese mixture. Refrigerate overnight.

To serve, unmold ring and ice with sour cream. Scoop out a trough on top and fill with caviar. Serve with melba toast. Yield: 1 (8-inch) ring.

Family Secrets

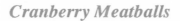

Cranberry Meatballs
Unusual and worth the trouble.

1/4 cup raisins	1/2 teaspoon salt
1/3 cup cranberry-flavored liqueur	1/4 teaspoon freshly ground pepper
1/2 cup finely chopped onion	1 tablespoon cornstarch
1 clove garlic, minced	1/2 cup water
1 tablespoon butter	1 1/2 pounds ground round
1 can (8-ounce) whole cranberry	or chuck
sauce	1 egg
3 tablespoons lemon juice	1/4 cup finely chopped onion
3 thin lemon slices, cut into quarters	3 tablespoons wheat germ
2 tablespoons sugar	1 teaspoon seasoned salt
2 tablespoons prepared horseradish	2 tablespoons butter

Combine raisins and liqueur in small bowl; reserve. Sauté 1/2 cup onion and the garlic in 1 tablespoon butter in large saucepan until soft. Add cranberry sauce, lemon juice, lemon quarters, sugar, horseradish, salt and pepper. Heat to boiling; reduce heat. Simmer uncovered 5 minutes. Add reserved raisin mixture. Dissolve cornstarch in water; stir into cranberry mixture. Cook, stirring constantly, until mixture thickens and bubbles for 3 minutes. Combine meat, egg, 1/4 cup onion, the wheat germ and seasoned salt in medium-size bowl; shape mixture into 1 inch balls. Sauté meatballs in 2 tablespoons butter in large skillet until brown on all sides, about 8 minutes. Pour off pan drippings. Stir in reserved sauce mixture. Heat to boiling; reduce heat. Simmer, uncovered, 10 minutes. Yield: 100.

Huntsville Entertains

Margaret's Tangy Meatballs
Wonderful for "open house" parties.

1 cup cornflakes, crushed
2 pounds ground chuck
2 tablespoons onion flakes
2 tablespoons soy sauce
1/2 teaspoon pepper

1/2 teaspoon garlic powder
Dash of salt
2 eggs
1/2 cup catsup

Mix above 9 ingredients together for meat balls, shaping the size of a quarter. Place in one layer in large baking pan.

SAUCE:
1 (12-ounce) jar chili sauce
1 (16-ounce) can jellied cranberry
   sauce

2 tablespoons sugar
2 tablespoons lemon juice

Mix sauce ingredients; pour over meatballs. Bake uncovered in 400° oven for 35 minutes. Serves about 16-18. Meatballs may be made and frozen ahead of time. Make very small if served as appetizer.

A Samford Celebration Cookbook

Nootsie's Party Pizzas

1 pound hot bulk pork sausage
1 pound ground beef
1 loaf Party Rye bread

1 pound Velvetta cheese
1 1/2 teaspoons dried oregano

Brown sausage and ground beef in skillet. Drain off fat. Stir in Velveeta cheese until thoroughly melted and mixed with ground meat/ sausage mixture. Add oregano and mix thoroughly. Spoon mixture on the tops of the rye bread. Bake in a pre-heated (350°) oven 10-15 minutes.

Heavenly Hostess

Mezza
(Lamb appetizers)
This is unusual and delicious.

1/2 pound lean ground lamb
1/2 cup bulghur, soaked 20
  minutes in water then squeezed
  dry (whole wheat bread crumbs
  may be substituted)
1/2 teaspoon salt
1/2 teaspoon allspice
1/2 teaspoon cinnamon
1 pinch of saffron or cumin

2 tablespoons dried currants
1 clove garlic, crushed
1 small onion, finely chopped
Salt to taste
Pepper to taste
1/4 cup olive oil
1 pound phyllo, cut in 4x5-inch
  rectangles

Preheat oven to 400°. Mix lamb and bulghur (or bread crumbs) with all the remaining ingredients except olive oil and phyllo. Cook mixture in olive oil over medium heat for 5 minutes. Cool slightly. Place 1 tablespoon of mixture on each phyllo piece. Turn shorter sides in slightly and starting with long side, roll as for a jelly roll. Place seam side down on ungreased cookie sheet. Bake at 400° fof 10 minutes or until slightly browned. May be frozen and cooked while still frozen adding 5 minutes to cooking time. There will be some phyllo left over. Wrap tightly and freeze for later use. Yield: 20 hors d'oeuvres.

Magic

Polish Sausage with Horseradish Sauce

1 can beets, drained and puréed
2 ounces horseradish
1 tablespoon sugar

1 tablespoon white vinegar
Salt and pepper
Ring of Polish sausage

Mix beets, horseradish, sugar, vinegar, salt and pepper. Let stand several hours to blend flavors. At serving time, broil sausage until brown, turning once. Quickly slice and arrange on platter with small container of the sauce for dipping. Serve with toothpicks.

An especially good hors d'oeuvre for the cooler months.

Loaves and Fishes

Tamale Bites
A real taste treat

2 cups crumbled corn bread	1 1/2 pounds ground beef
1 (10-ounce) can mild enchilada	1 (8-ounce) can tomato sauce
sauce	1/2 cup shredded Monterrey
1/2 teaspoon salt	Jack cheese

Combine bread crumbs, 1/2 cup of the enchilada sauce, and the salt. Add beef and mix well. Shape into 1-inch balls. Place in shallow baking pan. Bake, uncovered, in 350° oven for 18-20 minutes or until done. Meanwhile, in small saucepan, heat together tomato sauce and the remaining enchilada sauce. Place cooked meatballs in chafing dish; pour sauce over and top with shredded cheese. Keep warm over low heat. Serve with wooden picks. Make these ahead, chill and bake when you need them. Yield: 90 bites.

Huntsville Entertains

Salmon Pâté

1 (15 1/2-ounce) can red salmon	1/4 cup mayonnaise
1 package clear gelatin	2-4 tablespoons horseradish,
2 tablespoons onion, minced	depending on how hot you like it
very finely	

Drain salmon; remove all bones, skin and dark parts. Flake finely. Dissolve gelatin in 2 tablespoons of warm water. Add to salmon along with onion, mayonnaise, and horseradish. Press into mold and chill until firmly set. Garnish with fresh dill, if available. Yield: 8-10 servings. *Note:* May be sliced and served with melba toast as first course at dinner or with crackers as an appetizer.

Once Upon a Stove

Crab or Shrimp Mousse

1 1/2 cups shrimp (crab or lobster may be used--about 1 pound), chopped
1 cup chopped celery
1/2 cup chopped bell pepper
2 tablespoons grated onion
1 teaspoon salt
3 tablespoons lemon juice
1 tablespoon Worcestershire
1/2 teaspoon Tabasco
1 can tomato soup
3 (3-ounce) packages cream cheese
3 envelopes plain gelatin
1 cup cold water
1 cup mayonnaise

Combine shrimp, celery, bell pepper, onion, salt, lemon juice, Worcestershire and Tabasco. Mix well and let stand to blend flavors. Combine soup and cream cheese in double boiler. Heat and stir until cheese melts. Soften gelatin in water for 5 minutes. Add to soup mixture. Remove from heat and cool. When mixture begins to thicken, blend in mayonnaise. Stir in shrimp mixture, turn into mold and chill. Serve with crackers or may be used as a salad.

Made in a fish-shaped mold, garnished with lemon slices dipped in paprika and sprigs of parsley, our shrimp mousse is prettier than a picture in any magazine! Serve with candlelight and silver.

Cotton Country Cooking

Shrimp Mousse

2 envelopes unflavored gelatin
4 tablespoons water
4 cups Thousand Island dressing
1/2 cup diced celery
1/2 cup diced celery
2 tablespoons lemon juice
3 small cans tiny shrimp, washed or 1/2 cup chopped cooked shrimp

Soften gelatin in cold water and dissolve over hot water. Combine with remaining ingredients, mixing well. Pour into an oiled 6-cup mold and chill for 6-8 hours. Unmold on serving platter and serve with wheat crackers. Yield: 24-30 small servings.

Dining Under the Magnolia

Sea Island Shrimp Mold
This is addictive.

1 can she crab soup (Harris)
1 (8-ounce) package cream
  cheese (softened)
2 envelopes unflavored gelatin
1 cup mayonnaise
1 cup celery, finely chopped

4 green onions, finely chopped
1 tablespoon fresh lemon juice
1 teaspoon curry powder
1 pound cooked shrimp, cut up
  into small pieces

Heat soup and cream cheese until combined and creamy. Stir softened gelatin into soup-cheese mixture. Add other ingredients and pour into greased fish mold (or line mold with plastic wrap). Chill at least 4 hours. Unmold and garnish with whole shrimp and parsley. Serve with good crackers. Yield: 25 servings.

Huntsville Entertains

Ginger Shrimp

2 pounds shrimp
1/4 teaspoon salt
1/8 teaspoon Tabasco
1/4 cup celery, finely chopped
1/2 cup onion, finely chopped
1 tablespoon bell pepper,
  finely chopped
1 stick butter
1 (#2 1/2) can pineapple chunks

1 1/4 cups pineapple syrup
1 1/2 tablespoons cornstarch
3/8 cup granulated sugar
1/2 cup vinegar
1 1/2 tablespoons soy sauce
4 ounces snow pea pods
1 1/2 teaspoons grated ginger
  root, firmly packed

Prepare all ingredients before starting to cook. Peel shrimp and drain. Sprinkle 1/8 teaspoon salt and the Tabasco on drained shrimp. Sauté shrimp in butter one minute. Remove shrimp and set aside. Sauté onions, celery, and bell pepper in same butter one minute on medium heat. Stir fry to prevent burning. Add pea pods and pineapple chunks. Stir fry for 30 seconds. Add cornstarch dissolved in pineapple juice, sugar, vinegar, soy sauce, and 1/8 teaspoon salt. Simmer until the sauce is thick, stirring gently to prevent burning. Sauce should be thicker than regular sweet and sour sauce so that it will stick to the shrimp. Add shrimp and grated ginger root. Stir gently while heating until bubbly. Serve immediately.

Serve hot in a chafing dish with Melba toast or use toothpicks to spear pea pods, pineapple chunks, and shrimp.

The Alabama Heritage Cookbook

Marinated Shrimp

5 pounds headless fresh shrimp
4 tablespoons salt
2 cups sliced onions
7 or 8 bay leaves
3/4 cup white vinegar

1 1/2 tablespoons capers and juice
1 1/2 teaspoons celery seed
1 1/2 teaspoons salt
1 dash Tabasco sauce

Prepare this dish at least 24 hours ahead of time. It will keep 4-5 days in the refrigerator. In a large pot, bring to boil enough water to cover shrimp. Add 4 tablespoons salt and shrimp and cook until done (approximately 10 minutes). Drain and peel shrimp. In a large bowl alternate layers of shrimp, onions and bay leaves. Combine remaining ingredients and mix well. Pour over shrimp and place in refrigerator. Do not stir.

Variation: Marinated shrimp and mushrooms. Add 2 or 3 (8-ounce) cans whole mushrooms in layers with shrimp and onions. Serve as a salad or hors d'oeuvres.

Bravo! Applaudable Recipes

Artichoke Leaves with Shrimp or Crabmeat

4 artichokes
2 pounds shrimp or 1 pound
  crabmeat
1/2 cup homemade mayonnaise

Lemon juice
Relish, salt, pepper, and
  paprika to taste

Cook artichokes. Remove the individual leaves. If using shrimp, the medium size is advisable. Cook and clean shrimp. Put 1 teaspoon mayonnaise (with a little extra lemon juice added) in cup of each leaf. Top this with a shrimp. If using crabmeat, add 1/2 cup mayonnaise to each pound of crab. Mix well and season to taste. Place small amount of mixture on each leaf.

To arrange, start in center of serving platter with a small circle of individual leaves. Continue circling to form an overlapping pattern almost like water-lily leaves as you fill the plate. Have an empty dish on hand for discarded artichoke leaves. (*Note:* This is an excellent dish. Make plenty because they really go!)

Seconds Please!

Bacon Sticks

Bacon (1 slice per bread stick)   **Bread sticks**
Parmesan cheese, grated

Take one slice of bacon and put one side down onto a plate of grated Parmesan cheese. Wrap this strip around a bread stick, putting the side with the cheese on it next to the bread stick. Put in microwave until bacon is cooked. Remove and roll in Parmesan. (Be careful not to overcook.)

Gazebo I Christmas Cookbook

Strawberry Butter

3/4 cup finely chopped fresh   **3 - 5 tablespoons confectioners'**
    strawberries   **sugar**
1 pound sweet whipped butter

Combine all ingredients in food processor with steel blade. Process until light. Serve with warm biscuits or use as a spread for thin white bread cut in rounds or shapes. This is pretty to use for coffees, showers, or brunches. Yield: 2 1/2 cups.

Magic

Bread
and
Breakfast

The log cabin where W. C. Handy was born is now a restored museum established to contain his memorabilia. Florence.

Mrs. Hollowell's Egg Bread

2 cups corn meal
1 teaspoon salt
1/2 teaspoon soda

2 egg yolks, beaten
2 cups buttermilk
2 egg whites, beaten

Sift dry ingredients together. Add egg yolks to buttermilk and stir into dry ingredients. Fold in stiffly beaten egg whites. Pour into greased black iron skillet. Bake at 400° for 25 minutes or until brown. This recipe has stood the test of time since 1916. Many homemakers add a small amount of shortening, but it is good without it.

DOWN HOME In High Style

Caraway Rye Bread

2 1/2 cups rye flour
2 packages dry yeast
1/3 cup brown sugar
1 tablespoon salt
2 cups water

1/4 cup molasses or honey
1/4 cup margarine
2 to 3 teaspoons caraway seeds
3 1/2 to 4 cups all-purpose flour
1/2 to 1 1/2 cups flour

Combine the rye flour, dry yeast, brown sugar, and salt in the mixer. Heat water, honey or molasses, and margarine in a saucepan until very warm, 120°-130°. Add to the flour mixture and blend at low speed until moistened; beat 2 minutes at medium speed. Add caraway seeds and all-purpose flour and stir to form a sticky dough. Add additional flour and knead until no longer sticky, about 5 minutes.

Place in greased bowl. Let rise in warm place until not quite double in size, 45-60 minutes. Grease two loaf pans that are 8x4 or 9x5. Shape dough into loaves. Cover and let rise until light but not quite double in size. Brush loaves with beaten egg before baking. Bake at 375° for 25-30 minutes. Remove from pans and cool. Delicious when warm.

The Alabama Heritage Cookbook

Dill Bread

1 package dry yeast (dissolved
  in 1/4 cup lukewarm water for
  10 minutes)
1 cup large curd cottage cheese
  (heated)
2 tablespoons grated onion
1 tablespoon melted butter

1 tablespoon sugar
1 tablespoon dill seed
1 teaspoon salt
1/4 teaspoon baking soda
1 egg, lightly beaten
Flour

Sauté onion in butter till tender. Soften yeast in water. In a large warm bowl place cottage cheese, sugar, onion, dill seed, salt, soda, egg, and yeast, and mix well. Add enough flour to make a stiff dough. Beat well. Cover and let rise until double--about 1 1/2 hours. Stir down. Divide dough with sharp knife and place in 1 large or 2 small well-greased loaf pans. Let rise again (30-40 minutes). Bake at 350° for 50-55 minutes. Makes 1 large (9 1/2x5x2-inch) or 2 (7 1/2x3 1/2x2-inch) small loaves.

Auburn Entertains

Beer Bread
"Quick, easy, and so delicious."

3 cups self-rising flour
1 teaspoon salt

3 tablespoons sugar
1 (12-ounce) can beer

Mix all ingredients. Pour into greased 9x5x3-inch loaf pan. Bake 1 hour in 350° oven.

When Dinnerbells Ring

Short'nin Bread

1 cup light brown sugar   1 pound butter
4 cups flour

Combine sugar and flour. Add butter. Place on floured board and pat to thickness of 1/2-inch. Cut into shapes desired and bake in a moderate oven (325°-350°) for 25 minutes.

Most folks have heard of this but never eaten it. It is simple but delicious with tea or coffee.

Kum' Ona' Granny's Table

Orange Pecan Bread

1/4 cup butter or margarine,   2 1/2 teaspoons baking powder
  softened   1 teaspoon salt
3/4 cup sugar   3/4 cup orange juice
2 eggs, beaten   1/2 cup pecans, chopped
2 teaspoons grated orange rind   2 1/2 teaspoons orange juice
2 cups all-purpose flour   1/2 cup powdered sugar sifted

Cream butter. Gradually add 3/4 cup sugar, beating well. Add beaten eggs and grated orange rind. Mix well. Combine flour, baking powder and salt. Add to creamed mixture alternately with 3/4 cup orange juice, beginning and ending with flour mixture. Mix well after each addition. Stir in pecans. Pour batter into a greased 9x5x3-inch loaf pan. Bake at 350° for 50-55 minutes or until a wooden pick inserted in center comes out clean. Cool loaf in pan for 10 minutes. Remove from pan and cool completely.

Combine 2 1/2 teaspoons orange juice and 1/4 cup powdered sugar. Drizzle over loaf. Wrap and store overnight before serving. Can be frozen.

The Great Cookbook

Nancy's Hot Blueberry Bread

2 eggs
1 cup sugar
1 cup milk
1/4 cup butter, melted
3 cups flour

1 tablespoon plus 1 teaspoon
  baking powder
1 teaspoon salt
2 cups fresh blueberries
2 tablespoons flour

In a large bowl, beat thoroughly the eggs and sugar. Add milk and butter, mix together, and add dry ingredients. Stir just enough to moisten all ingredients. Add 2 tablespoons flour to blueberries, stirring well to coat. Fold into batter. Spoon into two greased and floured 7 1/2x3x2-inch loaf pans. Bake at 350° for 55-60 minutes or until bread tests done. Serve hot.

Heavenly Hostess

Apricot Nut Bread

1 cup dried apricots
1 cup sugar
2 tablespoons shortening
1 egg
1/4 cup water
2 cups flour

1/4 teaspoon soda
1 teaspoon salt
2 teaspoons baking powder
1/2 cup orange juice
1/2 chopped nuts

Chop the apricots and soak in water for 1/2 hour. Mix together the sugar, shortening, and egg. Stir in the remaining ingredients except the apricots and nuts and blend well. Stir in the apricots and nuts last and let batter stand for 20 minutes. Bake in a greased loaf pan for 1 hour at 350°.

Heirlooms From The Kitchen

Strawberry Bread

3 cups flour
2 cups sugar
1 teaspoon soda
1 teaspoon salt
3 teaspoons cinnamon
1 1/4 cups chopped pecans

2 (10-ounce) packages frozen
strawberries, thawed
1 1/4 cups vegetable oil
3 eggs, beaten
1 teaspoon vanilla

Sift dry ingredients into large mixing bowl; add pecans and mix. Combine remaining ingredients. Combine the two mixtures, stirring to just moisten. Pour into 2 greased loaf pans. Bake at 350° for 1 hour. Turn out on rack to cool.

Variation: To make Strawberry-Pineapple Bread, substitute 1 cup crushed pineapple for 1 (10-ounce) package strawberries.

Hallmark's Collection of Home Tested Recipes

Skillet Coffee Cake

3/4 cup butter or margarine
1 1/2 cups sugar
2 eggs
1 1/2 cups sifted all-purpose flour

Pinch of salt
1 1/2 teaspoons almond flavoring
Slivered almonds
Sugar

Melt butter and add to sugar in mixing bowl. Beat in eggs, one at a time. Add flour, salt and flavoring and mix well.

Pour batter into large iron skillet (9-11 inches) which has been lined with aluminum foil. (Leave excess foil on either side for later use.) Cover top with slivered almonds and sprinkle with granulated sugar. Bake 30-40 minutes in 350° oven.

Remove cake from the pan with foil and when cool, wrap tightly in the foil to store. Do not try to peel off the foil while cake is still warm, for it will stick.

This is a very rich, heavy, unleavened coffee cake. If you like coffee cake for Sunday morning breakfast though, forget this one or you'll kill yourself. It is perfect cut in tiny wedges or strips for a coffee or tea. Pecans may be used instead of almonds. Serves 10.

Loaves and Fishes

Honey Puffs
(Loukoumades or Svingous)

YIELD: 40-50 Honey Puffs:

Crisco or vegetable oil
1/4 teaspoon soda
1 teaspoon lemon juice
2 cups water
1 stick butter or margarine

1 cup plain flour
6 eggs
Honey
Ground cinnamon

YIELD: 250 Honey Puffs:

Crisco or vegetable oil
1 teaspoon baking soda
Juice of 1 1/2 lemons
3 quarts plus 2 cups water
2 1/2 sticks butter or margarine

3 pounds plain flour
4 dozen eggs
Honey
Ground cinnamon

METHOD:

Put Crisco or light vegetable oil in fryolator. Dissolve soda in lemon juice. In a deep saucepan, bring the water and butter to a boil. Quickly stir in the flour all at once. Add soda and lemon juice mixture. Keep stirring vigorously over low heat until the mixture forms a ball and no longer adheres to the sides of the pan. Place dough in a large bowl. Cool slightly, about 5 minutes. Add eggs, one at a time; blend thoroughly. Let dough rest.

At this point, you may refrigerate the dough. It will be ready for "Honey Puffs for breakfast" or any other occasion. Our daughter keeps this batter on hand. Anytime her family wants a snack, they make a few Honey Puffs and save the ramainder of the dough for the next time. This is also ideal for drop-in loved ones!

To fry the Honey Puffs, dip a spoon in a cup of oil. This will keep the batter from sticking to the spoon. Drop the dough by the teaspoonful into the hot grease. Fry; turn until the Honey Puffs are golden on all sides. Remove the Puffs with a slotted spoon. As many as six Honey Puffs may be fried at a time, depending on the size of the fryolator (for the larger yield, you will need several fryolators). Serve hot. Drizzle with honey; sprinkle with cinnamon. This is ideal for the hostess or host to prepare at the table at any and every occasion.

Note: This is a balanced recipe; never, never double this recipe.

A Southern Lady Cooks with a Greek Accent

Wilma's Cinnamon Rolls

2 packages dry yeast	1 teaspoon salt
4 tablespoons warm water	1 cup shortening
1/4 cup sugar, divided	2 cups warm milk
5 cups flour	Soft butter
3 teaspoons baking powder	Cinnamon

Dissolve yeast in warm water and add 2 tablespoons of sugar. Set aside. Combine dry ingredients and cut in shortening. Add yeast and warm milk. Mix well. Refrigerate mixture overnight or at least 6 hours.

Butter 4 round or square aluminum pans before kneading dough. Knead dough and divide mixture into thirds. Roll 1/3 of dough thin on floured surface. Spread soft butter on dough. Sprinkle sugar and cinnamon to cover butter. Roll as a jelly roll. Cut dough into 1-inch slices. Bake at 375° for 15 -20 minutes. Glaze rolls while warm, not hot.

GLAZE:

1 box powdered sugar	1/2 teaspoon imitation butter
1/2 cup butter	flavoring
1 teaspoon vanilla extract	Milk

Chop sugar and butter in food processor. Add vanilla and butter flavoring. Gradually add enough milk to mixture to reach spreading consistency. Glaze cinnamon rolls. These may be warmed for breakfast or snack. They freeze well, too! Yield: 3 or 4 dozen.

These cinnamon rolls are perfect for Christmas morning or anytime of the year. These rolls are a wonderful gift anytime! They are wonderful.

Cooks and Company

"Suffragettes" held their first American rally, the "Petticoat Rebellion," in Mobile in 1714.

Buttermilk Orange Rolls

2 cups sifted all-purpose flour	Grated rind of 2 large oranges
1 teaspoon sugar	1/2 cup sugar
1 teaspoon salt	1/4 cup light corn syrup
1 1/2 teaspoons baking powder	1/4 cup water
1/2 teaspoon baking soda	1/2 teaspoon rum flavoring
1/3 cup shortening	1/2 cup sugar
3/4 cup buttermilk	2 tablespoons melted butter

Blend dry ingredients. Cut in shortening with a pastry blender. Add buttermilk all at once. Stir until dough forms a ball. Turn onto lightly floured surface and knead 15-20 times. Roll dough into a rectangle and spread with 2 tablespoons melted butter. Set aside 1 tablespoon grated orange peel. Mix remaining orange peel with 1/2 cup sugar. Sprinkle over rectangle of dough. Roll up jelly roll fashion beginning with the long side. Press edges together to seal. Cut into 1-inch slices. Place on greased baking sheet and bake at 450° for 10 minutes. Cool slightly and spoon glaze over rolls.

GLAZE:
Combine 1/2 cup sugar and 1 tablespoon grated orange rind. Add corn syrup and water. Bring to a boil and boil for 2 1/2 minutes over medium heat. Remove from heat and add rum flavoring.

The Alabama Heritage Cookbook

Four Star Grain Muffins

1/2 cup cornmeal	1 1/4 teaspoons baking powder
1/4 cup regular oats, uncooked	1/2 teaspoon salt
1/4 cup all-purpose flour	1/2 cup buttermilk
1 1/2 teaspoons wheat germ	1/4 cup vegetable oil
2 tablespoons sugar	1 egg, beaten

Combine first four ingredients in a medium bowl. Stir in sugar, baking powder and salt. Add buttermilk, oil and egg, stirring until just moistened (batter will be lumpy). Grease muffin tin, fill until 2/3 full. Bake for 20-25 minutes. Yield: 10 muffins.

Huntsville Entertains

Jelly Gem Muffins

1/3 cup soft shortening (Crisco)	1/4 teaspoon nutmeg
1/2 cup sugar	1/2 cup milk
1 egg	1/2 cup currant jelly
1 1/2 cups sifted flour	6 tablespoons melted butter
1/2 teaspoon baking powder	1/2 cup sugar
1/2 teaspoon salt	1 teaspoon cinnamon

Combine first 3 ingredients and mix well. Mix and sift flour, baking powder, salt and nutmeg. Add alternately with milk and egg mixture. Fill greased small muffin tin half full. Put 1/2 teaspoon jelly in center of each cup. Add enough batter to fill 2/3 full. Bake at 350° for 20 minutes or until golden. Remove from pans at once. Roll in melted butter, then in mixture of remaining sugar and cinnamon. Makes 24 small muffins.

More Fiddling With Food

 Montgomery is the home of the Civil Rights Movement. Dr. Martin Luther King began preaching at that city's Dexter Avenue Baptist Church.

Velvet Vanilla Muffins

2 cups flour	3 eggs
4 teaspoons baking powder	1 cup milk
3 tablespoons sugar	2/3 teaspoon vanilla
1/4 teaspoon salt	1/4 cup melted butter

Sift dry ingredients together. Beat milk, eggs and vanilla until light and foamy. Pour into dry ingredients and stir just until liquid is absorbed. Add melted butter and beat one minute. Fill greased muffin rings two-thirds full and bake at 425° about 20 minutes or until delicately brown.

Treasured Alabama Recipes

Carrot Muffins

These rich-tasting muffins are super-delicious!

2 large eggs	3/4 cup wheat germ
3/4 cup instant nonfat dry milk powder	4 teaspoons baking powder
	1 1/2 teaspoons lemon peel, grated
3/4 cup water	1 1/2 cups carrots, grated
1/3 cup light molasses	3/4 cup pitted dates, finely diced
1/3 cup vegetable oil	
1 cup all-purpose flour, preferably unbleached	

Combine eggs, dry milk powder, water, molasses, and oil; beat with electric mixer on medium speed until well blended. Combine flour, wheat germ, baking powder, and lemon peel; add to liquid mixture, and stir until moistened. Stir in carrots and dates. Batter will be lumpy. Spoon batter into greased muffin pans, filling two-thirds full. Bake at 375° for 18-22 minutes or until done. Serve warm or cool. Yield: 12 muffins.

Once Upon a Stove

Cheeselette Rolls with Cream Cheese Pastry Dough

FILLING:
1/2 pound Feta cheese, grated on half moon side of grater
1 (3-ounce) package cream cheese, room temperature
2 eggs, beaten
Dash nutmeg

DOUGH:
1 (8-ounce) package cream cheese, room temperature
1 cup butter or margarine, room temperature
2 cups all-purpose flour

FILLING:
Combine Feta, cream cheese (3-ounce package), and eggs in bowl. Whip until smooth and creamy. Add nutmeg. Set aside.

DOUGH:
Mix cream cheese (8-ounce package) and butter well; add flour, keeping working until it all comes together; using your hands, form a ball. Refrigerate the dough for about an hour. Pinch off a piece of dough and roll it into a circle about 3 1/2 inches in diameter and 1/4-inch thick. Place a teaspoonful of cheeselette filling on the edge of the circle. Fold the sides to the middle; then roll pastry in a jelly roll fashion. Place seam side down on an ungreased pan; place on middle rack in 350° oven. Bake for 20-25 minutes or until done. Serve hot.

To freeze: Place in plastic containers with waxed paper between the layers of rolls. Seal and freeze. These will freeze up to 4 months at least. Do not defrost to bake.

A Southern Lady Cooks with a Greek Accent

Mother's Rusk Rolls, Streamlined

1 cup dried potato flakes	1/2 cup soft shortening
1 1/2 cups boiling water	4 eggs
3/4 cup sugar	Flour
2 envelopes yeast	1/2 stick butter
1 teaspoon salt	1/4 cup confectioners' sugar

Stir potato flakes into boiling water in large bowl. Add sugar and stir until dissolved. Add yeast, mix and let stand for 2-3 hours. Add salt, shortening and eggs. Stir in enough flour that the dough can be handled, but keep as soft as possible. Knead a few minutes, return to bowl, cover, and let rise until double in bulk. Punch down. Shape into rolls (pocket book is the classic shape) and place in greased pans to rise again until double in bulk. Bake at 350° until golden. Just before they are ready, melt butter and paint tops of rolls, sprinkle with powdered sugar and return to oven until browning is completed.

Loaves and Fishes

Spoon Yeast Rolls

1 package dry yeast	1/4 cup sugar
2 cups warm water	1 egg
1 1/2 sticks oleo, melted	4 cups unsifted self-rising flour

Dissolve yeast in warm water. Cream oleo and sugar. Add beaten egg. Add yeast to oleo mixture, then add flour. Stir until well mixed. Put in large bowl and refrigerate. To bake, drop by spoonfuls into greased muffin tins and bake at 425° until light brown. You do not have to wait for rolls to rise before refrigerating or after putting rolls in muffin pans.

Sumpthn' Yummy

Orville Wright established the first civilian pilot training school in Montgomery in 1910. The first night flight in aviation history also took place there.

Buttery Rolls

1/2 cup shortening	1/4 cup lukewarm water
1/3 cup granulated sugar	1 egg, beaten
1 teaspoon salt	4 cups sifted all-purpose flour
1/2 cup boiling water	1/2 cup ice water
1 package dry yeast	

Cream shortening, sugar, and salt; add boiling water. Combine yeast with lukewarm water; beat in egg and add to shortening mixture. Add sifted flour and ice water alternately to liquid, mixing well. Cover and set in a warm place to rise until double, about 1 1/2-2 hours. Shape as desired into Parker House, Clover Leaf, buns, or other rolls. Place on greased baking sheet. Let rise until double. Bake 400° for 10-12 minutes. Yield: 3 1/2-4 dozen.

Family Secrets

Birmingham's Vulcan statue, the largest iron figure ever cast, is one of the few monuments ever erected to symbolize an industry.

Buttercup Biscuits

1 (8-ounce) container sour cream   2 sticks butter or oleo
2 cups pre-sifted self-rising flour

Blend butter and sour cream until creamy. Add flour; mix. Place by teaspoon into buttercup-size biscuit pans. Makes 4 dozen. Bake 30-35 minutes at 350° or until golden brown.

    This recipe won first prize in our "Easter Brunch Contest."

Kum' Ona' Granny's Table

Buttermilk Biscuits

2 1/2 cups flour   2 teaspoons baking powder
1 teaspoon salt   3 tablespoons shortening
1/2 teaspoon soda   1 cup buttermilk

Sift dry ingredients together. Work in shortening, add buttermilk slowly, mixing well. Roll out on lightly floured board, cut into desired shape and bake in 425° oven 10 to 12 minutes.

Recipe Jubilee!

Tomato Gravy

1/4 cup Crisco   1 1/2 cups stewed (canned)
6 level tablespoons flour   tomatoes
1 cup milk   1 teaspoon salt
1 cup water

In large skillet, melt Crisco on high heat. Add flour and stir constantly until it is slightly brown. Remove from heat. Let cool. Mix together the milk and water. Add to Crisco-flour mixture and stir until well blended. Add tomatoes. Put back on heat and stir until thickened. Add salt.

    To make Old-Fashioned White Gravy, use the same recipe, but omit the tomatoes. Black pepper is also good in this gravy. This was always an old standby when food was scarce during depression days. Some of those "necessities" turned out to be favorite foods.

Kum' Ona' Granny's Table

Garlic Grits

1 cup grits, cooked
1 stick butter
1 1/2 tablespoons Worcestershire
   sauce

3/4 pound grated American cheese
1/2-1 clove garlic, minced
Tabasco sauce to taste
2 egg whites

To hot grits add all remaining ingredients except egg whites. Cool.
When cool, add stiffly beaten egg whites and bake 20 minutes in 400°
oven. Serves 6.

Recipe Jubilee!

Creole Grits

1/4 cup bacon grease
1 medium onion, chopped
2 small bell peppers
1 (16-ounce) can tomatoes
   undrained and chopped

1/4 teaspoon sugar
1 teaspoon garlic salt
Dash of pepper
1 1/2 cups uncooked grits

Sauté onions and bell pepper in bacon grease, stir in tomatoes, sugar,
salt and pepper. Simmer for 30 minutes. This can be done in advance.
Then add to the 1 1/2 cups grits that have been cooked according to
package directions. Serves 10.

Heavenly Hostess

Deluxe Cornbread

1 cup self-rising cornmeal mix
1/2 cup margarine or butter
2 eggs

1 cup sour cream
1 cup cream-style corn

Combine all ingredients and mix well. Pour into a hot, well-greased skillet and bake at 325° for about 30 minutes or until firm and light brown.

Kitchen Sampler

Corn Spoon Bread
Absolutely marvelous!

3 cups milk
1 cup white corn meal
1 1/2 teaspoons salt
3 cups whole kernel corn
   (fresh or frozen)

3 tablespoons margarine or butter
5 eggs, separated

Scald milk. Add corn meal, salt and corn. Cook until thick, about 5 minutes. Add margarine and slightly beaten egg yolks. Fold into stiffly beaten egg whites. Pour into greased 13x9-inch casserole dish. Bake at 350° for 50-60 minutes. Serves 8.

Cookbook

Corn Fritters

1 cup sifted flour
1 teaspoon baking powder
1 tablespoon melted fat
1 2/3 cups fresh cut corn,
   (or 1 [12-ounce] can)

1 egg
1/2 teaspoon salt
5 tablespoons milk
4 tablespoons sugar

Sift dry ingredients together; add beaten egg to milk and melted fat; mix with dry ingredients; beat until smooth, stir in corn. Drop by tablespoon into hot fat, 375°-385°, fry until golden brown. Makes 24.

Treasured Taste

Macadamia Nut Pancakes

1 cup all-purpose biscuit mix	3/4 cup sour cream
1 egg, beaten	1/3 cup Macadamia nuts,
1 cup milk	finely chopped

Combine first 3 ingredients and beat until smooth. Spoon about 3 table-spoons of batter (scant 1/4 cup at a time) onto hot greased skillet. Bake until bubbles appear. Turn pancakes gently and finish baking. Put pancakes between folds of a towel until ready to use. Make a filling by combining sour cream and nuts. Spread 1 tablespoon of filling in center of each pancake. Roll up and place close together in lightly greased baking pan. Just before serving reheat in hot oven. Yield: 12 pancakes. Serve the following syrup over pancakes:

PINEAPPLE SYRUP:

2 cups sugar	1 (6-ounce) can frozen pineapple
1/2 cup butter	juice or medium can pineapple
1/4 cup water	sauce for sundaes

Combine all ingredients in saucepan and boil 5 minutes.

Seconds Please!

Baked Sausage in Crescent French Toast

8 link sausages
1 can crescent rolls
3 eggs

2 tablespoons cream
4 tablespoons melted margarine
Warm maple syrup

Bake sausage on baking sheet in a 400° oven for about 15-20 minutes. While the sausage is cooking, lay each crescent roll out flat on a baking sheet and bake for about 7 minutes. Place sausage on wide end of crescent roll; roll up rather gently but not too tightly.

Whisk eggs; add cream and dip each roll into this mixture. Melt margarine in a large saucepan; brown rolls on all sides. Serve warm with warm maple syrup. Serves 8.

Gazebo I Christmas Cookbook

Easy Never-Fail Cheese Soufflé

3 tablespoons quick-cooking Tapioca
2 tablespoons onion, minced
1 teaspoon salt
1 cup milk

1 cup American cheese, grated
3 egg yolks, well beaten
1 tablespoon parsley, minced
3 egg whites, stiffly beaten

Combine Tapioca, onion, salt and milk. Cook in a double-boiler for 10 minutes, stirring frequently. Add cheese and stir until the cheese melts. Add a little of the hot mixture to egg yolks. Stir a minute, then add back to the remaining hot mixture. Cool slightly and add parsley. Fold in the egg whites and pour into an ungreased 1-quart baking dish. Bake the soufflé in a pan with 1 inch of hot water surrounding it at 350° for 1 hour. Serves 4.

One of a Kind

Fort Conde at Mobile was the headquarters for French, English, and Spanish military rule of the coastal area. The fort was built in 1711, and now serves as the official City of Mobile Visitor Welcome Center.

Breakfast Pizza

1 pound bulk pork sausage
1 (8-ounce) package refrigerated
   crescent rolls
1 cup frozen loose-pack hash
   brown potatoes, thawed
1 cup shredded sharp Cheddar
   cheese
5 eggs, beaten

1/4 cup milk
1/2 teaspoon salt
1/2 teaspoon pepper
2 tablespoons grated Parmesan
   cheese
Pimiento (optional)
Fresh oregano (optional)

Cook sausage in medium skillet until brown; drain and set aside. Separate crescent dough into 8 triangles. Place with elongated points toward center of greased 12-inch pizza pan. Press bottom and sides to form a crust. Seal perforations. Spoon sausage over dough. Sprinkle with hash brown potatoes and Cheddar cheese. Combine eggs, milk, salt and pepper; pour over sausage mixture. Bake at 375° for 25 minutes. Sprinkle with Parmesan cheese and bake an additional 5 minutes. Garnish with pimiento and fresh oregano, if desired. Yield: 6-8 servings.

Cooks and Company

Sausage Ring

1 pound bulk sausage, hot
1 pound bulk sausage, mild
1 large onion, chopped

2 apples, peeled and chopped
1 cup corn flakes, crushed

Mix all ingredients together and pack into 1 1/2-quart ring mold. Place mold on cookie sheet and bake (350°) for 20 minutes. Drain grease off mold and bake another 20 or 30 minutes or until done. Fill center with scrambled eggs. Serves 10-12.

Heavenly Hostess

Alabama has about one million acres of water for recreational purposes.

Men's Breakfast

SCRAMBLED EGGS CASSEROLE (make day ahead):

1/4 cup green onions, chopped
2 tablespoons parsley, minced
3 tablespoons butter
14 eggs, beaten
Cheese Sauce (recipe below)

1/4 cup melted butter
1 (10-ounce) can Italian Bread
  Crumbs
1/8 teaspoon paprika

CHEESE SAUCE:

2 tablespoons butter
2 tablespoons flour
3/4 cup milk
1/4 cup cooking sherry

1/2 teaspoon salt
1/8 teaspoon pepper
4 ounces Velveeta, cubed

Make white sauce with flour, butter, milk and wine. Stir in cheese, salt and pepper, stirring until cheese melts. Sauté onion in butter until tender. Stir in eggs and scramble to the soft curd, set stage. Stir in Cheese Sauce. Spoon into 3-quart casserole. Combine 1/4 cup melted butter with Italian bread crumbs. Mix well and sprinkle evenly over egg mixture. Sprinkle with paprkia. Cover and chill overnight.

Bake uncovered at 350° for 30 minutes. Remove from oven and let sit 5 minutes to firm up. Serves 12.

Heavenly Hostess

Bacon and Egg Breakfast Pie

Pastry for (9-inch) 2 crust pie
12 slices bacon, fried
6 eggs
1/4 teaspoon salt
1/8 teaspoon pepper

2 tablespoons chopped parsley
1 tablespoon chopped chives or
    green onion tops
1 can cream of mushroom soup
3 tablespoons milk

Place 1/2 the bacon strips in the bottom of a pastry lined pie pan. Carefully break each egg, keeping yolk whole, into cup. Slip, one at a time, on top of bacon. Sprinkle with salt, pepper, parsley and chives. Top with remaining bacon slices. Spoon 1/2 cup mushroom soup in small dots over top. Cover with top crust, flute edges and cut steam vents. Bake at 425° for 30 minutes, or until lightly browned. Cut in wedges and serve hot with mushroom sauce made by combining remaining mushroom soup with milk and heating. Yield: 6 servings.

Kitchen Sampler

Breakfast Ambrosia

This is a delightful way to start the day. This recipe keeps for about a week in the refrigerator.

2 cups oranges, peeled, sectioned,
    (all the white and seeds removed),
    cut into bite-size portions
1 (8-ounce) can pineapple chunks
    (save juice)

1 small can mandarin oranges
1 banana, sliced
2 tablespoons coconut
1 teaspoon vanilla extract
1 cup plain or vanilla yogurt

Mix all together; cover; refrigerate until serving time.

When You Can't Cook

Tramp Eggs

Back during the Depression, those lean, grey years stretching from 1929 through the late 1930's, tramps came often to our house to ask for a meal.

Mother never turned one away; whatever we had to eat, she shared with the shabby strangers who stopped at our kitchen door.

A favorite Sunday breakfast dish at our house was eggs baked in a casserole with rich milk, dabs of butter and generous sprinkles of grated cheese. We were having this breakfast one Sunday when a hungry tramp appeared at the back door. As always, Mother fixed him a plate, including a generous serving of the eggs.

We thought he had eaten and gone (tramps usually put their empty plates on the back porch and left hurriedly after they'd eaten, possibly wishing to avoid any involvement with the wood pile near the back gate) when we heard him knock at the door again.

Mother went to see what he wanted. "Lady," he said as he handed her the empty plate, "Would you please give me the recipe for those eggs? They're the best I ever ate!"

So ever since then, our Sunday morning eggs have been called Tramp Eggs. The recipe follows.

1 egg per person   **Butter**
Salt   **Grated Cheddar cheese**
Milk

Butter a shallow baking dish and break into it the number of eggs needed to serve the eaters. Sprinkle salt on the eggs and pour milk around them until the yellow tops are peeping out. Dot with dabs of butter. Grate cheese over the top. Bake in a slow oven (300°) until cheese is bubbly and eggs are of desired doneness. Serve atop crisp toast or in a nest of grits.

Treasured Alabama Recipes

Instructor's Salary Sandwich

2 tablespoons butter or margarine
2 tablespoons all-purpose flour
1/4 teaspoon salt
Dash freshly ground pepper
1 cup milk
1 slightly beaten egg
3/4 cup (3-ounces) shredded
   natural Cheddar cheese

1 tablespoon lemon juice
1 (10-ounce) package frozen
   broccoli, cooked and drained
6 slices white bread, toasted or
   English muffins
6 slices bacon, crisp-cooked,
   drained, and crumbled

In saucepan, melt butter or margarine; blend in flour, salt, and pepper. Add milk all at once. Cook and stir till mixture thickens and bubbles. Stir a moderate amount of hot mixture into egg. Return from heat. Stir in cheese and lemon juice, stirring to melt cheese. Arrange cooked broccoli on split English muffins or toast, spoon lemon-sauce over. Garnish with bacon. Makes 6 sandwiches. This is a great luncheon dish served with fruit salad.

Auburn Entertains

Spinach Sandwiches

1 package frozen spinach, cooked,
  drained well
1/2 cup dehydrated onion chips
1/4 cup dried parsley, chopped
  or fresh
1 pint Hellman's mayonnaise

1 tablespoon lemon juice
1 teaspoon Tabasco
1 (3-ounce) cream cheese
1 1/2 loaves very thin sliced
  white bread

Mix thoroughly; let stand overnight. Spread on thin sliced bread, crusts removed. Slice diagonally. These are especially good for parties or to take to the beach. Serve with a cool summer salad.

Try Me

Watercress Sandwiches

Watercress
Salt and pepper
Few drops vinegar

Cottage cheese
White bread

Wash watercress and chop coarsely. Season with salt, pepper, and a few drops of vinegar. Blend with cottage cheese and spread between slices of white bread.

Heirlooms From the Kitchen

Grated Carrot Sandwiches

2 (8-ounce) packages cream cheese
4 small carrots, grated fine
1/2 cup chopped pecans
1 tablespoon onion juice

Salt
Pepper
Mayonnaise
Brown bread

In mixer, cream the cheese and add grated carrots, onion juice, salt and pepper and enough mayonnaise to moisten. Add pecans. Trim bread. Spread filling and roll like jelly roll. Chill or freeze before slicing. Freezes well. Excellent tea sandwiches.

Eufaula's Favorite Recipes

Pimento Cheese

1/2 pound sharp Cheddar cheese	1 ounce pimentos, finely chopped
1/2 cup Kraft mayonnaise	1 tablespoon sweet pickle,
1/2 teaspoon salt	chopped
2 dashes Accent	1/4 teaspoon garlic or
1 tablespoon sugar	onion salt

Allow cheese to reach room temperature. Cream grated cheese in electric mixer, adding mayonnaise until soft and fluffy. Then add salt, Accent, sugar. Mix well. Add pickles and garlic salt. Very important to beat in electric mixer much longer than you think necessary to make smooth and fluffy. Refrigerate. Makes about 1 pint.

If you think pimento cheese is a spread you buy at the grocery in a plastic carton with dear Mrs. Doe's name on top, please think again. Then whip up a batch of Mrs. McCrary's. She advises that for family, you use very little garlic salt (if any)--but that you pour on the garlic for parties.

Cotton Country Cooking

Salads

The Winged Victory statue, one of many works of art found at Jasmine Hill Gardens and Outdoor Museum. North of Montgomery.

Asparagus with French Mustard Dressing

Steam asparagus in 1/2 cup boiling water for about 12 minutes or until tender. Remove and pat dry.

FRENCH MUSTARD DRESSING:

2 tablespoons Dijon-style mustard	**3 tablespoons red-wine**
1 teaspoon salt	**vinegar**
Pepper to taste	**1/2 cup olive oil**

In a bowl combine mustard, salt, and pepper. Stir in red-wine vinegar. Add olive oil in a stream, beating, and continue to beat until the dressing is well combined. Yield: about 3/4 cup.

The Alabama Heritage Cookbook

Oriental Salad

1 can bean sprouts, drained
Ice water
1 bunch spinach
1 head lettuce
1 can water chestnuts, drained
   and sliced

1 can chow mein noodles
4 hard boiled eggs, sliced
1/2 pound bacon, crumbled

Soak bean sprouts 30 minutes in ice water and drain. Then mix all other ingredients together. Yields 12 servings.

DRESSING FOR ORIENTAL SALAD:
1/3 cup white vinegar
1 cup corn oil
3/4 cup sugar
1 teaspoon salt

1 teaspoon Worcestershire sauce
1 bunch green onions,
   finely chopped

Combine above ingredients in blender and blend until creamy. Yields 12 servings.

The Great Cookbook

Marinated Artichoke

1 green pepper, sliced thin
1 small onion, sliced thin
1 (8 1/2-ounce) can artichoke
   hearts, drained and cut up
1/2 cup diced celery
1 cucumber unpeeled, sliced thin
1 cup mozzarella cheese, cubed
1/2 pound fresh mushrooms, sliced

1 teaspoon salt
1/4 teaspoon pepper
1/4 teaspoon dill seed
3/4 cup salad oil
1/4 cup cider vinegar
1/4 teaspoon garlic salt
1 tablespoon Dijon mustard
1 tablespoon Parmesan cheese

Combine first 7 ingredients in bowl. Combine remaining 8 ingredients in jar and shake well. Yields about 1 cup. Pour over vegetables, marinate for 4 hours or longer. When ready to serve, drain and put on bed of lettuce. Sprinkle crumbled bacon on top.

Hint: Serve as salad with entrée or as an appetizer.

Kitchen Sampler

Avocado Ring Salad

1 (3-ounce) package lemon Jello
1 cup hot water
3 tablespoons lemon juice
1/2 teaspoon salt
1/2 cup mayonnaise

1 cup avocado, mashed
1/2 pint whipping cream,
  whipped
Grapefruit sections
French dressing

Pour hot water over lemon Jello. Add lemon juice and salt. Set aside to cool and when it is slightly congealed, whip it with a rotary beater. Add mayonnaise, avocado and whipped cream. Put in ring mold to congeal. Marinate grapefruit sections (entirely free from membrane) in French dressing. Drain the sections and heap in center of molded ring. Garnish with lettuce.

Old Mobile Recipes

Brussels Sprout Salad

1 box fresh Brussels sprouts
1 cup mayonnaise
2 tablespoons lemon juice
2 teaspoons grated onion

2 teaspoons sugar
1 teaspoon curry powder
Orange slices, halved

Cook sprouts in salted water to cover for 6 minutes. Drain and refrigerate. Mix mayonnaise, lemon juice, onion, sugar and curry powder. Add sprouts and toss. Let stand at least 2 hours. To serve, surround sprouts on a platter with orange slices. May also be used as an hors d'oeuvre, served with toothpicks.

Loaves and Fishes

The Appalachian Mountain chain originates in Alabama, forming the front side of Lookout Mountain in the northeast part of the state.

Creamy Broccoli and Cauliflower Salad

VEGETABLE MIX:

1 (2-ounce) jar pimiento, drained
  and chopped
1 bunch broccoli flowerets
1 head cauliflower flowerets

2 hard-cooked eggs, chopped
20 ripe olives, sliced
1 small onion, sliced

Combine all ingredients in a large bowl. Pour dressing over vegetables and toss to coat. Refrigerate overnight.

DRESSING:

1 cup mayonnaise
1 (8-ounce) carton sour cream
1 teaspoon parsley flakes

1 teaspoon dill weed
1 teaspoon onion salt
1 teaspoon Beau Monde

Combine ingredients. Mix well and set aside.
Yield: 12 servings.

Cooks and Company

Layered Salad

1/2 head of lettuce
1 cup diced celery
4 boiled eggs, chopped
1 can English peas

1/2 cup diced bell pepper
1 small onion
Bacon bits

Place in large bowl in layers as listed above; repeat until all ingredients are used.

TOPPING:

2 cups mayonnaise
2 tablespoons sugar

Shredded Cheddar cheese

Spread mayonnaise over top and sprinkle with sugar and cheese. Set overnight.

Calling All Cooks

Ritz Cracker Slaw
"Try this flavorful slaw stuffed in a tomato."

1 medium cabbage, grated	2 tablespoons pickle relish
1 medium onion, chopped finely	2 cups mayonnaise
2/3 cup celery, chopped	4 tablespoons mustard
2/3 cup bell pepper, chopped	Salt and pepper to taste
2 packages Ritz crackers, crushed	1 cup sharp cheese, grated
(2 out of 3 stack-box)	

Grate or chop cabbage; chop onion, celery and bell pepper. Crush crackers. Mix all ingredients together except cheese. Place grated cheese on top of slaw. Chill. Serves 12-15.

When Dinnerbells Ring

Stay Crisp Salad

8 cups shredded cabbage (use knife)
2 carrots (shredded or grated)
1 green pepper cut in thin strips
1/2 cup chopped onion
3/4 cup cold water
1 envelope unflavored gelatin

2/3 cup sugar
2/3 cup vinegar
2 teaspoons celery seed
1 1/2 teaspoons salt
1/4 teaspoon pepper
2/3 cup salad oil

Mix cabbage, carrots, green pepper and onion; sprinkle with 1/2 cup cold water--chill. Soften gelatin in 1/4 cup cold water. Mix sugar, vinegar, celery seed, salt and pepper in saucepan; bring to boil. Stir in softened gelatin. Cool until slightly thickened. Beat well. Gradually beat in salad oil. Drain vegetables; pour dressing over top. Mix lightly until well coated. May be served immediately or stored in refrigerator. Toss before serving. Serves 8.

Guaranteed to live up to its name, this slaw brought cheers from all who tasted it. It is unusually delicious!

Cotton Country Cooking

Sweet and Sour Slaw

1 large cabbage, shredded
3 stalks celery, chopped
1 bell pepper, chopped
1 (4-ounce) jar pimiento, chopped
1 large red onion, shredded
1/2 cup red wine vinegar

1/2 cup white vinegar
3/4 cup sugar
1 1/2 teaspoons salt
3/4 cup salad oil
Coarsely ground black pepper

Layer cabbage, celery, bell pepper, pimiento, and onion in bowl. Boil vinegar, sugar, and salt for 2 minutes. Remove from heat; add salad oil and coarsely ground black pepper; return to heat and bring to a boil. Pour over vegetables while hot. Cover tightly. Refrigerate overnight. If refrigerated, this will keep indefinitely. Serves 10-12.

When Dinnerbells Ring

"Daughter-in-law" Potato Salad

4 cups diced, cooked potatoes	1/2 cup chopped celery
2 hard-cooked eggs	Diced pimiento (optional)
1/2 cup chopped pickle or salad cubes	1/4 cup chopped green pepper
	Salt and pepper to taste
1/4 cup minced green onion or mild white onion	Mayonnaise
	Prepared mustard

A secret to a good potato salad is to add the mayonnaise, salt, and pepper to the potatoes while they are still hot and will absorb the flavors. Add a small amount of mustard to the mayonnaise to give a nice color. Add remaining ingredients and toss lightly with 2 forks until coated with mayonnaise. Yield: about 8 servings.

At the Thomas Reunion, this is made in much larger amounts and is referred to as "Daughter-in-law" salad because the task generally falls to some of the daughters-in-law!

Family Secrets

Aunt Sadie's Potato Salad

1 head cabbage - green or red or mixed (shredded)	Onions - in rings (about 3)
	Green peppers - in rings (about 3)
10 potatoes (boiled in jackets, peeled and sliced)	Hard boiled eggs - sliced
Salt and pepper (on each layer of potatoes)	1 quart jar mayonnaise or salad dressing
	Paprika - for decorating top of salad
Celery seed	

Begin with layer of shredded cabbage in bowl. Add layer of sliced potatoes. Salt and pepper, and sprinkle with celery seed. Add onion rings and pepper rings (your own preference for onion and pepper will determine how much to use. Men love lots of onion!) Add sliced eggs and then spread mayonnaise over all. Be sure to use enough to cover mixture. This is the magical ingredient. Now start all over and add as many layers as needed, ending with mayonnaise and eggs. The above amount will serve about 10. This mixture must be refrigerated at least 24 hours before serving.

A Decatur favorite, Aunt Sadie's Potato Salad never fails to be a crowd pleaser. Watch the men -- they sometimes even go for thirds!

Cotton Country Cooking

70

Molded Gazpacho

3 envelopes gelatin	2 large tomatoes, chopped
3 cups V-8 juice	and drained
1/4 cup tarragon vinegar	1 medium onion, finely chopped
1 clove garlic, crushed	1/4 cup pimento chopped
2 teaspoons salt	1 large cucumber, chopped
1/4 teaspoon pepper	and drained
Dash of Tabasco	

DRESSING:

1/2 cup sour cream	1/3 cup mayonnaise
1/2 teaspoon salt	2 teaspoons horseradish

Heat 1 cup V-8 juice with the gelatin until completely dissolved. Add remaining juice, vinegar, garlic, 2 teaspoons salt, pepper and Tabasco. Cool mixture, then add tomatoes, onion, green pepper, cucumber, pimento and pour into a 6-cup mold that has been sprayed with Pam. Chill until set. Unmold on salad greens and top with dressing, or serve dressing on the side. Serves 8.

Auburn Entertains

Tomato Aspic

Chili sauce gives this salad a delicious flavor.
Great with or without the shrimp.

1 (12-ounce) bottle Heinz chili sauce	Pinch of salt
2 tablespoons plain gelatin	1/2 cup chopped celery
1/2 cup cold water	1/2 cup sliced olives
1/2 cup boiling water	1 pound shrimp, boiled (optional)
Dash of Tabasco	

Pour chili sauce and same bottle filled with water into a bowl. Soften gelatin in cold water; dissolve in boiling water. Cool. Add gelatin and rest of ingredients to chili sauce. Pour into 8 individual molds.

Cookbook

Easy Tomato Aspic

1 (14 1/2-ounce) can Del Monte	1 box lemon Jello
stewed tomatoes	1/4 cup chopped olives

Heat stewed tomatoes. Add Jello. Stir until thoroughly dissolved. Add chopped olives, pour into molds, and chill until congealed. Serves 6.

Florence Cook Book

Dill and Roquefort Green Bean Salad

DILL DRESSING:

1 cup vegetable oil
1/4 cup white vinegar
3 tablespoons lemon juice
1/2 teaspoon cracked black
  pepper

1 tablespoon dill seed
1/4 teaspoon paprika
1/2 teaspoon dry mustard
1 or 2 garlic cloves

THE DAY BEFORE:

Put all ingredients in a jar and shake well. Refrigerate. Makes 1 1/2 cups.

SALAD:

2 pounds green beans or 4 cans
  cut Blue Lake beans
Ham hock
1 onion

Lawry's seasoning salt
Salt and pepper to taste
1 clove garlic

THE DAY BEFORE:

Cook beans with all the seasonings in a small amount of water. When tender, drain and cool. This is important for a well flavored dish.

THE DAY OF SERVING:

1/2 pound bacon
1 bunch green onions, chopped
1/4 pound Roquefort or bleu
  cheese, crumbled

1/4 cup Dill Dressing
1/4 cup Hellman's mayonnaise
2 tablespoons sour cream

Fry bacon until crisp. Crumble. Mix the drained beans with onions, 1/2 of the crumbled bacon and remaining ingredients. Chill several hours. Garnish top with remaining bacon. Serves 8.

Twickenham Tables

The Huntsville Herb Society's Annual Herb Fair offers for sale herb plants, jelly, mixes, potpourris, sachets, vinegars, and herb wreaths.

Steak Salad

2 1/2 pounds beef tenderloin
1 (8-ounce) package mushrooms, sliced
1/2 cup chopped green onion
1 (8-ounce) can artichoke hearts
1 cup sliced celery

1 package Good Seasons Old Fashioned French Salad Dressing
1 teaspoon dill weed
1 pint cherry tomatoes
Green leafy and Iceberg lettuce

Cook whole tenderloin until medium rare. Let stand 1 hour or until cool, then slice into bite-sized strips. Prepare salad dressing according to package directions, adding dill weed. Marinate mushrooms, onions, artichoke hearts, and celery in dressing. Using large salad bowl, layer lettuces, tomatoes, marinated ingredients and meat, making 2 or more layers ending with meat. Pour remaining dressing over all. No need to toss, just serve. May be prepared ahead.

Magic

Creamy Cucumber Salad

2 cups cucumbers (peeled, shredded, drained thoroughly (press out liquid with a spoon)
3/4 cup boiling water
1 (3-ounce) package lime gelatin

3 tablespoons vinegar
1/2 cup sour cream
1 teaspoon onion juice
1/2 cup mayonnaise

Pour boiling water over gelatin; stir until gelatin is dissolved. Stir in vinegar, sour cream, onion juice, and mayonnaise. Add cucumbers. Pour into 4 or 5-cup mold. Chill in refrigerator until firm. Cover. This can be served as soon as firm, or can be done the night before, but it should not be kept longer than 24 hours.

Gazebo I Cookbook

Rice Artichoke Salad

1 1/3 cups rice
4 cups chicken broth
4 green onions, chopped
1 jar marinated artichokes, drained
   and chopped

16 stuffed green olives, chopped
1 bell pepper, chopped
1/2 teaspoon curry powder
2/3 cup mayonnaise
Salt and pepper to taste

Cook rice in chicken broth. Cool and add remaining ingredients, mix well. Put in oiled mold and chill. To serve, unmold on a bed of lettuce.

Hallmark's Collection of Home Tested Recipes

Hot German Rice Salad

3 cups water
1 1/2 cups uncooked rice
1 1/2 teaspoons salt
8 strips of bacon
3/4 - 1 cup sugar
1 cup apple cider vinegar
Black pepper
3 hard boiled eggs, sliced

2 tablespoons flour
3 tablespoons water
1 teaspoon celery seed
3 tablespoons chopped onion
1/4 cup chopped bell pepper
1/4 cup diced celery
1/4 cup diced pimento

Cook rice barely done. Cook bacon until crisp. Make gravy from bacon drippings, flour, vinegar, sugar, salt and pepper. Bring to boil; pour over all ingredients, reserving eggs for garnish.

Sumpthn' Yummy

Crab Rice Salad

1 pound crab meat
1 (6-ounce) can English peas
2 tablespoons oil
1 1/2 teaspoons lemon juice
3 cups cooked rice

3/4 cup plain yogurt
1/8 teaspoon hot pepper sauce
Salt
White pepper
1/2 teaspoon powdered onion

Combine all ingredients and keep refrigerated. Serve on a bed of lettuce. Garnish with lemon wedges. Yield: 12 (1/2 cup) servings.

Cooks and Company

Cold Pasta Salad

2 cups pasta (cooked and drained)	**Freshly ground black pepper**
3 tablespoons vinegar	**1/2 cup cut-up green pepper**
2 tablespoons olive oil (no substitute)	**1/2 cup garbanzos (chickpeas)**
2 tablespoons chopped chives	**Large cut-up tomato**
1/4 teaspoon oregano	**1/2 cup sliced black olives**
Pinch basil	**2 or 3 tablespoons sour cream**
Salt to taste	

Toss pasta (I use the twisted kind) with vinegar and olive oil. Chill well. Then add rest of ingredients. Toss and chill so that flavors mingle.

This is best when made the day before it is needed.

Heavenly Hostess

Chicken Salad in Raspberry Ring

2 cups cubed cooked or canned
  chicken
1 teaspoon salt
2 hard cooked eggs

3/4 cups sliced celery
1 teaspoon lemon juice
1/2 cup Creamy Mayonnaise

Lightly toss ingredients together. Chill. Serve in Raspberry Ring.

RASPBERRY RING:

3 (10-ounce) packages frozen red
  raspberries
2 envelopes plain gelatin
1/2 cup lemon juice

1 1/4 cups boiling water
3/4 cup sugar
1/4 teaspoon salt
3/4 cup cantaloupe balls

Thaw raspberries. Drain, reserving 2 cups syrup (use berries for garnish). Soften gelatin in lemon juice. Dissolve in boiling water. Stir in sugar, salt, and reserved raspberry syrup. Chill til partially set. Add cantaloupe balls. Pour into 5-cup ring mold. Chill til firm. Pass additional mayonnaise.

CREAMY MAYONNAISE:

Combine 1 cup mayonnaise and 1/2 cup heavy cream whipped. Makes 1 2/3 cups.

    Serve this on a large silver platter surrounded with fruit. So pretty.

Old Mobile Recipes

Crunchy Hot Chicken Salad

3 cups diced cooked chicken	1/2 teaspoon salt
1 cup finely chopped celery	1/4 teaspoon pepper
2 teaspoons chopped onion	3/4 cup mayonnaise
1/2 cup sliced almonds	1/4 cup water
1 (10 3/4-ounce) can cream of	3 hard-cooked eggs, sliced
chicken soup, undiluted	2 cups crushed potato chips
1 1/2 cups cooked rice	3/4 cup shredded Cheddar cheese
1 tablespoon lemon juice	

Combine first 9 ingredients; toss gently and set aside. Combine mayonnaise and water; beat with a wire whisk until smooth. Pour over chicken mixture; stir well. Add eggs, and toss gently. Spoon into a greased 2-quart shallow baking dish; cover and refrigerate 8 hours or overnight.

Bake at 450° for 10-15 minutes or until thoroughly heated. Sprinkle with potato chips and cheese; bake an additional 5 minutes. Yield: 6-8 servings.

Treasured Taste

Cheese Puffs with Chicken Salad

2 tablespoons butter	Dash of salt
1/4 cup boiling water	1 egg
1/4 cup all-purpose flour	1/4 cup shredded Swiss cheese

Melt butter in boiling water. Add 1/4 cup flour and a dash of salt. Stir rapidly until mixture leaves sides of pan and forms a ball that does not separate. Remove from heat and cool slightly. Add egg and beat until smooth. Stir in shredded cheese. Drop from a teaspoon onto a greased baking sheet and bake in a 400° oven for 20 minutes. Cool and split. Fill with chicken salad. Unfilled puffs may be kept in freezer.

PARTY CHICKEN SALAD:

2 cups chopped, cooked chicken	1/4 cup mayonnaise
1/4 cup minced celery	1/2 teaspoon salt
2 tablespoons minced green onion	Dash of pepper
2 tablespoons minced pimiento	1/4 teaspoon lemon juice
2 tablespoons white wine	1/4 cup sliced almonds

Mix chicken with celery, green onion, pimiento, wine, mayonnaise, salt, pepper, lemon juice, and sliced almonds. Fill puffs with chicken salad.

The Alabama Heritage Cookbook

Curry Chicken Salad

5 whole chicken breasts
2 stalks celery, chopped
2 teaspoons onion, grated
1/2 cup seedless grapes, halved
1/3 cup toasted almonds
1 heaping teaspoon curry powder

1 cup mayonnaise
1/3 cup sour cream
Salt and pepper (white
    preferably) to taste
Lettuce
Tomato wedges

Cook chicken until tender; debone and cut into large chunks. Add celery, onion, grapes, and almonds; toss together. Combine curry powder, mayonnaise, and sour cream; salt and pepper to taste. Add mayonnaise mixture to chicken mixture; mix thoroughly. Chill and serve on lettuce with tomato wedges. Yield: 6 servings.

Once Upon a Stove

One More Tuna Salad

2 (6 1/2-ounce) cans tuna, drained
2 tablespoons lemon juice
1 teaspoon Worcestershire sauce
1/2 cup Vidalia onion, chopped
    (if you can't get Vidalia onion,
    get some sweet, mild onion)

1/2 cup plain yogurt
1 (14-ounce) can artichoke hearts,
    drained
1 cup water chestnuts, sliced
Hollandaise sauce to hold together
1 tablespoon sweet pickle relish

Gently mix together, using as much hollandaise sauce as you need to hold the salad together. Buy hollandaise in the jar; make it from a dry mix; or make your own. Chill until serving time or serve immediately at room temperature.

When You Can't Cook

West Indies Salad

1 medium onion, chopped fine
1 pound fresh lump crabmeat
4 ounces Wesson oil

3 ounces cider vinegar
4 ounces ice water
Salt and pepper

Spread half of onion over bottom of large bowl. Cover with separate crab lumps and then remaining onion. Salt and pepper. Pour oil, vinegar, ice water over all. Cover and marinate for 2 to 12 hours. Toss lightly before serving.

Recipe Jubilee!

Shrimp and Caper Salad

2 pounds shrimp, peeled and
  deveined
Liquid crab boil
2 tablespoons fresh lemon juice
3/4 cup green onions, chopped
1 1/2 cups celery, chopped

3 tablespoons capers, drained
1 cup black olives, sliced
1/2 cup oil and vinegar salad
  dressing
3/4 cup mayonnaise
1 tablespoon celery seed

Boil shrimp, using liquid crab boil and lemon juice. Drain shrimp, discarding liquid. Combine all ingredients and chill. This is better if made the night before. Serve on crisp salad greens and garnish with tomato wedges and hard cooked egg wedges. Serves 6.

One of a Kind

Fresh Cranberry Salad

2 cups fresh cranberries, washed and picked	2 packages Knox plain gelatin
1 orange, washed and seeded	2 tablespoons sugar
1 cup sugar	1 cup hot water
1 small can crushed pineapple, juice and all	Juice of 1 lemon
	1 cup pecans, chopped

Run cranberries and entire orange (peel and all) through a meat chopper (or chop in food processor). Add 1 cup sugar. Let stand for 2 hours. Soften gelatin and 2 tablespoons sugar in 3 tablespoons cold water. Add the rest of the water, boiling to soften gelatin. Add pineapple, lemon juice, and pecans to cranberry mixture. Then add gelatin. Refrigerate in greased salad mold.

PINEAPPLE SALAD DRESSING:

1 (6-ounce) can pineapple juice	3/4 cup sugar
2 eggs, separated	2 tablespoons butter
1 tablespoon flour	

Heat juice. Blend together egg yolks, sugar, and flour. Add juice. Stir in a double boiler until thick. Remove from heat and blend in the butter. Beat egg whites until they hold soft peaks. Fold into the egg yolk mixture. Chill and serve with Fresh Cranberry Salad.

The Alabama Heritage Cookbook

Christmas Salad

1 tablespoon gelatin	2 orange-grind peel, separate sections
2 (3-ounce) packages Jello, any flavor	1 small can crushed pineapple
3 cups water (boiling)	1/2 cup (or more) chopped pecans
1 can whole cranberry sauce	Pinch of salt

Soak gelatin in small amount of cold water. Dissolve Jello and gelatin in boiling water and cool. Add remaining ingredients. Mold in small pointed paper drinking cups. Stand each cup in orange juice glass. Unmold on lettuce and decorate with whipped cream.

Old Mobile Recipes

Apricot Salad
A favorite at W.O.C. luncheons.

2 (16-ounce) cans apricot halves
1 (3-ounce) box orange gelatin
1 (3-ounce) box lemon gelatin
1 tablespoon plain gelatin
1 (6-ounce) can frozen orange juice
2 tablespoons lemon juice

Dash of salt
1 cup lemon-lime carbonated
  drink
Avocado and pineapple slices
  (optional)

Drain apricots, reserving juice. Purée apricots in blender. Bring 1 1/2 cups reserved juice to a boil. Add gelatins and mix until dissolved. Add orange juice, lemon juice and salt. Then add puréed apricots. Pour carbonated drink slowly down side of bowl into mixture; stir gently. Pour into 2-quart mold or 2 smaller molds. Refrigerate until congealed. Garnish with avocado and pineapple slices. Serves 12.

Cookbook

Blueberry Salad I

3 packages raspberry Jello   1 large can crushed pineapple
3 cups hot water   1 can blueberries

Dissolve Jello in hot water. Drain pineapple and blueberries, reserving juice. Add enough water to juice to make 3 cups. Add water mixture to dissolved Jello. Reserve 2 cups of juice and Jello mixture for topping. Add fruit to the 4 cups of Jello and juice.

TOPPING:
1 (8-ounce) package cream cheese   1 large carton Cool Whip
2 cups Jello mixture

Combine. Let Jello congeal a little before adding the topping.

More Fiddling With Food

Pickled Peach Salad

1 jar pickled peaches   Juice of 1 lemon
1 1/2 packages lemon gelatin   Pinch of salt
1/2 cup water   1 jar white cherries, drained
1/2 cup orange juice   1 cup chopped pecans

Drain peaches, saving 1 cup juice. Heat juice and dissolve gelatin. Add water, orange juice and lemon juice. Add fruit which has been cut up, then add nuts. Put in ring mold and chill. Optional: Soak fruit in sherry for several hours before making salad. Serves 10.

Huntsville Heritage Cookbook

 The Mound State Monument, which includes 317 acres on the Black Warrior River, used to be a large, powerful Southeastern Indian community.

Fruit-Horseradish Salad

1 package lime-flavored gelatin	3 tablespoons horseradish
1 package lemon-flavored gelatin	1 cup mayonnaise
1 (20-ounce) can crushed pineapple	1 carton creamed cottage cheese
3 tablespoons chopped pimento	1/2 cup chopped nuts

Dissolve gelatins in 2 cups boiling water. Cool. Add pineapple, pimento, horseradish, cottage cheese, nuts, and mayonnaise. Mix well and mold.

Kitchen Sampler

Frozen Salad

1 (8-ounce) package cream cheese
1/2 pint sour cream
1/2 cup sugar
1/4 teaspoon salt
1 can Bing cherries, drained
1 (11-ounce) can mandarin oranges,
    drained

1 (8-ounce) can crushed pineapple,
    drained
2 cups miniature marshmallows
1/2 cup pecans, chopped

Beat cream cheese until fluffy. Add sour cream, sugar and salt. Mix together all other ingredients with cream cheese mixture.

Pour into individual paper baking cups or casserole dish. Freeze at least 6 hours or overnight.

Cooks and Company

Winter Peaches

Canned peach halves   Mincemeat

Lay drained peach halves on broiler pan. Spoon a tablespoon or two of mincemeat in the center of each peach half. Heat in oven briefly, just until warm. Allow 1 or 2 per person.

These make an easy salad for a luncheon or a pretty garnish to accompany meat. The addition of a little butter, rum or brandy makes the peaches special.

Family Secrets

Poppy Seed Dressing

3 tablespoons dry mustard
1 1/2 teaspoons salt
2 cups sugar
1 cup vinegar

2 tablespoons grated onion
3 cups Wesson oil
1/2 box (3 teaspoons)
    Poppy seed

Mix mustard, salt, sugar and vinegar and beat well. Add slowly 1 tablespoon at a time the Wesson oil. When thick, add grated onion and poppy seed. Will keep. This recipe can be halved or quartered, and is delicious.

Ole Mobile Recipes

Horseradish Dressing

1 cup mayonnaise	4 teaspoons undrained horseradish
1/2 cup sour cream	2 pods garlic, pressed
1/4 teaspoon dry mustard	2 teaspoons chives

Put in blender. Then add two teaspoons chives and refrigerate. Serve on frozen tomato salad or fried shrimp.

Recipe Jubilee!

French Dressing

Shake 2 buds garlic with the following ingredients:

1/2 cup sugar	1/2 cup tomato catsup
1 teaspoon mustard	1 teaspoon salt
1 tablespoon Worcestershire sauce	1/2 onion, grated
1 cup salad oil	1/4 cup lemon juice
1 teaspoon black pepper	

Mix thoroughly, remove garlic buds. Store in a jar in refrigerator.

Florence Cook Book

Thousand Island Dressing

1 1/2 cups mayonnaise	1 teaspoon sweet pickle relish
1/2 cup chili sauce	Worcestershire sauce
2 tablespoons catsup	

Combine all ingredients until well blended. Yield: 2 1/2 cups.

Dining Under the Magnolia

Curry Mayonnaise

1 egg, room temperature	1 small clove garlic, crushed
5 teaspoons lemon juice	1/4 teaspoon salt
1 1/2 teaspoons curry powder	1/4 teaspoon pepper
1 teaspoon Dijon mustard	3/4 cup oil

In a food processor or blender on high, blend egg, lemon juice, curry powder, mustard, garlic, salt and pepper. Then add oil in a stream, blending while adding. Serve the sauce with meat, poultry, fish or vegetables. Yield: 1 cup.

One of a Kind

Soups

Alabama's Capitol. Montgomery.

Curried Zucchini Soup

5 - 6 zucchini	1 1/2 teaspoons curry powder
1 large onion, thinly sliced	3 cans chicken broth
(1 cup) or 1 bunch green onions,	1 1/2 cups half-and-half
sliced	Salt and white pepper to taste

Rinse zucchini and pat dry. Trim ends. Cut half of 1 zucchini into thin matchsticks, blanch, and set aside. Slice remaining zucchini and place in pan. Add onion and sprinkle with curry, stirring to coat pieces. Add broth; boil and simmer covered, 45 minutes. Spoon into blender and purée. Add half-and-half, salt and pepper. Add reserved zucchini strips, chill and serve. Serves 8.

Magic

Cream of Broccoli Soup

1 bunch broccoli, trimmed	1 cup milk
1/2 cup butter	Salt and pepper
1 1/2 cups chicken broth	1/2 teaspoon cumin
1 cup flour	

Wash broccoli, and cut into bite-size pieces. Melt butter in a medium-size saucepan. Cook broccoli until just tender in boiling chicken broth in a medium-size boiler. Add flour to butter; whisk, stirring constantly, for 3 minutes. Slowly add broth and broccoli to cooked roux, should be thick, thin out with milk and add seasonings to taste. Serve hot. Yield: 4 servings.

Dining Under the Magnolia

Cauliflower Soup

1 cauliflower	Salt
1 medium onion, chopped	1 teaspoon pepper, black
1 cup dry rice	or white
1 tablespoon parsley	1 cup shrimp, boiled
1 pinch curry	2/3 cup half-and-half scalded
1/2 stick butter	

Parboil cauliflower in 2 quarts water with salt and pepper. Remove cauliflower. Add next four ingredients to water. Cook 25 minutes. Put cauliflower back in soup in lumps. Add sprimp. Turn heat off and add half-and-half that has been scalded. Serve immediately. Serves 6.

Try Me

Cream of Wild Rice Soup

1/2 cup wild rice	1/2 teaspoon dried basil
1 (10 3/4-ounce) can condensed	1 (4-ounce) can sliced mushrooms,
chicken broth	drained
1 cup water	1/4 cup snipped parsley (optional)
1/4 cup chopped onion	2 cups light cream or milk
1/4 cup shredded carrot	1 tablespoon flour
1 small bay leaf	

Rinse rice. In a 3-quart saucepan combine rice, broth, water, onion, carrot, bay leaf, and basil. Bring to a boil; reduce heat. Cover and simmer 45 minutes. Remove bay leaf. Add mushrooms and parsley. Stir cream or milk into flour; add to soup. Cook and stir mixture till thick and bubbly. Season to taste with pepper. Makes 4 servings.

Twickenham Tables

 Alabama's rich black heritage is celebrated in a number of annual events, including a Martin Luther King, Jr. Pilgrimage, a seven-day tour of historic sites, the W.C. Handy Music Festival, and the African Extravaganza.

Black Belt Butterbean Soup

2 cups shelled fresh butterbeans
2 tablespoons butter
2 tablespoons flour
1 cup scalded milk

1 tablespoons onion juice
2 cups chicken stock or chicken
  consommé
Salt and pepper to taste

Cook butterbeans in salted water until tender. Drain and put through colander. Melt butter in heavy skillet, stir in flour and add scalded milk, stirring constantly. Add stock or consommé and blend until smooth. Combine with prepared beans and add onion juice and seasonings. Heat and combine well. Sprinkle each serving with paprika. A pat of butter may also be added to each bowl of soup, if desired.

Treasured Alabama Recipes

Black Bean Soup

2 cups black beans
5 cups water
1 meaty ham hock with skin
3/4 cup olive oil
1 large onion, chopped
2 bell peppers, chopped

2 pods (not cloves) garlic,
  crushed
4 tablespoons salt
1/3 cup wine vinegar
Yellow rice
Chopped purple onions

Soak beans in water overnight. Do not use aluminum container. Next morning, using the same water, add next 7 ingredients. Pour into heavy pot; bring to a boil . Cook covered over low heat until beans are tender and liquid is thick (several hours). Remove meat from bones; cut into bite size pieces and return to soup. One-half hour before serving, add the wine vinegar. Cook yellow rice according to directions. Serve soup over rice. Season with olive oil and wine vinegar to suit taste. Sprinkle generously with chopped onions. Serve with Cuban bread.

Sumpthn' Yummy

Onion Soup

3 onions, sliced thinly
1/4 cup margarine
2 (10 1/2-ounce) cans beef broth
1 cup hot water
1/2 cup dry white wine

1/8 teaspoon cayenne pepper
1/4 teaspoon black pepper
6 slices French bread
1 cup muenster cheese, shredded

Slice onions in bowl with margarine. Cover with stretch plastic wrap, vent and cook 10 minutes on HIGH. Add beef broth, hot water, wine, peppers, and stir. Cook on HIGH again for 10 minutes, covered. Serve in individual bowls, top with French bread, then cheese, and serve. The heat of the soup will melt the cheese.

Kitchen Sampler

Peanut Soup

1 medium onion, chopped
1 cup celery, chopped
1/2 cup butter
2 tablespoons flour
2 quarts chicken broth

1 cup creamy peanut butter
1 cup half-and-half cream
1/4 cup chopped parsley
1/4 cup chopped, salted peanuts

Sauté onion and celery in butter until tender. Stir in flour; blend. Add broth. Strain. Blend in peanut butter; reduce heat and add cream. Simmer for 5-10 minutes. Serve with parsley and chopped peanuts. Serves 10.

A Samford Celebration Cookbook

Shoppers travel hundreds of miles to browse in the factory outlet stores in Boaz, about 20 miles north of Gadsden. Downtown Boaz is the home of VF Factory Outlet Mall, Boaz Outlet Center, Reading China and Glass, Fashion Outlets, and the Downtown Mall.

Curried Chicken and Apple Soup

2 apples, peeled, cored
  and diced
2 onions, peeled and sliced
2 tablespoons butter
1 tablespoon curry powder
1 teaspoon flour

2 cups chicken stock
1/8 teaspoon red pepper
Salt and pepper
1 cup half-and-half
1/2 chicken breast, diced

Sauté apples and onions in butter until onions are translucent. Stir in curry powder and flour and cook 5 minutes. Add chicken stock, salt, and red pepper. Stir in wine and simmer for ten minutes. Strain and purée solids in food processor. Combine and chill mixture. Just before serving, add cream and chicken. Yield: 4 servings.

Huntsville Entertains

Lime Soup

3 to 3 1/2 pounds chicken
10 cups water
6 peppercorns
1/2 teaspoon coriander
1 stalk celery
1 medium onion, quartered
2 teaspoons salt
Pepper
1/2 teaspoon thyme

2 tablespoons vegetable oil
1 medium onion, chopped
1 medium green pepper,
    chopped
3 large tomatoes, chopped
Juice of 3 or 4 limes
3 tablespoons fresh coriander
    or parsley

Simmer chicken in uncovered Dutch oven in water, peppercorns, coriander, celery, quartered onion, salt, pepper and thyme until chicken is tender, about 1 1/2 hours. Remove chicken; strain broth, cool chicken, remove from bones and cut in bite-sized pieces. Sauté chopped onions and green pepper in oil until tender--3 or 4 minutes. Add tomatoes; cook 5 minutes. Add strained broth and lime juice. Stir in coriander and simmer 20 minutes. Add chicken. Heat thoroughly. Serves 8. This may be served over crisp tortilla wedges. Garnish with lime slices and coriander leaves. This is good and different.

Seconds Please!

Marion's Chicken Soup

1 (4-pound) fryer or hen, cut
    into pieces
6 cups water
3 sprigs parsley
1 medium onion, quartered
8 peppercorns
1/2 teaspoon ginger

2 teaspoons salt
2 large carrots, sliced
2 ribs celery, sliced
1 can sliced mushrooms
1 cup fine egg noodles, cooked
    according to directions on
    package and drained

Place chicken in a large boiler, add water and bring to a boil. Place parsley, onion, peppercorns on a square of cheese cloth; sprinkle with ginger. Tie cheese cloth and add to chicken; add salt, cover and cook until chicken is tender. Remove chicken from broth. Cool. Remove skin and bones, cut into chunks and return to broth. Add vegetables, simmer until tender. Add cooked noodles. Serves 6-8.

Hallmark's Collection of Home Tested Recipes

Cream of Shrimp Soup
Superb shrimp soup!

3 cans mushroom soup
3 cups milk
1 bunch green onions, chopped
5 stalks celery, finely chopped
1 (3-ounce) can mushroom caps
1/2 teaspoon garlic powder
1 teaspoon salt
1/2 teaspoon white pepper

1/4 teaspoon cayenne pepper
Dash Tabasco
1 tablespoon Worcestershire sauce
1 pound cooked shrimp, may
   use frozen
1/4 cup vermouth
2 tablespoons heavy cream
   (optional)

Combine soup and milk in a medium saucepan over medium heat. Add onions, celery, mushroom caps and seasonings; simmer about 30 minutes. *Do not boil.* Add shrimp and vermouth and cook until shrimp are well heated, about 15 minutes. If desired, heavy cream may be added during last 5 minutes of cooking for a richer, creamier taste. Serves 6-8.

Birdies in the Oven/Aces in the Kitchen

Flawless Oyster Stew

2 cups milk
2 cups thin cream
2 dozen small oysters
4 tablespoons butter

Salt
Celery salt
White pepper
Paprika

Combine milk and cream and scald (this means heating to the point where a film forms on top, not boiling). Drain off nearly all of the juice from oysters, leaving about 2 tablespoons on oysters. Heat the drained-off oyster juice to the boiling point only in a separate pan. Add the butter to oysters (a few drops of Worcestershire sauce, if you like a dash of piquancy) and place over high heat just long enough for oysters to fatten up and edges to begin to curl—no longer or they will be as tough as shoe leather. Take oysters off stove, add both liquids, stir in salt, celery salt and pepper to taste. And be sure to taste. Serve immediately, sprinkle with some merry paprika accompained by oyster crackers. Serves 6.

Old Mobile Recipes

Crab Gumbo Point Clear Style

4 tablespoons bacon fat	2 small cans tomato paste
6 tablespoons flour	2 quarts chicken stock or stock
1 green pepper	made with bouillon cubes
1 stalk celery	2 bay leaves
2 large onions, chopped	2 pounds crabmeat
2 pounds okra	6 cups boiled rice
2 cups canned tomatoes	Salt and pepper to taste

Brown flour in bacon fat. Add pepper, celery, onions and okra, all cut into small pieces. Cook about 20 minutes, stirring constantly. Add tomatoes and tomato paste. Mix well. In a large container, add mixture to stock. Simmer gently one hour. Add crabmeat with bay leaves and simmer half an hour more. Season to taste. Serve with rice. This quantity makes 12-15 generous servings. More crabmeat may be added if gumbo is to be the main course of meal.

Treasured Alabama

Bayou La Batre's Seafood Festival is a July extravaganza for seafood-lovers. Approximately 250 gallons of gumbo, along with shrimp and other seafood delights, tempt festival goers. Unique activities, such as shrimp picking and live crab races, combine with the food offered to make the festival a favorite.

Gazpacho
(Cold Vegetable Soup)

1 or 2 garlic cloves	1 slice bread (2 if greater
2 pounds fresh tomatoes (about 5)	thickeness desired)
1 green pepper	1 cucumber
3 tablespoons oil	2 tablespoons vinegar
Few cumin seeds	Dash pepper
1/2 teaspoon salt	

Put bread, garlic, tomatoes (except 1), a small piece of green pepper (put rest aside), 2 or 3 slices of cucumber (put rest aside), oil, vinegar, cumin, salt in blender. Whirl until completely liquid. Strain. Add 1 pint water. Mix well. Taste test and add salt and vinegar as desired. Put in refrigerator. Serve very cold in individual cups. Garnish with remaining pepper, cucumber and tomato, all finely chopped. Small cubes of bread and chopped hard boiled eggs may be added.

Eufaula's Favorite Recipes

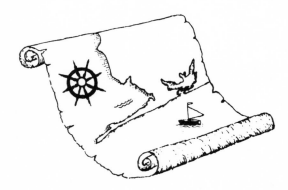

Vegetables

Bald Rock, a popular vantage point on Mount Cheaha (at 2,407 feet, Alabama's highest point), looks out over miles of Appalachian Valley. Northeast.

Asparagus Amandine

1 (20-ounce) can asparagus spears	1 cup grated American cheese
1 can cream of mushroom soup	1 cup fresh bread crumbs
1/2 teaspoon salt	1/2 cup blanched almonds
1/4 teaspoon pepper	1/4 cup butter or margarine

Grease a 10x6x1 1/2-inch baking pan. Drain asparagus; reserve 1/2 cup liquid. Arrange asparagus in pan. In bowl blend soup, reserved liquid, salt and pepper. Pour over asparagus; sprinkle with cheese. Sprinkle crumbs and almonds on top; dot with butter or margarine. Bake at 375° for 35 minutes. Yield: 6 servings.

Kitchen Sampler

Asparagus Egg Casserole

2 tablespoons butter or oleo	1 cup grated cheese
2 tablespoons flour	1 small can pimento, chopped
Salt and pepper	1 (#1) can green asparagus tips
1 cup liquid (mixed asparagus juice and milk)	3 hard boiled eggs
	Grated almonds (optional)

Melt butter and heat to bubbling point; add flour, salt and pepper. Add liquid gradually and cook until thick. Add cheese and pimento. In a greased baking dish arrange a layer of asparagus, then a layer of eggs, then sauce. Repeat. Grated almonds are good sprinkled over the top. Bake in 350° oven long enough to heat thoroughly. Can be made the day before serving.

Sumpthn' Yummy

Magnolia Springs, Alabama, is one of the few places in the United States still using postal service by boat.

Asparagus and Tomato Slices
An easy, colorful dish for luncheons or buffet dinners.

4 medium, firm, ripe tomatoes
1 (15-ounce) can asparagus spears,
   drained
1/2 cup mayonnaise

2 cups grated sharp cheese
Tabasco sauce to taste
1/2 teaspoon Worcestershire sauce
3 tablespoons grated onion

Preheat oven to 350°. Cut stem ends off tomatoes and slice each into 3 thick slices. Cut asparagus spears in half and arrange on top of tomato slices in a buttered, shallow baking dish. Combine remaining ingredients and spoon over asparagus. Bake for 10-15 minutes or until cheese is melted. Do not overbake. Tomatoes may be prepared early in the day and refrigerated before baking. Serves 6-8.

Magic

Country Baked Beans
"An absolute necessity with barbecue."

4 pieces bacon, fried and drained
1 (1-pound 15-ounce) can pork
   and beans, drained
1 (16-ounce) can kidney beans,
   drained
1 (8-ounce) can lima beans,
   drained
1 small bell pepper, chopped
   (optional)

1 medium onion, chopped
2 tablespoons bacon drippings
3/4 cup brown sugar
1 tablespoon mustard
3 tablespoons Worcestershire sauce
1/3 cup catsup
1/4 teaspoon pepper
Salt to taste

Fry bacon and crumble. Mix all beans and chopped bell pepper and place in a 2 1/2 to 3-quart casserole dish. Brown onion in bacon drippings. To browned onion, add remaining ingredients and cook over medium heat for 10 minutes. Add cooked mixture and crumbled bacon to beans. Bake, covered, at 350° for 30 minutes. Remove cover and bake an additional 15 minutes. May be prepared a day or two in advance and refrigerated. Serves 16.

When Dinnerbells Ring

Green Bean Casserole

4 boxes frozen French style green beans	3/4 pound sharp Cheddar cheese, grated
1/2 pound mushrooms, sliced	1/8 teaspoon Tabasco
1 large onion, chopped	2 teaspoons soy sauce
1 stick margarine	Salt and pepper
1/4 cup flour	1 can water chestnuts, chopped
1 pint half-and-half cream	1 tablespoon Worcestershire sauce

Cook beans, drain well. Cook mushrooms and onions in butter until done but do not let onions brown. Add flour, mix well, then add cream and let thicken. Add cheese and stir until smooth. Add seasoning. Mix in beans and chestnuts. Sprinkle top with either chopped almonds or cracker crumbs and butter. Bake at 350° until thoroughly heated. Serves 14.

This is excellent to make ahead and freeze. It is a delicious casserole.

Eufaula's Favorite Recipes

Green Beans with Bacon Dressing

1/2 pound bacon
2 eggs
1/3 cup vinegar
1/2 cup water
3 tablespoons sugar

1/4 tablespoon salt
2 cans (1-pound each) whole
   green beans
1 tablespoon diced pimiento

Cook bacon until crisp; reserve 1/4 cup drippings; crumble bacon. Beat eggs, vinegar, water, sugar and salt together until blended. Return reserved drippings to skillet; add egg mixture. Cook over low heat, stirring constantly until thickened. Heat beans in can liquid; drain; arrange on serving dish. Pour hot dressing over beans; sprinkle with crumbled bacon and diced pimiento. Serve at once as a hot vegetable or chill and serve as salad with crisp greens.

Use this vegetable to "fancy up" a special dinner. An attractive dish.

Kum' Ona' Granny's Table

Sweet and Sour Green Beans

1 quart cooked green beans
1 meduim onion, chopped
8 slices bacon, fried crisp and
   crumbled

1/2 cup vinegar
1/2 cup sugar
1/2 cup bacon grease

Place a layer of beans in flat casserole, then a layer of onion and a layer of bacon. Repeat. Pour sauce of vinegar, sugar and bacon grease over casserole. Cook uncovered at 350° for 30 minutes. Cover and cook an additional 30 minutes. Serves 8.

Sumpthn' Yummy

The battleship *USS Alabama*, now resting in Mobile, survived many major World War II battles without being injured by enemy fire.

Broccoli Casserole

2 packages frozen broccoli
2 eggs, slightly beaten
1 cup mayonnaise
1 can cream of mushroom soup

2 tablespoons chopped onion
Salt and pepper to taste
1 cup rolled cracker crumbs
1 cup grated cheese

Cook broccoli and drain. Place in bottom of casserole dish. Mix remaining ingredients together except cracker crumbs and cheese. Pour on top of broccoli and top with cheese. Put cracker crumbs on last. Bake at 400° for 20 minutes.

Variation: Cheese crackers, crushed, margarine, melted. Combine and top instead of cracker crumbs.

Kitchen Sampler

Broccoli Bleu Cheese Casserole

2 tablespoons oleo
2 tablespoons flour
1 (3-ounce) package cream cheese, softened
1/4 cup crumbled bleu cheese

1 cup milk
2 (10-ounce) packages chopped broccoli
1/3 cup crushed Ritz crackers

Cook and drain broccoli. In a saucepan melt oleo; blend in flour and cheeses. Add milk. Cook and stir until mixture boils. Stir in broccoli. Put in buttered casserole. Top with cracker crumbs. Bake in 350° oven for 30 minutes. Serves 8.

Sumpthn' Yummy

Broccoli Rice Casserole

1 cup chopped onions
1 cup chopped celery
1 stick oleo
1 large package frozen chopped
  broccoli, cooked according to
  directions, drained

1 cup Minute Rice, uncooked
1 can cream of mushroom soup
1 can cream of chicken soup
1/2 soup can of water
Grated Cheddar cheese

Sauté onions and celery in oleo until tender. Combine all ingredients. Pour into buttered casserole. Sprinkle grated cheese on top. Bake at 350° for 35 minutes. Serves 6.

Hallmark's Collection of Home Tested Recipes

Broccoli Tart

1 (10-ounce) package frozen
  chopped broccoli, cooked
  according to package directions
2 eggs
1/2 cup milk

Salt
Black pepper
1 cup gruyère, finely grated
30 (2-inch) tartlet shells, unbaked

Drain cooked broccoli and press to remove moisture. Place broccoli in food processor. Blend for a few seconds, or chop the broccoli with a knife. In a bowl beat together the eggs and cream. Season with salt and pepper to taste. Stir in the broccoli. Place 1 teaspoon cheese in each tart shell, then fill with the egg mixture to top of shell. Bake at 400° 12-15 minutes, or until puffed and golden. These can be frozen and re-heated before serving. Yield: 2 1/2 dozen tartlets.

Huntsville Entertains

Futuristic space technology is on display at the Space and Rocket Center in Huntsville. Some exhibits give visitors a taste of astronaut training, while others teach the history of space exploration.

Southern Fried Cabbage

4 tablespoons rendered bacon
  fat
1 small green cabbage, cored
  and shredded

2 teaspoons red pepper
  flakes
Salt

Heat the bacon fat in a skillet, toss in the cabbage and stir until it is glistening. Lower the heat, add the pepper flakes, season with salt to taste, and continue cooking and turning the cabbage until it is barely tender, about 10 minutes. Yield: 4 servings.

Dining Under the Magnolia

Carrots with Walnuts and Green Onions

6 carrots, peeled and juliened
2 bunches green onion, sliced with
  some green stem

1 1/2 cups chopped walnuts
1 stick butter
Fresh ground pepper to taste

Melt butter and sauté carrots, onions and walnuts for about 15 minutes. Add fresh pepper to taste. Serves 6.

   The green onions add a wonderful flavor to the carrots--the dish adds beautiful color to your plate!

Twickenham Tables

Spiced Carrots

12 medium carrots, sliced crosswise
1 cup sugar (better to use 1/2 cup
  white and 1/2 cup light brown)
1 stick butter
1 tablespoon cinnamon

1 tablespoon nutmeg
Approximately 1/2 cup whole, fresh
  mint leaves
3 tablespoons grated orange rind

Cook carrots in salted water until tender. Drain off all but about 1/2 cup water. In a saucepan melt the butter and stir remaining ingredients into the melted mixture. Pour this mixture over the cooked carrots and stir well. Simmer carrots in spice mixture for about 20 minutes. If more water is needed add just a little at a time. Serves 12.

More Fiddling With Food

Candied Carrots

1 pound carrots, steamed and
  peeled

1 cup peach preserves
1/4 cup melted butter

Cut carrots in slices. Add peach preserves and butter in shallow pan.
Bake for 30 minutes at 325°. Serves 6.

A Samford Celebration Cookbook

Cheese-Topped Cauliflower

1 large head cauliflower
1 cup mayonnaise
2 teaspoons prepared regular
  or Dijon mustard

1 1/4 cups shredded sharp
  Cheddar cheese
Paprika

Preheat oven to 350°. Remove leaves and stem end from cauliflower.
Soak in salted water to cover for 15-20 minutes. Drain well. Steam
cauliflower in a small amount of boiling salted water for 10-15 minutes,
being careful not to overcook. Drain thoroughly. Place cauliflower in
shallow 2-quart buttered casserole. Combine mayonnaise and mustard
and spread over cauliflower. Sprinkle with cheese and paprika and bake
for 10 minutes or until cheese melts. Serves 4-6.

Magic

Celery Casserole

1 quart diced celery
1/2 pound sharp Cheddar cheese,
  grated
1 cup slivered almonds

1 cup cracker crumbs (Waverly or
  Escort crackers)
1 teaspoon salt
1/2 teaspoon sugar

WHITE SAUCE:
9 tablespoons butter
9 tablespoons flour

4 cups warm milk
1 teaspoon salt

TOPPING:
1/4 pound butter, melted

1 1/2 cups cracker crumbs

Parboil celery 5 minutes, drain and set aside. Prepare White Sauce in top of double boiler by melting butter, slowly adding flour, stirring constantly. Slowly add milk and salt and cook until smooth and heated thoroughly. Combine topping ingredients and set aside. Mix celery, White Sauce, cheese, casserole and cover with reserved topping of buttered cracker crumbs. Bake at 350° for 35 minutes. Serves 10-12.

Bravo! Applaudable Recipes

Corn Chowder

1/3 cup chopped salt pork or bacon
1 onion, chopped
3 tablespoons butter
1 quart cooked potatoes

1 can corn
1 quart scalded milk
Salt and pepper

Fry salt pork in 1 tablespoon of butter. If using bacon, chop and fry about 6 slices. Drain grease, reserving 1 tablespoon. Add chopped onion and brown. Put in a stew pan and add cubed cooked potatoes, corn, hot milk, seasoning and remaining butter. Heat to a boiling point and serve.

Heirlooms From the Kitchen

White Corn Casserole

10 strips bacon	1 medium onion, chopped
2 (12-ounce) cans white corn, drained	1 (8-ounce) carton sour cream

Fry bacon crisp. Sauté onions in bacon grease. Combine 8 strips bacon, corn, sour cream and onions. Cook at 350° for 20 minutes or until bubbly. Top with remaining bacon. Yield: 5-6 servings.

Kitchen Sampler

Corn Quiche
Cinnamon and brown sugar give a different taste to corn.

1 (9-inch) deep dish pie shell	1/2 teaspoon salt
1 (12-ounce) can whole kernel white corn, drained	1/8 teaspoon white pepper
	1/8 teaspoon nutmeg
4 ounces Swiss cheese, shredded	1 1/2 tablespoons butter, melted
3 eggs, beaten	1 1/2 tablespoons brown sugar
1 cup half-and-half	1/4 teaspoon cinnamon

Preheat oven to 425°. Bake pie shell for 5 minutes. Reduce oven temperature to 350°. Place corn in pastry shell and sprinkle with cheese. Combine eggs, half-and-half, salt, pepper, and nutmeg and pour over corn and cheese. Bake for 30 minutes. Drizzle melted butter over top of quiche and sprinkle combined brown sugar and cinnamon on top. Return to oven for 5 minutes or until center is firm. Quiche can be made ahead and frozen by omitting topping and the last 5 minutes of baking time. Defrost and bring quiche to room temperature, add topping, and bake in preheated 350° oven for 15 minutes. Delicious alternative to sweet potatoes or can be sliced into small wedges and served instead of bread with a meal. Serves 6.

Magic

Eggplant Casserole

1 medium eggplant	1 egg, well-beaten
1-2 slices white bread, diced	1 cup cubed cheese
2 tablespoons butter or margarine, melted	Milk
	Salt, pepper, paprika

Peel and cut eggplant. Cook in salted water until tender. Drain and put in greased 2-quart casserole. Add bread. Melt butter and pour over eggplant. Add egg, cheese and enough milk to make thick soupy mixture. Salt and pepper to taste. Sprinkle well with paprika. Bake at 350° until set. Serves 3-4. Canned squash may be substituted for eggplant.

Huntsville Heritage Cookbook

Sophia's Mousaka

1 large or 2 small eggplants	Oil as needed
Salt	

Prepare eggplants; slice into 1/4-inch circles. Salt each slice and place in colander. Weight down the slices with a heavy plate so that all excess water will drain from eggplant slices; drain for 30 minutes. Wipe dry with paper towels. Pour 1/4 inch of oil into a large frying pan. When oil is *hot,* quickly fry dried eggplant slices, turning to brown quickly on each side. Drain fried eggplant slices on layers of paper towels to absorb all excess oil. Set aside.

MEAT SAUCE:

22 ounces ground lean beef or lamb	1/2 cup tomato sauce
Salt to taste	2 tablespoons fresh minced parsley
Pepper to taste	or 2 teaspoons dried parsley
1 small onion, finely chopped	1/2 teaspoon sugar
1 clove garlic, mashed	1/2 teaspoon dried leaf oregano
2 tablespoons grated Romano cheese	1/4 teaspoon ground allspice

Combine all ingredients in a large dutch oven; sauté over medium heat stirring with a wooden spoon. Continue to sauté in its own juice for 30 minutes very low heat.

CONTINUED

CONTINUED

CREME SAUCE:

4 large eggs

2 cups cold milk

Salt to taste

Pepper to taste

2 tablespoons Romano cheese

Dash nutmeg

In a large mixing bowl beat the eggs and milk together. Add salt and pepper. Add cheese and nutmeg. Mix well. Set aside.

ASSEMBLING THE CASSEROLE:

(Sprinklings of Romano Cheese and paprika as needed.) Spray baking pan or casserole with non-stick spray. Lightly sprinkle the bottom of the pan (11 1/2x9 1/2x2 inches) with cheese. Layer 1/2 eggplant slices evenly. Place all of the simmering meat sauce over the eggplant and cheese layers. Place remaining eggplant slices attractively over the meat mixture. Then ladle the creme sauce over the Mousaka being sure the sauce soaks all the way to the bottom. Top the casserole by at least 1/4 inch. Sprinkle the top of Mousaka with cheese and paprika for color. Bake in 375° oven for 45-50 minutes. Let stand for 10 minutes before cutting into 2-inch squares for serving. Serves 6 generously.

To Freeze: This Mousaka freezes well, so double or triple this recipe. Bake 20 minutes. Seal well and freeze. Finish baking on day you wish to serve. This may be made in individual ramekins for luncheons. For ramekins, slice eggplants thin and use less baking time. Be sure your ramekin allows space for the Mousaka and full measure of creme sauce.

A Southern Lady Cooks with a Greek Accent

Crispy Eggplant

1/2 cup Hellmann's mayonnaise	1/3 cup grated Parmesan cheese
1 tablespoon instant minced onion	1/2 teaspoon dried Italian seasoning
1/2 teaspoon salt	1 eggplant (about 1 pound) cut
1/3 cup fine dry bread crumbs	crosswise in 1/2-inch slices

In small bowl stir together first 3 ingredients. In shallow dish or on sheet of waxed paper, combine bread crumbs, Parmesan, and Italian seasoning. Brush both sides of eggplant slices with mayonnaise mixture; dip in crumb mixture and coat well. Place in shallow greased baking pan or on baking sheet. Bake at 425° for 15-17 minutes or until crisp and browned. Serves 4.

Loaves and Fishes

Alabama Eggplant

1 large eggplant	1/2 teaspoon salt
1/4 cup chopped onion	1/8 teaspoon pepper
2 tablespoons parsley	1 cup cracker crumbs
1 can cream of mushroom soup	2 tablespoons butter
1 teaspoon Worcestershire sauce	

Remove stem end of eggplant and cut in half lengthwise. Cut and remove inside pulp, being careful to leave 1/4 inch inside shell. Cook pulp about 10 minutes. Drain. Mix pulp with remaining ingredients, except butter, using enough cracker crumbs to make filling of stuffing consistency. Return eggplant to shells. Cover with cracker crumbs. Dot with butter and put in baking dish with 1/2 inch boiling water. Bake at 375° for 30-35 minutes until set. Yields 6-8 servings.

Huntsville Entertains

Fresh Mushrooms Polish Style
Absolutely delicious! Everyone who tries them raves.

3/4 pound fresh mushrooms,
  thinly sliced
1 tablespoon fresh lemon juice
4 tablespoons butter or margarine
1/4 teaspoon salt
1/4 teaspoon pepper

1 tablespoon flour
1 tablespoon minced onion
2 tablespoons Parmesan cheese
1 cup heavy cream
2 egg yolks, slightly beaten
2 tablespoons soft bread crumbs

In saucepan sprinkle mushrooms with lemon juice. Cover and simmer lightly. Add 3 tablespoons of butter, salt, pepper, flour, onion and cheese. Simmer for 3 minutes. Place in buttered 1 1/2-quart baking dish. Beat together cream and egg yolks; pour over mushrooms. Sprinkle top with bread crumbs. Dot with remaining butter. Bake at 375° for about 15 minutes. Serves 6.

Cookbook

Broun Hall Mushrooms

1 pound fresh mushrooms	1/8 teaspoon ginger
4 tablespoons oleo or butter	4 tablespoons all-purpose flour
1 tablespoon finely chopped onion	1/2 cup milk
3/4 teaspoon salt	3 dashes Tabasco
1/4 teaspoon ground nutmeg	2 large eggs, well beaten

Wash, dry and coarsely chop mushrooms. Melt 4 tablespoons butter in heavy skillet and sauté onion until transparent. Add mushrooms and stir constantly for 5 minutes. Add flour and seasonings, blend, then take pan off fire and blend in milk and Tabasco. Return to heat and stir until mixture thickens. Cool. Then add well-beaten eggs. Oil 1-quart casserole or 8-cup ring mold and pour in mushroom mixture. Bake in 350° oven 30 minutes or until top lightly browns. The mushroom ring can be filled with peas for variation.

Auburn Entertains

The unique King Shell is a seashell that is found only on Dauphin Island, Alabama.

Italian Stuffed Mushrooms

16 large mushrooms
1 1/2 teaspoons Cavender's
  Greek seasoning
1 cup chopped tomatoes
1/2 teaspoon dried parsley
1/8 teaspoon garlic powder

1/8 teaspoon white pepper
1/2 teaspoon salt
6 tablespoons mayonnaise
1/3 cup grated fresh Parmesan
  cheese

Remove stems and scrape out inside of mushrooms. Wash gently. Peel tomatoes and cut off top to expose seeds. Squeeze tomatoes to remove seeds. Chop tomatoes and add seasonings. Fill mushrooms. Make paste of mayonnaise and cheese. Put about 1 teaspoon on top of each mushroom. Place in 375° oven and bake about 15 minutes or until mushrooms are done and top is brown. Serve immediately. Yields 8 servings.

Huntsville Entertains

Mushroom Pie

2 pounds fresh mushrooms
1/4 cup plus 2 tablespoons butter,
  divided
Salt and freshly ground pepper
Juice of 1/2 lemon

3 tablespoons flour
1/2 cup Madeira wine
1/2 cup heavy cream, heated
Your own pie crust recipe
1 egg, beaten

Trim mushroom and heat in a large skillet with 1/4 cup butter. Add salt, pepper, and lemon juice. Cover the skillet and cook mushrooms for 10 minutes, shaking the pan frequently. Arrange mushrooms in a buttered baking dish. To the juice remaining in the pan, add remaining 2 tablespoons butter, flour, wine, and hot cream. Season with salt and freshly ground pepper. Pour sauce over mushrooms and cover with flaky pie crust. Brush crust with beaten egg, and make a few slits in top. Bake in hot oven (450°) for 15 minutes. Reduce heat to moderate (350°) and bake for 10-15 minutes longer.

Heavenly Hostess

French Onion Casserole

5 medium onions, sliced
5 tablespoons butter or margarine,
   divided
2 tablespoons all-purpose flour
Pepper to taste
1 cup beef bouillon

1/4 cup dry sherry
1 1/2 cups plain croutons
1/4 cup shredded Swiss cheese
2 tablespoons grated Parmesan
   cheese

Cook onions in 3 tablespoons butter till tender. Blend in flour and dash of pepper. Add bouillon and sherry; cook and stir till thick and bubbly. Turn into 1-quart casserole; cover. Toss croutons with remaining 2 tablespoons melted butter; chill croutons until needed.

Bake casserole, covered, in 350° oven for 30 minutes. Sprinkle with buttered croutons, then cheeses. Bake, uncovered, 5-10 minutes more. Serves 6.

Try Me

Onion Casserole

The secret is that you make this ahead and refrigerate it until needed. Men especially like it.

4 large mild onions, sliced
5 tablespoons butter
1 loaf French bread, cut in
   1/2-inch slices

1 pound Swiss cheese, sliced
1 (10 3/4-ounce) can cream of
   mushroom soup
1 soup can milk

Sauté onions in butter until clear; remove from heat. In a buttered 9x13x2-inch casserole dish, place a layer of French bread; cover with half the onions and half the cheese. Repeat layers. Combine soup and milk; pour over casserole. Refrigerate, covered, overnight or longer (will keep 2 or 3 days).

To serve, bake in a 350° oven for 30 minutes or until bubbly and only slightly brown. Yields 8-10 servings.

Family Secrets

Baked Black-Eyed Peas

2 pounds dried black-eyed peas
5 ounces celery, diced
5 ounces green pepper, diced
1/2 cup red peppers, diced
1/4 teaspoon ground camino seed
3/4 teaspoon garlic powder

3/4 stick margarine
3 1/4 teaspoons Seasonall
1 teaspoon black pepper
1 tablespoon salt
Dash cayenne pepper
Pinch of salt

Cover peas with water and soak overnight. Drain; add remaining ingredients and cover with water. Place in oven at low temperature (250°) and simmer, covered, for at least 2 hours. Add more water if necessary. The peas can be served cold as a relish or hot as a side dish.

More Fiddling With Food

Black-Eyed Pea Patties

Cooked black-eyed peas
Chopped onion
Chopped bell pepper
Dash of mace

Few mustard seeds
Beaten egg
Heavy cream

Personally, my favorite is black-eyed pea patties. You take cooked black-eyed peas, add a very little chopped onion and chopped green pepper, a dash of mace, a few mustard seeds, some beaten egg, a very little heavy cream and you make patties which you bake at 350° for about 20 minutes, and serve hot with green tomato pickles and a good cucumber salad.

If pepper and onion are chopped fine, there's no need to blanch them, but some cooks prefer to toss these into simmering salted water for 10 minutes, then drain well and add to peas. Some like a bit of tomato paste added, others a bit of hot mustard, but not too much.

Delectable Dishes from Termite Hall

Cinderella's Golden Potato Casserole

6 large potatoes
2 cups shredded Cheddar cheese
6 tablespoons margarine, divided
2 cups sour cream

1 teaspoon salt
1/3 cup chopped green onion
1/4 teaspoon white pepper

Boil potatoes in skins. Cool, peel and coarsely shred. Melt 4 table-spoons of margarine and cheese in a saucepan over low heat. Stir until melted. Remove from heat. Blend in sour cream, salt, onion and pepper. Add potatoes, stirring lightly. Place in buttered 1 1/2-quart baking dish. Dot with remaining margarine. Bake at 350° for 30 minutes. Yield : 6-8 servings.

Cooks and Company

Potato Boats

6 huge baking potatoes
1 pound ground meat (beef or
  mixed beef and pork)
1 onion, chopped
1/2 cup milk
2 tablespoons unsalted butter
6 or 8 capers, chopped
Pinch dill

Pinch mace
Freshly-ground black pepper
Salt to taste
Chopped parsley to sprinkle
  on before serving
Parmesan or sharp American
  cheese
Sunflower seed kernels (optional)

Wash, bake potatoes at 425° about 45 minutes. Brown beef, add onion, cook 5 minutes. Cut lid off potatoes, scoop out flesh, leaving enough to leave firm shell and lid. Add milk, butter and seasonings to cooked potaotes, beat until fluffy, add browned meat mixture, beating well. Refill potato skins and top with cheese or kernels or both. Sometimes a mix of ground-up Triscuits and some sharp cheese is good. Bake about 20 minutes at 350°, garnish with parsley and serve. Schoolboys like this particularly, but so do their papas.

Delectable Dishes from Termite Hall

Potato Casserole

1 (2-pound) bag frozen hash
 brown potatoes
1/2 cup melted oleo
1 tablespoon salt
1/2 teaspoon pepper
1 can cream of chicken soup

1/2 cup chopped onion
1 carton sour cream
1 (10-ounce) package sharp
 Cheddar cheese, grated
2 cups crushed corn flakes
1/4 cup melted oleo

Mix first 8 ingredients together and pour into buttered casserole. Top with corn flake crumbs mixed with oleo. Bake uncovered for 1 hour at 300°. Serves 12.

Sumpthn' Yummy

Cheese Potato Balls

2 2/3 cups instant mashed potato
 puffs (dry)
1 1/2 cups water
2 tablespoons butter or margarine
1 teaspoon salt

1/2 cup milk
16 (1/2-inch) cubes processed
 American cheese
3 tablespoons butter or margarine,
 melted

Heat oven to 400°. Measure 1/2 cup of the potato puffs; set aside. Heat water, 2 tablespoons butter and the salt to boiling in large saucepan. Remove from heat; stir in milk and the remaining potato puffs. (Potatoes will be stiff). Form into 16 balls, shaping each heaping tablespoon of potatoes around a cube of cheese. Stir reserved potato puffs into melted butter. Roll balls in buttered potato puffs; place on ungreased baking sheet. If desired, sprinkle with paprika. Bake 10-15 minutes or until light brown. Serves 8.

Note: Potatoes can be prepared, shaped and stored in refrigerator several hours ahead of serving time. Roll in buttered potato puffs just before baking. This recipe won first place in our "Finger Foods Contest."

Kum' Ona' Granny's Table

Creamy Scalloped Potatoes

2 pounds potatoes (about 6 medium)   1/4 teaspoon pepper
3 tablespoons butter   2 1/2 cups milk
3 tablespoons all-purpose flour   1 small onion, finely chopped
1 teaspoon salt   1 tablespoon butter

Pare and cut potatoes into enough thin slices to measure about 4 cups. Heat 3 tablespoons butter in saucepan over low heat until melted. Blend in flour, salt, and pepper. Cook over low heat, stirring constantly, until mixture is smooth and bubbly; remove from heat. Stir in milk; heat to boiling, stirring constantly. Boil and stir 1 minute.

Arrange potatoes in greased 2-quart casserole dish in three layers, topping each of the first two with 1/2 of the onion and 1/3 of the white sauce. Top with remaining potatoes and sauce. Dot with 1 tablespoon butter. Cover and cook at 325° for 40 minutes or 350° for 30 minutes. Uncover and cook until potatoes are tender, 60-70 minutes longer. Let stand 5-10 minutes before serving. Yield: 6 servings.

Once Upon a Stove

Sour Cream Grilled Potatoes

1 1/2 cups sliced, cooked potaotes   1 package onion soup mix
Salt and pepper   1/4 cup light cream
1 pint sour cream   Broiler foil

Place sliced potatoes in center of a 14-inch square of foil. Season with salt and pepper. Combine sour cream, onion soup mix and cream and pour over potatoes. Seal foil and place on grill for 20 minutes. Serves 6. (Sliced raw potatoes may be used-cook 45 minutes to an hour.)

Recipe Jubilee!

 The Coon Dog Cemetery near Tuscumbia is a unique tribute to man's best friend, dedicated to a special breed of hound—the coon dog. There are nearly 100 graves with markers.

Orange Sweet Potatoes

6 large sweet potatoes
1/2 pound butter
1 1/2 cups sugar

3/4 cup orange juice
1 cup chopped pecans
1 bag miniature marshmallows

Peel and slice potatoes. Cook until tender and drain. Whip until fluffy. Add other ingredients, reserving a few marshmallows for topping. Put in 2-quart casserole and top with marshmallows. Bake at 350° until bubbly and marshmallows browned. May be made ahead and refrigerated until time to bake and serve. Serves 8. May use canned sweet potatoes.

Variation: Scoop out orange shells and fill with potato mixture.

Huntsville Heritage Cookbook

Ambrosia Sweet Potato Bake

1/2 lemon, sliced thin
1/2 orange, sliced thin
7 cups cooked or canned sweet
 potatoes
1 cup crushed pineapple

1/2 cup brown sugar
1/2 cup melted butter
1/2 teaspoon salt
1/2 cup shredded coconut
Cherries for decoration

Alternate in a 13x9-inch Pyrex dish the sliced sweet potatoes, lemons and oranges. Combine pineapple, sugar, butter and salt; pour over all. Sprinkle with coconut and cherries. Bake at 350° about 30 minutes. Serves 8-10.

Twickenham Tables

Spanakopitakia
(Spinach Puffs)

(From a truly great international star, Madame Elena Nikolaida, who was born in Turkey and is a permanent resident of the United States by a special act of Congress.)

1 medium onion, finely chopped	1/2 cup evaporated milk
1 bunch scallions, chopped	3 eggs, well beaten
1/4 cup olive or salad oil	1 pound Feta cheese (or 1/2 pound
1/4 cup chopped parsley	cottage cheese and 1/2 pound
1/4 cup fresh dill chopped fine, or	Feta)
1 teaspoon dry dill weed	1 pound filo (phyllo) pastry leaves
1/2 teaspoon salt	1 pound butter, clarified
White pepper to taste	
2 pounds fresh spinach, chopped and	
drained well, or 3 (10-ounce) packages	
frozen chopped spinach, thawed and	
well drained	

Sauté onions and scallions in oil until soft and transparent. Add parsley, dill and seasonings. Cook 5 minutes. (If frozen spinach is used, squeeze to remove all water.) Add drained spinach to sautéed mixture and cook until almost dry, stirring often. Add milk and cool. Crumble Feta cheese into beaten eggs; add to spinach mixture, mix well and set aside. (Filo pastry dries out very quickly and must remain covered with a barely damp towel. The leaves are about 16x14 inches.) Stack 2 leaves of pastry on work surface and cut through both leaves, making 8 strips, 2x14 inches. Brush top layer of each strip with melted butter. Place a scant tablespoon of spinach mixture at top of each strip and fold into a triangle (folding as a flag is folded). Repeat with remaining filo leaves and spinach mixture. Place on ungreased cookie sheets and bake at 350° for 25-30 minutes or until golden brown. Serve hot. (May be frozen before baking. Thaw completely before baking.) Yield: 7 dozen.

Bravo! Applaudable Recipes

Hot Spinach Molds on Tomatoes

2 (10-ounce) packages frozen
   chopped spinach
3 tablespoons butter
6 eggs, slightly beaten
1 medium Bermuda onion, grated
1 1/3 cups milk

1 1/2 teaspoon salt
1/4 teaspoon pepper
1 tablespoon white vinegar
1/4 teaspoon dried savory
8 tomato slices (2 inches thick)

About 2 hours before meal, cook spinach and drain well. Mix with all ingredients except tomatoes. Place mixture in 8-9 buttered (6-ounce) custard cups. Place in shallow pan in 1 inch hot water. Bake at 350° only until firm. Ten minutes before serving, sprinkle tomato slices with salt and pepper. Place slices over custard cups and invert on serving dish.

Huntsville Heritage Cookbook

Tomatoes Stuffed with Spinach and Ricotta Cheese

1 cup onion, finely chopped
3 tablespoons olive oil
1 (10-ounce) package frozen
   chopped spinach, thawed and
   squeezed dry
1 cup ricotta cheese
2 egg yolks

1/2 cup Parmesan cheese, grated
1/2 cup parsley, chopped
Nutmeg to taste
Salt and pepper to taste
1/2 cup pine nuts, toasted
6 firm ripe tomatoes

Sauté onions in olive oil until tender. Add spinach; mix and cover. Simmer on low heat about 10 minutes. In mixing bowl, combine ricotta cheese and egg yolks. Add Parmesan cheese, parsley, seasonings, and tomatoes; hollow out, leaving thick sides. Salt the inside and pat dry with paper towels. Fill tomato shells with spinach mixture. Bake tomatoes in a preheated 350° oven for 20 minutes. Sprinkle a small amount of Parmesan cheese on top. Serve immediately or chill. Yield: 6 servings.

Once Upon a Stove

Spinach Quiche

2 frozen pie crusts, partially baked
2 ounces Gruyére cheese, grated
2 cups heavy cream or 2 cups milk
1/2 cup flour
6 eggs
1 medium onion, minced

1 1/2 teaspoons salt
1/2 teaspoon pepper
1 (10-ounce) package frozen
    spinach; let thaw and
    dry with towel

Preheat oven to 400°. Sprinkle grated cheese onto pie crusts. Beat cream with flour, onion, seasonings, and beat well. Add spinach and blend. Pour into pie crusts. Bake at 400° for 40 minutes, or until a knife inserted near the center comes out clean. Serves 12-16.

One of a Kind

Spinach Casserole

2 packages frozen chopped
    spinach
1 (8-ounce) package cream
    cheese

1 stick butter divided in half
1 cup Pepperidge Farm Herb
    Stuffing
Salt and pepper (cayenne) to taste

Cook spinach according to directions on package. Drain and add softened cream cheese and 1/2 stick butter. Mix well and season in casserole and cover with herb stuffing to form a top crust. Pour on the melted butter. Bake in moderate (350°) oven 20-30 minutes, until thoroughly hot. Serves 6.

Old Mobile Recipes

 Country cooking takes the spotlight at the Annual Sorghum Festival, which takes place in Springville. The event also includes a reconstructed pioneer homestead, with cooking and crafts demonstrations.

Italian Zucchini Casserole

6 medium zucchini, sliced
1 bay leaf
2 eggs, slightly beaten
1 cup sour cream
1 cup shredded Cheddar cheese
1 teaspoon dried basil
1/2 teaspoon oregano
1/2 teaspoon garlic powder
1/4 teaspoon salt

1/2 teaspoon pepper
2 tomatoes, chopped
4-5 slices bacon, cooked and
   crumbled
1/3 cup dry Italian seasoned
   bread crumbs
2 tablespoons grated Parmesan
   cheese

Boil zucchini in water with bay leaf until tender crisp, about 6-8 minutes. Drain. Set aside. Combine eggs, sour cream, cheese, basil, oregano, garlic powder, salt and pepper in a large bowl. Stir to mix. Add zucchini, tomatoes and bacon. Stir gently to mix. Spoon mixture into a greased 7x11-inch baking dish. Combine bread crumbs and Parmesan cheese. Sprinkle over mixture. Bake at 350° for 30 minutes. Yield: 8 servings.

Cooks and Company

Baked Squash

3/4 pound yellow squash, sliced
10 scallions, chopped
   (including tops)
2 tablespoons butter
Salt, to taste

1 egg, beaten
1 can cream of celery soup
Cheese Ritz crachers, crumbled
Parmesan cheese

Cook squash, scallions, and butter with salt until tender. (Add a little water, if needed.) Cool squash, add beaten egg and celery soup. Then add Cheese Ritz crackers (enough to thicken mixture for baking) and much Parmesan cheese. Pour in buttered casserole and bake at 350° until top is brown. Serves 4.

Thank Nabisco and their cheese Ritz crackers for this taste treat.

Cotton Country Cooking

Squash Casserole

2 cups fresh or frozen squash
2 medium onions, chopped
1 cup chopped celery
1 bell pepper, chopped

1 pound ground beef
1 can cream of mushroom soup
1 egg, beaten
1/2 cup grated cheese

Sauté onions, pepper and celery. Add beef and brown. Cook squash until tender, mash. Salt and pepper to taste. In buttered dish put in squash and top with beef mixture. Top with beaten egg, cheese and soup. Top with bread crumbs. Bake 20 minutes.

Treasured Taste

Jeri's Squash Casserole

2 pounds squash, cooked and
   drained
1 large onion, chopped
1 cup sour cream
1 can cream of mushroom soup

1 can water chestnuts, chopped
   (optional)
1 stick butter
1 package plain stuffing mix

Cook squash and onion together and drain. Mash up and add sour cream, soup and chestnuts. Melt butter and pour over dressing crumbs. Line pan with 1/2 crumbs. Pour in squash mixture. Cover top with remainder of crumbs. Bake at 350° for 30 minutes. Salt and pepper to taste. Yields: 8 servings.

   Hint: Recipe can be frozen or halved.

Kitchen Sampler

Stuffed Squash

8-10 medium yellow squash
1/2 cup chopped green pepper
1 medium, chopped tomato
2 tablespoons chopped onion
2 slices bacon, fried and crumbled
1/2 cup shredded Cheddar cheese
   or Ritz cracker crumbs

1/2 teaspoon salt
1/4 teaspoon pepper or to taste
Dash of Worcestershire sauce
Butter

Cook squash until barely tender. Drain. Cool slightly and cut a slice from each. Carefully remove the seeds. Combine remaining ingredients, except butter. Mix well. Spoon into shells. Top each with a pat of butter. Bake at 400° for about 20 minutes. Yield 8-10 servings.

The Alabama Heritage Cookbook

Mardi Gras originated in Mobile, Alabama, long before the event began in New Orleans.

Helen's Tomato Mess

Corn bread	Butter
Tomatoes	Cumin seeds
Salt, pepper, mace	Parmesan cheese

Mix up a batch of yellow meal corn bread by your favorite recipe. Butter a pan well. Put in enough ripe red tomato slices to cover bottom of pan about 3/4-inch deep. Season with salt, pepper, touch of mace. Dot with butter. Squash them down to fill space. Pour your batter over this. On top put good handful of cumin seeds, thin slices of tomato, dots of butter and grated Parmesan cheese. Bake at 350° about 30 minutes. Serve hot.

Delectable Dishes from Termite Hall

Broiled Tomatoes

Tomatoes	1/4 teaspoon thyme
Margarine	1/4 teaspoon oregano
1/2 teaspoon salt	1/4 teaspoon sugar
1/8 teaspoon pepper	Parmesan cheese, grated
1/4 teaspoon basil	

Purchase firm ripe tomatoes according to how many you are going to feed. Slice tomato in fairly thick slices and place on foil-lined baking sheet. Dot with a little margarine.

Combine the salt, pepper, spices, and sugar, Parmesan cheese on top. Grill or bake at 300° for about 20 minutes. Check frequently.

Gazebo I Christmas Cookbook

Gingered Turnips

2 pounds yellow turnips, pared and cubed	1/2 teaspoon ground ginger
	1/2 teaspoon sugar
1 tablespoon minced onion	2 teaspoons soy sauce
1 1/2 cups beef broth	

Combine all ingredients in a saucepan; simmer covered until turnips are tender, about 15 minutes. Drain; mash turnips with potato masher or electric mixer until fluffy. Add cooking liquid as needed for desired consistency. Yield: 6 servings.

Dining Under the Magnolia

Green Tomato Pie

Baked pie crust
Philadelphia cream cheese
Unsalted butter
2 strips bacon
1 onion
5 - 6 green tomatoes

Dash of salt and freshly ground
  pepper
Dash of powdered mace
Dill
Grated lemon peel
Chopped capers (optional)

Line a pre-baked crust with cream cheese. In a skillet melt some un-salted butter, finely chopped bacon, one finely chopped onion, green tomatoes cut in fingernail-size thick slices, pinch of salt, some freshly-ground black pepper, dash of mace, nice bit of dill, a little grated lemon peel. Add chopped capers if you like. Cook this mixture until tomatoes are soft but not mushy, then pile all into pie crust. Put in moderate oven either open-face or with a bit of pastry lattice. If open-face, for 10 min-utes; if lattice must bake, tomatoes need not be cooked all the way, but finished off in oven. You judge, 15-20 minutes.

Delectable Dishes from Termite Hall

Turnip Greens with Cornmeal Dumplins

3 pounds fresh turnip greens
1 tablespoon bacon drippings
  or 1/4 pound salt pork

1 teaspoon salt
1 teaspoon sugar

Wash and stem greens, discarding stems and tough leaves. Put an ample amount of water in large boiler (enough to more than cover greens after they cook down). Simmer bacon drippings or salt pork in water 10-15 minutes. Add greens, salt and sugar. Cover and simmer 30-45 minutes (depending on their tenderness).

CORNMEAL DUMPLINS:
2 cups self-rising meal
1/2 small onion, grated

Sprinkling of black pepper
1 cup pot "likker"

When greens are thoroughly done, make a stiff dough of the above in-gredients. Roll into small balls. Be sure there is plenty of pot "likker" (liquid in which greens were cooked) remaining in kettle to cover dumplings. Drop dumplins in "likker." Cook, covered, 20 minutes.

Seconds Please!

Baked Deviled Egg Casserole

6 hard-cooked eggs
2 teaspoons mustard
3 tablespoons sour cream
1/4 teaspoon salt
2 tablespoons margarine
1/2 cup chopped green pepper

1/3 cup chopped onion
1/4 cup chopped pimento
1 can mushroom soup
3/4 cup sour cream
1/2 cup grated Cheddar cheese

Cut eggs in half lengthwise; remove yolks. Mash yolks together with mustard, sour cream and salt. Fill whites with yolk mixture. Melt margarine in large skillet, sauté green pepper and onion until tender. Remove from heat, stir in pimento, soup and 3/4 cup sour cream. Place 1/2 of soup mixture in 1 1/2-quart shallow baking dish. Arrange eggs, cut side up, in single layer in dish. Pour remaining soup mixture over top. Sprinkle with cheese. Bake at 350° for about 20 minutes or until thoroughly heated. Casserole may be made in advance and refrigerated until ready to bake. Yield: 12 servings.

Anniversary Collection of Delectable Dishes

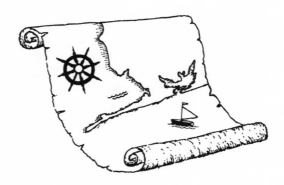

Macaroni and Cheese

1 (8-ounce) package macaroni
1 cup shredded Cheddar cheese
  (mild)
1 cup sour cream

2 cups cottage cheese
1 egg
Paprika

Cook macaroni according to directions. Drain and rinse. Combine next 4 ingredients with cooked macaroni. Place in a baking dish and sprinkle with paprika. Cook at 350° for 45 minutes.

Note: The cheese, cream and egg can be mixed and kept in the refrigerator a day or two.

Dinner on the Ground

Garlic Cheese Souffle

4 slices bread, buttered
1 (5-ounce) jar Kraft Old English
  garlic cheese spread
1 package Italian salad dressing mix

3 eggs
2 cups milk
1 teaspoon dry mustard

Tear bread into cubes and layer bottom of 1 1/2-quart casserole dish. Crumble cheese spread over bread. Sprinkle lightly with dressing mix. Add eggs beaten with milk and mustard. Place casserole in pan of hot water and bake 45 minutes at 325°. Serve immediately. Serves 4.

Huntsville Heritage Cookbook

Southern Rice Casserole

1 cup uncooked rice
1/2 cup butter

1 can beef consommé
1 can water

Melt butter, add rice and cook for 5 minutes. Pour into casserole dish consommé, water, rice and butter. Bake uncovered at 350° for one hour. Serves 6.

In cotton country, rice is more than a staple--it's almost a necessity, and is served, in one form or another, *very* frequently. A favorite southern rice dish is made with beef bouillon or consommé--a modified pilaf. Add mushrooms, toasted almonds, or seedless green grapes the last 15 minutes if you want.

Cotton Country Cooking

Chili Sauce

28 ripe tomatoes, peeled and
   chopped
6 medium onions, diced
8 jalapeño peppers or hot peppers,
   diced (optional)
4 green peppers, diced

4 banana peppers, diced
3 cups vinegar
2 cups sugar
1 tablespoon salt
1 teaspoon each cloves, allspice,
   cinnamon and mustard

Mix tomatoes with diced peppers and onions. Add vinegar, sugar and seasonings. Bring to a boil and simmer until desired consistency. Put into sterilized jars and give hot-water bath for at least 10 minutes.

(*Note:* Be sure to watch as mixture tends to stick toward the end. Timing cannot be given as tomatoes vary but it usually takes about 2 hours.)

Seconds Please!

Gizrum

16 large ripe tomatoes
6 large white onions
6 green peppers
1 red hot pepper

2 cups sugar
6 tablespoons salt
1 pint vinegar
Spices to taste

Scald and skin tomatoes. Peel onions and run them and peppers through food chopper. Tomatoes may be put through chopper too, if desired, but they usually cook to pieces. Combine all ingredients in large, heavy kettle and cook slowly for one hour or longer, until thick. Stir often to prevent scorching. Pour into small jars and seal while hot. This Gizrum is excellent served with black-eyed peas (either fresh or dried) and with turnip greens.

Treasured Alabama Recipes

Sweet Pickled Okra

3 pounds fresh small pods okra
6 cloves garlic
6 teaspoons dill seed
6 teaspoons celery seed
Hot pepper pods as you wish
   (6 pods for fanatic, 4 for
   convinced, 2 or 3 for the
   undecided)

1 quart white wine vinegar
1 quart water
1/2 cup salt *not* oxidized
1 cup sugar

Pack washed okra into 6 pint jars (leave stem ends). Divide garlic, dill, celery, pepper among your jars. Put vinegar, water, salt, sugar into big saucepan; bring to boil. Pour into jars, to within 1/2 inch of top. Seal jars, place in hot water bath (jars must be covered) 7 or 8 minutes. Remove to wire racks or whatever to cool. About 6 pints.

(Chopped peeled baby turnips and celery, with some of these okra sliced, on a bed of lettuce hearts, with a lemony mayonnaise, make a delicious and unforgettable salad in mid-winter.)

Delectable Dishes from Termite Hall

Squash Relish

10 cups squash	2 cups vinegar
3 cups onion	3 cups sugar
2 cups bell pepper, red and green	2 teaspoons whole celery seeds
3 tablespoons salt	

Before measuring vegetables, chop peppers and cut other vegetables thin. Mix vegetables and salt and let stand, covered, in cool place at least 1 1/2 hours. Stir 2 or 3 times. Drain well. Bring sugar, vinegar, and spices to a full boil. Pour over drained vegetables and bring back to full boil. Can seal in sterilized jars. Makes 4 pints. Refrigerate before serving.

A Samford Celebration Cookbook

Artichoke Relish

6 quarts Jerusalem artichokes	4 tablespoons tumeric
6 pounds white cabbage	3 pounds brown sugar
4 quarts cider vinegar	3 pounds white sugar
3 pounds onions	2 (16-ounce) jars prepared
12 green bell peppers	mustard
1 cup salt	1 1/2 cups flour
2 tablespoons black pepper	
8 tablespoons white mustard seed	

Cut vegetables. Soak in salt and water overnight. Drain well next day and boil with vinegar, sugar and spices for 20 minutes. Remove from heat. Add paste, made of flour and mustard. Cook 10 minutes, stirring constantly. Place jars in sauce pan of boiling water.

Boil tops and rings in separate pan. Fill jars while hot. Screw hot top on.

Eufaula's Favorite Recipes

Beck's Hot Pear Casserole

6 whole cooked or canned pears (drained)
1 1/2 cup sharp cheese, grated
1 cup sugar

3/4 stick butter or oleo
3 tablespoons flour
Ritz crackers, crumbled

Cut pears in chunks. Make a heavy sauce of flour, sugar, butter and 1 cup of juice cooked over medium heat. In greased casserole place cut pears. Pour sauce over. Add cheese and cover with crumbled Ritz crackers. Bake at 350° until cheese is melted and sauce is bubbling.

Heavenly Hostess

Hot Fruit Compote

1 cup (heaping) dried prunes, pitted
2 cups dried apricots
1 1/2 cups pineapple chunks, undrained

1 can cherry pie filling
1/2 cup sherry
1 1/2 cups water

Combine prunes, apricots, and pineapple, and put in buttered baking dish. Combine cherry pie filling, sherry, and water, and pour over fruit. Cook at least one hour at 350°. Serve hot. This is a very good accompaniment for ham or turkey.

Treasured Alabama Recipes

The first fig trees in America were planted by Isabella DeSoto at Fort Morgan. The trees came from Spain.

Scalloped Apples

6 large apples

1/2 teaspoon cinnamon

1/4 teaspoon salt

1 tablespoon lemon juice

1/2 cup water

1/2 cup flour

3/4 cup brown sugar

1/2 cup butter

Pare, core and slice apples. Place in buttered casserole. Mix cinnamon, salt, lemon juice and water. Work sugar, flour, butter together until crumbly. Spread over the apples. Bake 30 minutes in 400° oven.

More Fiddling With Food

Seafood

*Alabama's Gulf Coast has thirty-two miles of beautiful, uncluttered,
pure white beaches for get-away-from-it-all fun in the sun.*

Shrimp Remoulade

6 tablespoons olive oil
2 tablespoons vinegar
1 tablespoon paprika
1 teaspoon salt
2 1/2 tablespoons Creole Mister
   mustard

2 celery stalks, finely chopped
1 small white onion, grated
2 tablespoons chopped parsley
2 pounds cooked, cleaned shrimp

Mix first 8 items well. Marinate shrimp in mixture. Refrigerate for several hours, stirring occasionally before serving. Serve on shredded lettuce.

Old Mobile Recipes

Bob's Barbecued Shrimp

5 pounds medium to large shrimp,
   headless
1/2 pound butter
1/2 pound margarine
1/2 teaspoon rosemary
3 ounces Worcestershire sauce

2 1/2 tablespoons black pepper
2 tablespoons salt
2 lemons, sliced thin
3 cloves garlic, minced
1/2 tablespoon Tabasco
1 ounce soy sauce

Wash shrimp and place in a large baking dish. Combine remaining ingredients; bring to a boil. Pour over shrimp. Bake at 400° for 20 minutes. Serve hot with plenty of garlic bread.

Hallmark's Collection of Home Tested Recipes

Hot Shrimp

2-5 pounds shrimp
1 bottle of Kraft Italian dressing
1 stick margarine

Salt
Garlic

Melt margarine in large roasting pan. Put in shrimp and seasoning to taste. Pour over dressing. Cover tightly and bake at 350° until done...about 45 minutes to 1 hour.

More Fiddling With Food

Fried Shrimp

Fresh shrimp
Lemon juice
Cayenne pepper
Flour seasoned with salt
   and pepper

Beaten egg
Cracker meal

Peal and devein shrimp and put in a bowl. Squeeze lemon juice over all
and sprinkle with cayenne. Let sit for a half-hour. Dredge in flour to
which salt and pepper have been added. Let sit another half-hour. Dip
in beaten egg and dredge in cracker meal. Fry in hot fat until golden
brown, 3 to 5 minutes depending on size of shrimp. Drain on paper
towel and serve with horseradish dressing, catsup or tartar sauce.

Recipe Jubilee!

Shrimp Tetrazzini

2 tablespoons butter
1 medium onion, minced
8 ounces shrimp, peeled and
  deveined
8 ounces fresh mushrooms,
  sliced
1/4 cup all-purpose flour

1/4 cup mayonnaise
2 cups milk
1/4 cup sherry
1/2 (8-ounce) package thin
  spaghetti, cooked and drained
Parmesan cheese

Sauté onion in butter until tender. Add shrimp and mushrooms. Cook 5 minutes, stirring often; remove from skillet. Add flour and mayonnaise to skillet; blend well. Add liquids; cook until thickened. Toss with shrimp mixture and spaghetti. Pour into a 1 1/2-quart casserole. Top generously with cheese. Bake in 350° oven for 30 minutes. Yield: 4 servings.

Once Upon a Stove

Wild Rice and Shrimp Creole

1/2 cup chopped onion
1/2 cup diced bell pepper
1/4 cup butter or margarine
1 (16-ounce) can tomatoes,
  cut up
1 3/4 cups water
1/2 teaspoon salt
1/4 teaspoon pepper

1/4 teaspoon garlic salt
1/4 teaspoon dried rosemary,
  crushed
1/4 teaspoon paprika
1 (6-ounce) package Uncle Ben's
  long grain and wild rice
1 pound shrimp, peeled and cleaned
Tabasco

Sauté onion and bell pepper in butter until tender. Add the tomatoes, undrained, water, and seasonings. Stir in rice and add rice seasoning packet. Simmer covered for 20 minutes on top of stove. Add shrimp; cover and simmer 10 more minutes. Season to taste with Tabasco. Serves 6-8.

DOWN HOME In High Style

Shrimp and Rice Casserole

2 packages Uncle Ben's wild
   and white rice
2 tablespoons butter
1 cup celery, bias cut
2 (2 1/2-ounce) jars sliced
   mushrooms, drained
1/2 cup green onions, sliced

2 tablespoons pimento, chopped
2 cups shrimp, cooked and cleaned
1/2 teaspoon salt
1 teaspoon pepper
1 1/2 teaspoons Accent
1/2 green pepper chopped

Cook rice according to directions. Sauté in butter, celery, onions, green pepper. Stir in mushrooms, pimento, seasoning and shrimp. Fold into cooked rice. Put in buttered 2-quart casserole. Add topping. Serves 8-10.

TOPPING:
1 can cream of celery soup
1 1/3 cups sour cream
2 tablespoons butter

2/3 cup bread crumbs
2 tablespoons parsley,
   snipped fresh

Combine soup and sour cream. Spoon over casserole. Toss bread crumbs in butter and add to top, then add parsley. Bake in 325° oven for 40 minutes.

Try Me

Seafood booths and outdoor activities highlight the Annual National Shrimp Festival, held each October in Gulf Shores.

Shrimp Casserole

3 pounds shrimp, cooked, peeled
   and deveined
1 (8-ounce) package green noodles,
   cooked and drained

1 bunch green onions, chopped
1 cup grated sharp cheese

SAUCE:
1 cup sour cream
1 cup mayonnaise
1 (10 1/2-ounce) can mushroom soup

2 tablespoons prepared mustard
2 eggs, well beaten

Combine all ingredients for sauce. Add shrimp, noodles and green onions. Pour into a greased casserole; top with cheese and bake at 300° for 30 minutes. Serves 10.

Bravo! Applaudable Recipes

Shrimp-Egg Casserole

Make ahead for your luncheon--even the day before--then bake while you set the table and welcome your guests.

1 1/2-2 cups cooked shrimp	**2 tablespoons margarine or butter**
1/4 cup crumbs	

SAUCE:

2 teaspoons minced onion	**1/4 teaspoon pepper**
1/3 cup margarine	**2 1/2 cups milk**
1/3 cup flour	**2 tablespoons sherry**
1/2 teaspoon salt	**3/4 cup shredded sharp cheese**

To make sauce, slightly cook but do not brown onions in margarine. Blend in flour, salt and pepper. Stir in milk and sherry. Cook until thickened then add cheese. Add shrimp and distribute through sauce.

DEVILED EGGS:

6 boiled eggs, halved	**1 teaspoon prepared mustard**
1/4 cup Miracle Whip	**1/4 teaspoon salt**
1 teaspoon lemon juice	**1/4 teaspoon pepper**

Remove yolks from eggs and mix with other ingredients. Adjust seasoning to taste, but filling should be fairly highly seasoned. Stuff egg whites with filling and place in 7 1/2x12-inch baking dish. Distribute sauce over eggs then top with buttered crumbs. Bake at 350° for about 30 minutes. Serves 6.

Cookbook

Quick Shrimp Casserole

1/2 stick butter
1 (16-ounce) carton sour cream
Cavender's or seasoned salt
  to taste
1/2 teaspoon mace
1 pound cooked shrimp,
  shelled and deveined

2 (14-ounce) cans artichoke hearts,
  heated, drained and kept warm
4 (10-ounce) packages frozen
  chopped spinach, cooked,
  squeezed dry and kept warm
Paprika
Parsley for garnish

Melt butter in double boiler. Fold in sour cream and gently heat until warm. Season with Cavender's or seasoned salt and mace. Add shrimp. Arrange artichoke hearts in casserole. Top with spinach and pour sour cream/shrimp mixture over this. Sprinkle with paprika and garnish with parsley flakes. Serve immediately. Do not try to reheat before serving.

Magic

Elly's Shrimp Spaghetti

1 stick butter
2 cloves garlic, crushed
1 pound mushrooms, sliced
5 sprigs parsley, chopped
1 pound shrimp, cooked and
  cleaned

1/4 cup sherry
1/2 teaspoon salt
3 cups cooked spaghetti
Parmesan cheese

Sauté mushrooms, garlic and parsley in butter until tender. Add shrimp, sherry and salt and toss until heated. Pour over spaghetti and toss with parmesan to taste. Serves 4.

Heavenly Hostess

Foster's Crab Omelet

2 tablespoons butter or oil
2 tablespoons chopped onion
1/2 rib celery, chopped
2 teaspoon parsley, chopped
2 tablespoons chopped sweet
  green pepper

2 eggs, separated
Salt and pepper to taste
Meat from 2 large crabs

Sauté onion, celery, parsley and pepper in butter until tender-crisp, but not brown. Remove from pan and combine with beaten egg yolks, salt and pepper. Fold crabmeat in gently. Beat egg whites stiff and fold in. For each omelet, drop about 3 tablespoons of mixture into heavy frying pan which contains about 1/4-inch of melted fat. A large pan should be able to cook 4 omelets at a time. Fry until golden brown on one side, turn carefully and brown on other side. Drain on absorbent paper and serve immediately. Serves 2.

To anyone who grew up around the shores of Mobile Bay, the words "crab omelets" conjure up an entirely different picture than they do to anyone else. Foster's, swimming pavilion and restaurant south of Mobile in the days just before World War II, elevated crab omelets to fine art.

Loaves and Fishes

Christopher's Favorite Shrimp, Crab, and Cheese Casserole

A delightful luncheon or brunch dish when accompanied by fresh asparagus and fresh seasonal fruit.

8-9 slices white bread, trimmed and cubed	1/2 cup butter
2 pounds fresh, small or medium shrimp, cooked and peeled	2 1/2 cups milk (or cream)
	4 eggs, beaten
2 pounds fresh crabmeat, drained and well picked	3/4 teaspoon Colman's Dry Mustard
	Salt to taste
3/4-1 pound sharp Cheddar cheese, grated	Cayenne pepper to taste
	Dash of Tabasco sauce

Arrange bread, shrimp, crab, and cheese in layers in a 3-quart casserole. Pour melted butter over these layers. Mix milk (or cream), egg, dry mustard, salt, pepper, and cayenne pepper. Pour this mixture slowly over layers. Lightly cover. Refrigerate for 4 hours or overnight. Bake, lightly covered with foil tent, at 350° for 1 hour or until bubbly. Remove foil and brown top by placing under broiler. Serves 6-8.

Note: I usually sprinkle top with grated bread crumbs before placing under broiler.

A Samford Celebration Cookbook

Shrimp Crabmeat Galore

1 cup finely chopped bell pepper	1/2 teaspoon pepper
2 cups finely chopped celery	1 1/2 tablespoons Worcestershire
3 tablespoons finely chopped fresh onion	1/4 teaspoon Tabasco
	2 teaspoons Accent or monosodium
1 1/2 cups crabmeat	glutamate
4-5 cups boiled shrimp, cut into 2 or 3 pieces	1 1/4 to 1 1/2 cups mayonnaise
	1-2 cups buttered cracker crumbs

Mix all ingredients listed except mayonnaise and cracker crumbs. Then add mayonnasie and mix well. Pour into casserole and top with buttered cracker crumbs. Bake at 350° until hot, bubbly and brown.

Cotton Country Cooking

Swiss Quiche with Crabmeat Sauce

1 unbaked (9-inch) pie shell
4 slightly beaten egg yolks
1 1/2 cups light cream
1/2 teaspoon salt

1/8 teaspoon ground nutmeg
4 egg whites
1 1/2 cups shredded Swiss cheese

Bake pastry shell in 450° oven for 7 minutes. Remove. Reduce heat to 350°. Combine egg yolks, cream, salt and nutmeg. Beat egg whites until stiff. Fold into yolk mixture. Fold in cheese. Pour into shell. Bake 350° for 40-45 minutes or until knife inserted just off-center comes out clean. Let stand 5 minutes. Serve with Crabmeat Sauce.

CRABMEAT SAUCE:

1 (6-7-ounce) package frozen,
   drained crabmeat
2 tablespoons margarine

2-4 teaspoons flour
1/8 teaspoon salt
1 cup light cream

Heat crabmeat in margarine. Blend in flour and salt. Add cream; cook and stir until thick. Serves 6-8.

Auburn Entertains

Crabmeat Imperial

1 green pepper, finely diced
2 pimientos, finely diced
1 tablespoon Dijon mustard
1 tablespoon salt
2 teaspoons white pepper
2 eggs, slightly beaten

1 cup mayonnaise
3 pounds lump crabmeat
1 tablespoon mayonnaise, for
   topping
Paprika, for topping

In a large mixing bowl combine green pepper, pimientos, mustard, salt, white pepper, eggs and mayonnaise. Mix well. Add crabmeat and stir carefully so that lumps are not broken. Place in a well-greased 2-quart casserole. Top lightly with mayonnaise and sprinkle with paprika. Bake at 350° about 30 minutes. Serves 8-10.

Bravo! Applaudable Recipes

Crab au Gratin

4 tablespoons butter
1 onion, finely chopped
4 tablespoons flour
2 cups hot milk
1 1/2 cups sharp cheese, grated
3 drops Tabasco
1 tablespoon Worcestershire
Salt and pepper, to taste

1/2 cup mushrooms, sautéed in
   butter (or more mushrooms
   if you like)
1/4 cup Chablis
1 pound lumb crabmeat, picked
   over
Buttered bread crumbs
Additional grated cheese, for crepes

Melt butter in a 2-quart saucepan and sauté onion until it is limp. Stir in flour and cook 2 minutes. Add hot milk all at once and stir until mixture comes to a boil. Add cheese, seasonings, mushrooms, wine and crabmeat. Stir gently. Pour into a greased 2-quart casserole dish and top with buttered bread crumbs. Bake in a 350° oven for 30 minutes. The sauce may be strained to remove the sautéed onion if you like, but do this before you add seasonings, cheese, etc. Instead of baking this in a casserole dish, it may be used nicely as a crepe filling. In this case, omit bread crumbs, and use additional grated cheese to sprinkle over the top of crepes, returning them to the oven just long enough to let the cheese melt. Mixture should fill at least 12 crepes. Serves 6.

One of a Kind

Crab Souffle

1 1/2 cups crabmeat	2 tablespoons brandy
4 tablespoons butter	1/8 teaspoon white pepper
4 tablespoons flour	1/4 teaspoon salt
3/4 cup milk	4 eggs, separated
1/4 cup dry sherry	Paprika

Pick over crabmeat and set aside. In medium saucepan, melt butter, take off heat and add flour, then the milk and sherry, stirring to keep sauce smooth. Put back on low fire and cook until thickened. Add brandy, pepper and salt; beat in egg yolks one at a time. Cook a few more minutes, but do not let boil. Remove from heat and fold in crabmeat. Beat egg whites stiff. Beat in 1/4 of egg whites to lighten mixture, then fold in the rest. Turn into buttered 1-quart souffle dish. Bake at 375° for 30 minutes. Sprinkle top of souffle with paprika. Serves 4.

Fresh fish or canned tuna may be substituted for the crab.

Loaves and Fishes

Crab Cakes a la Mobile Bay

1 pound crabmeat	1/2 teaspoon salt or Old Bay
1 egg	Seasoning if available
1 tablespoon prepared mustard	2 tablespoons mayonnaise
1 tablespoon baking powder	1 cup bread crumbs
1 tablespoon parsley, minced	

Mix all but crabmeat and bread crumbs to form a paste. Add crabmeat and enough bread crumbs to hold mixture together. Shape into flat cakes about 2 1/2-inches in diameter. Refrigerate about 2 hours. Fry in iron skillet with 1/4-inch medium hot oil until brown on both sides. Serve with beer, slaw and crackers. Allow two per person. Serves 4-6.

Heavenly Hostess

Scallop Sauté

The large sea scallops are best, but even the small bay scallops make this dish outstanding!

3 tablespoons butter
3 tablespoons olive oil
8 ounces fresh mushrooms,
  washed and dried, sliced
1 bunch green onions, chopped
2 pounds fresh scallops, rinsed
  and drained

2 tablespoons lemon juice
1/2 teaspoon salt
1/2 teaspoon black pepper
1/4 teaspoon white pepper
Dash Tabasco
Rice, preferably wild rice

In a large skillet or sauté pan, heat butter and oil until sizzling; add mushrooms and onions and sauté about 6 minutes. Add scallops and sauté an additional 5-6 minutes. Add lemon juice and seasonings. Remove from heat and serve over wild rice. Serves 6.

Birdies in the Oven/Aces in the Kitchen

Scallops with Pine Nuts
Wonderful!

1 pound fresh bay scallops
12 tablespoons butter
3 tablespoons finely chopped
  shallots
Salt

2 tablespoons pine nuts
1 tablespoon chopped parsley
1/3 cup fine bread crumbs
1 tablespoon lemon juice

Preheat oven to 500°. Rinse the scallops and pat them dry. Work the butter with the fingers until it is soft. Add the salt to taste, pine nuts, parsley, bread crumbs and lemon juice. Place scallops in 2-quart Pyrex. Top the scallops with spoonfuls of the butter mixture. Bake for 10 minutes or until piping hot and bubbling. Yield: 8 servings.

Huntsville Entertains

Polynesian Tuna

1 (9-ounce) can pineapple tidbits	1/4 cup cold water
1 tablespoon butter or margarine	2 tablespoons soy sauce
1 cup green pepper, cut in strips	2 tablespoons cider vinegar
1 chicken bouillon cube	2 tablespoons sugar
3/4 cup boiling water	1/4 teaspoon pepper
2 tablespoons cornstarch	1 (7-ounce) can solid pack tuna

Drain pineapple and reserve the syrup. Melt margarine or butter in saucepan over low heat; add pineapple and cook for about 3 minutes until lightly browned. Measure 1/2 cup of the pineapple juice and add to pineapple with the green pepper. Cover and simmer for 10 minutes. Dissolve bouillon cube in boiling water and add to pineapple mixture. Stir in cornstarch mixed with cold water until smooth. Add soy sauce, vinegar, sugar and pepper. Cook, stirring constantly, until thickened and clear. Drain tuna; break into chunks; fold gently into pineapple mixture. Heat and serve over crisp chow mein noodles. Serves 4.

Auburn Entertains

Creole Fish

1 green pepper diced	1 1/2 tablespoons onion flakes
2 stems diced celery	(dried)
5 tablespoons water	Salt and pepper
1 chicken bouillon	1 1/2 cups tomato juice
1 small can sliced mushrooms	5 fish fillets

Combine all ingredients in baking dish and bake uncovered until fish is flaky. Do not overcook, about 1 hour 15 minutes at 350°.

Treasured Tastes

Both fresh- and saltwater fishing waters are located within a quarter mile of each other at Gulf Shores.

Trout Amandine

SAUCE:

1/2 cup butter

Juice of 1/2 lemon

2 tablespoons Worcestershire

2 tablespoons chopped parsley

1/4 cup browned, blanched,
   chopped almonds

Melt butter. Add lemon juice, Worcestershire and cook, stirring, for two minutes. Add parsley and almonds.

FISH:

Trout fillets

2 egg yolks

1/2 cup milk

Flour

Beat egg yolks and add milk slowly, mixing well. Dip fillets in this mixture and roll in flour. Heat fat and cook fish three to five minutes or until brown. Pour sauce over fish and serve.

Recipe Jubilee!

Little River, in north Alabama, is the farthest south that freshwater trout can be caught.

Seafood Batter

1 can beer
1 teaspoon salt
2 cups plain flour

1 teaspoon paprika
1/8 teaspoon cayenne pepper

Blend all ingredients together. Great batter for crab claws and shrimp.

The Great Cookbook

Poultry and Game

Ivy Green, the birthplace and childhood home of Helen Keller. Tuscumbia.

Southern Fried Chicken

1/2 cup all-purpose flour	2 1/2 to 3 pound broiler-fryer
1 teaspoon salt	chicken, cut up
1/4 teaspoon pepper	Vegetable oil

Mix flour, salt and pepper. Coat chicken with flour mixture. Heat oil (1/4-inch in 12-inch skillet over medium high heat until hot. Cook chicken in oil until light brown on all sides, for about 10 minutes; reduce heat. Cover tightly and simmer, turning once or twice, until thickest pieces are done, for about 35 minutes longer. If skillet cannot be covered tightly, add 1-2 tablespoons water. Remove cover during last 5 minutes of cooking to crisp chicken. Makes 6 servings.

Mama used to have the kids run down a chicken. She would chop or wring his neck off. The next step was to dip him in hot water, and then dress him for the frying pan. A chicken could be in the yard one hour and on the table the next hour. As soon as "Thanks" was offered, everyone grabbed for the chicken plate to try and be lucky enough to get the breast or pulley bone. If company happened to be present, only the chicken gravy was left for the little folks. Fried chicken was a favorite dish for breakfast in those days.

Kum' Ona' Granny's Table

Spicy Fried Chicken

3 pounds chicken parts or 1	1 teaspoon paprika
(2 1/2-pound) fryer, cut up	1/2 teaspoon cayenne pepper
1/2 cup flour	1/4 teaspoon freshly ground
1 teaspoon salt or garlic salt	black pepper
1 teaspoon dry mustard	Corn oil
1 teaspoon chili powder	

Dry chicken pieces on paper towels. Combine flour and seasoning in paper bag. Place chicken pieces a few at a time in bag, twist end, and shake vigorously to coat chicken well. Heat 1 1/2-inches corn oil in deep skillet until temperature reaches 365°. Lower chicken into hot oil and cook 8-10 minutes to a side or until golden brown. Lift out and drain well on paper towels. Serves 3-4.

Loaves and Fishes

Glazed Butterfly Chicken

8 whole chicken breasts
6 tablespoons butter or margarine
1 teaspoon ground ginger

Curry glaze
1/4 cup flaked coconut

Cut away rib bones from chicken with sharp knife or scissors, leaving the V-shaped bone at neck; save bones to simmer for broth. Melt butter in large shallow baking pan; stir in ginger. Roll chicken in mixture to coat well; arrange, skin side up, in single layer in pan. Tuck edge of each breast under to give a rounded shape. Spoon Curry Glaze over to make very thick coating. Bake, uncovered, at 350° for 1 hour and 20 minutes or until richly glazed and tender. Baste often with glaze mixture. Top each breast with a sprinkle of coconut; bake 10 minutes longer or until lightly toasted.

CURRY GLAZE:

8 slices bacon, diced
1 large onion, chopped
2 tablespoons flour
1 tablespoon curry powder
1 teaspoon sugar
1 teaspoon salt
1 teaspoon bottled steak sauce

1 (4-ounce) jar baby-pack
   strained apples and apricots
1 cup water
3 tablespoons lemon juice
2 envelopes instant beef broth or
   2 beef bouillon cubes

Fry bacon slowly in medium saucepan until fat starts to cook out; stir in onion and sauté just until soft. Blend in flour, curry powder, sugar, salt and steak sauce until mixture bubbles; stir in remaining ingredients. Heat, stirring constantly to boiling. Simmer, uncovered, 15 minutes or until thickened. Yield: 8 servings.

    This chicken is very good and makes a very attractive dish to serve on special occasions. The coconut and baby food makes this dish.

Kum' Ona' Granny's Table

French Chicken with Sherry Nutmeg Sauce
(Low-Cal)

3 broiler chicken breasts, split
1 onion, minced
1 cup fat skimmed chicken broth,
   fresh or canned (put can in
   refrigerator and discard
   congealed fat that
   rises to the top)
1/2 teaspoon ground nutmeg
3 teaspoons dry sherry wine or
   cooking sherry

Pinch of red cayenne pepper
Salt and pepper
   (if cooking sherry is
   used, cut down on
   amount of salt)
1 teaspoon minced parsley
   (optional)
3/4 cup skim milk
2 teaspoons flour

Put chicken skin-side-down in a non-stick skillet or electric frying pan. Brown slowly over moderate heat with no fat added, until skin is well browned. Drain melted fat. Put chicken skin side up and add onion, broth and wine. Sprinkle with seasonings. Cover and simmer over very low heat until nearly tender, 40-50 minutes. Uncover. Skim fat off if necessary. Continue to simmer uncovered until liquid is reduced by half. Whisk milk and flour together and stir into pan. Cook and stir until thickened. Serves 4, about 215 calories each.

More Fiddling With Food

Mustard Chicken

4 chicken breasts	1/2 pound mushrooms, sliced
Flour	1 tablespoon parsley, chopped
4 tablespoons butter	Salt and pepper
Dijon mustard	1 cup heavy cream
2 tablespoons oil	
1/2 medium onion, chopped	

Dredge chicken breasts in flour, sauté in butter until lightly browned. Spread lightly with mustard and place in 11x7x2-inch baking dish. Sauté onions and mushrooms in oil; add parsley, salt, and freshly ground pepper. Blend in cream, pour over chicken. Cover and bake at 325°-350° for 25 minutes. Uncover and continue baking for an additional 5-10 minutes. Yield: 4 servings.

Once Upon a Stove

Over 150 antique dealers from throughout the United States are collected in the Olde Mill Antique Mall and Village. The complex, which covers 31 acres, is located just off I-20 at the Oxford/Anniston exit.

Chicken a la King

4 tablespoons butter	2 eggs
1 cup mushrooms	1 cup sour cream
1 bell pepper, chopped	1 cup chopped pimento
2 tablespoons flour	2 tablespoons sherry
1 cup chicken broth	Salt and pepper to taste
2 cups chopped chicken	

Melt butter in skillet. Add mushrooms and bell pepper. Stir. Add 2 tablespoons flour, mix thoroughly, add chicken broth, chicken. Cook on low heat 10 minutes. Beat eggs and add sour cream. Add pimento. Heat--do not boil. Add salt and pepper and sherry. Serve in pastry or on rice. Serves 6 or 7.

Heavenly Hostess

Baked Chicken Breasts

1/2 cup grated Parmesan cheese	3 tablespoons sesame seeds
2 cups seasoned bread crumbs	3-4 chicken breasts

Mix above ingredients. Dip pieces of chicken breasts into 1/2 cup melted butter and then into crumb mixture. Freeze or refrigerate until ready to cook. (Use 3-4 chicken breasts cut in half.) Bring to room temperature to cook. Place in shallow pan, dot with butter and bake 1 hour at 350°. Serve with Cumberland Sauce.

CUMBERLAND SAUCE:

1 cup red currant Jelly	1 teaspoon dry mustard
1 (6-ounce) frozen orange juice	1/4 teaspoon ginger
4 tablespoons dry sherry	1/4 teaspoon hot pepper sauce

Combine and simmer until smooth.

More Fiddling With Food

Chicken Breasts with Dried Beef

2 jars dried beef	1 1/2 cans mushroom soup
8 whole chicken breasts, boned	1 1/2 cups sour cream
8 slices bacon	Paprika

Line large flat 2-3-quart casserole with dried beef. Place in oven to dry out beef. Roll each chicken breast and wrap with slice of bacon. Place chicken on top of beef. Combine soup and sour cream and pour over chicken. Sprinkle with paprika. Cover casserole with foil and bake 3 hours or more in 300° oven. Remove foil for last 1/2-hour to brown. Do not cook too fast or sauce will boil away. Good for luncheons. Serves 8.

Variation: Add 2 tablespoons sherry to soup mixture.

Huntsville Heritage Cookbook

Athens College Chicken Souffle

3 tablespoons butter
3 tablespoons flour
1 cup milk
1/4 teaspoon salt
2 egg yolks (beaten)
1 1/2 cups cooked chicken cut
   in tiny pieces

1 teaspoon onion juice
2 well-beaten egg whites
1/4 teaspoon cornstarch
1/4 teaspoon sugar

Make cream sauce of butter, milk, flour and salt. Add egg yolks, chicken and onion juice. Cool. Fold in beaten egg whites to which cornstarch and sugar have been added. Put mixture in buttered casserole, place in pan of hot water and bake at 325° for an hour.

Treasured Alabama Recipes

Chicken Almondine

2 sticks butter or oleo
8 chicken breasts, or more
2 cans sliced mushrooms and juice
4 tablespoons flour

1 1/2 cups water
1/2 cup dry white wine
Salt and paprika
1 package slivered almonds

Melt butter in skillet. Rub chicken with salt and paprika. Brown well. Put in roaster with lid. Add flour to butter and brown. Add water, wine, mushrooms and juice. Pour over chicken. Cook in 350° oven for 1 hour. Add almonds just before serving.

Sumpthn' Yummy

Ave Maria Grotto, sometimes called "Little Jerusalem," features over 150 miniature replicas of the world's best-known religious shrines. Built by a Benedictine monk, the shrine is located one mile east of Cullman.

Chicken and Artichoke Casserole

1 (3-pound) fryer and 2 or 3 extra
  breast halves
1 cup butter
1/2 cup flour
3 1/2 cups milk
3 ounces Gruyére or Swiss cheese
1/8 pound rat cheese
  (mellow Cheddar)

1 tablespoon Accent
2 cloves garlic, pressed
1/2 tablespoon red pepper
  (or less)
2 large cans button mushrooms,
  drained
2 large cans artichoke hearts,
  drained

Boil chicken in seasoned water. Remove skin and bones and cut meat into large pieces. Set aside. Melt butter, stir in flour until blended. Slowly add milk and stir until the sauce is smooth. Add cheese (cut into small pieces or grated) and seasonings. Stir until cheese melts and sauce bubbles, then add chicken, mushrooms, and artichokes to the sauce. Check the seasonings. Put the combined mixture in a casserole dish and bake 30 minutes at 350°. Lobster, crab, or shrimp may be substituted. This is good served with buttered noodles. Serves 10.

One of a Kind

Broccoli and Chicken Casserole

2 packages broccoli
6 chicken breasts, cooked and
  boned
2 cans cream of chicken soup,
  (undiluted)

1 cup mayonnaise
1 teaspoon lemon juice
1 teaspoon curry powder
Cheddar cheese, grated
Ritz crackers, grated or crushed

Cook broccoli for a few minutes and put on bottom of casserole dish. Top with bite-size pieces of chicken. Mix next 4 ingredients together and pour sauce over chicken and broccoli. Sprinkle with cheese and top with Ritz crackers. Bake 30-40 minutes at 350°.

Calling All Cooks

Cheese Chicken Casserole

6 chicken breasts
2 (10-ounce) packages chopped
  broccoli
2 cups milk
1 (8-ounce) package cream cheese

1 teaspoon salt
1/8 teaspoon garlic powder
1 1/2 cups Parmesan cheese
1 can onion rings

Cook chicken and remove from bones. Cook broccoli only until crisp, tender. Drain. Arrange in bottom of a large casserole dish (9x13). Blend milk, cream cheese, salt and garlic powder in double boiler until smooth. Stir in 3/4 cup Parmesan cheese. Pour 1 cup of sauce over broccoli. Top with chicken. Cover with remaining sauce. Sprinkle rest of Parmesan on top. Bake at 350° for 25 minutes. Top with onion rings. Let stand 5 minutes before serving. Yields 8-10 servings.

The Great Cookbook

Cheesy Chicken
(Microwave)

1/4 cup butter or margarine
3/4 cup cornflake crumbs
1/3 cup grated Parmesan cheese
2 tablespoons chopped chives

2 tablespoons chopped parsley
1 broiler-fryer chicken, 3 pounds,
  cut in serving pieces

Place butter in an 8-inch square microproof baking dish. Cook on MEDIUM power for 1 1/2 minutes, or until butter is melted. Combine corn flake crumbs, cheese, chives, and parsley in a shallow dish. Dip pieces of chicken in butter and roll in crumb mixture. Place chicken pieces in an 8-inch square microproof baking dish, skin-side-up with thickest pieces of chicken toward outside of dish. Cover with waxed paper and cook on HIGH for 15-17 minutes, or until chicken in tender. Let stand, covered, about 15 minutes before serving. Yield: 4 servings.

Hint: Rotate crumb-coated chicken. Arrange coated chicken with the most attractive side up. Rotate the dish during microcooking, but do not turn chicken over. This helps keep the crumbs crisp.

Kitchen Sampler

Polynesian Chicken

6 chicken breasts (halves)
1 bottle Russian salad dressing
1 jar apricot preserves

1 package Lipton dry onion
  soup mix

Place chicken breasts in baking dish. Mix dressing, preserves, and soup mix and pour over chicken. Bake at 350° for 1 1/2 hours. Serves 6.

Gazebo I Cookbook

Chicken Rockefeller

1 (10-ounce) package frozen,
  chopped spinach
1 beaten egg
1/4 cup grated Parmesan cheese

1 cup Italian-style bread crumbs
6 whole split, boned chicken breasts
3 tablespoons melted butter
Salt and pepper to taste

Cook spinach per package directions. Drain well. Cool. Combine spinach, egg and 1 tablespoon Parmesan. Set aside. Combine breadcrumbs and remaining Parmesan in shallow pan. Sprinkle breasts with salt and pepper, roll each in breadcrumb mixture and drizzle with butter. Place equal amounts of spinach mixture on top of each breast. Cover and bake 40 minutes at 350°. Serves 6.

Try Me

Chicken Crescent Roll

1 (3-ounce) package cream
  cheese, softened
3 tablespoons melted butter
2 cups cooked cubed chicken
1/4 teaspoon salt
1/8 teaspoon pepper

2 tablespoons milk
1 tablespoon chopped onions
1 tablespoon chopped pimientos
1 (8-ounce) can crescent rolls
1 tablespoon butter

Blend cream cheese and butter, then add chicken, salt, pepper, milk, onions and pimientos. Mix well. Spoon 1/2 cup chicken mixture to each
rectangle crescent roll. Pull up four corners and twist. Brush tops with
butter. Place in 9x9-inch glass baking dish at 350° for 20 minutes.
Yield: 6-8 servings.

Cooks and Company

Chicken Tetrazzini For a Crowd

2 (2 1/2 to 3-pound) fryers, cut up
Water to cover
Salt and Pepper
1 (12-ounce) package spaghetti
1 green pepper, chopped
1 onion, chopped
1 stick margarine

2/3 cups flour
4 cups milk
1 can cream of mushroom soup
1 pound sharp Cheddar cheese,
  grated (reserve 1 cup for top)
Salt and pepper

Place fryers in a large boiler; cover with water. Add salt and pepper to
taste, cook until tneder. Remove from broth. Cool; remove skin and
bones. Set chicken aside. Cook spaghetti in chicken broth until tender.
Sauté pepper and onion in margarine until clear. Add flour, milk, soup,
cheese, salt and pepper to taste. Cook until thickened. Add sauce and
chicken to cooked spaghetti. Pour into a large shallow baking dish.
Sprinkle top with cheese. Bake at 400° for 30 minutes. Makes 4
quarts. Freezes well.

Hallmark's Collection of Home Tested Recipes

First Place Chicken Casserole

2-3 cups cooked chicken, diced
4 hard-boiled eggs, chopped
2 cups cooked rice
1 1/2 cups celery, chopped
1 small onion, chopped
1 cup mayonnaise
2 cans mushroom soup

1 (3-ounce) package slivered
  almonds
1 teaspoon salt
2 tablespoons lemon juice
1 cup bread crumbs
2 tablespoons margarine

Mix all ingredients except bread crumbs and margarine. Place mixture in buttered 9x12-inch pan or casserole. Brown bread crumbs lightly in margarine. Sprinkle over casserole, refrigerate overnight. Remove from refrigerator 1 hour before cooking. Bake 40-45 minutes at 350°. Serves 8.

Superlatives are definitely in order for this make-ahead dish which came to us already aptly named. We suggest cooking the rice in the broth left from the chicken. We promise rave notices to you, too!

Cotton Country Cooking

Grandma Hallmark's Chicken and Dumplings

1 large fryer, cut into serving pieces
2 quarts water

Salt and pepper to taste

Put chicken and water into a large boiler; add salt and pepper. Cook until tender; remove from broth, bone and set aside. Make dumplings.

DUMPLINGS:
4 cups flour
1 teaspoon salt

Shortening size of a large egg
1 cup cold water

Sift flour and salt into bowl. Make a well in center of flour; put shortening and water into well. Mix with your hands. Knead until firm and smooth. Place dough on lightly floured surface, cover and let rest for 1-2 hours. Roll paper thin with rolling pin. Cut into small squares. Drop one at a time into boiling chicken broth. Stir chicken into dumplings; let simmer for 5-10 minutes, covered.

Hallmark's Collection of Home Tested Recipes

Bill's Famous Barbeque Sauce and Chicken

SAUCE:

2 sticks butter	1 tablespoon catsup
1/2 cup lemon juice	1/2 cup orange juice
1-2 tablespoons Worcestershire sauce	1 - 2 tablespoons lemon pepper
	Garlic salt
1/2 cup cider vinegar	Salt and pepper

Mix all ingredients; boil for 2-3 minutes and then simmer 10 minutes. Keep warm for basting chicken.

CHICKEN:
4 whole fryers, split

Salt and let stand for 15 minutes, then pepper. Brown for 15 minutes and begin turning and basting.

WHITE TABLE BARBEQUE SAUCE:
Add 1 1/2 tablespoons mayonnaise (more or less) to remaining red barbeque sauce and serve at table. Serves 8.

Twickenham Tables

Hickory-Smoked Turkey

Select a 10-12 pound ready-to-cook turkey. Rinse bird; pat dry with paper toweling. Soak in salt brine overnight.

BRINE: (to each 2 cups water add):

5 tablespoons salt	**Dash lemon juice**
1 tablespoon brown sugar	**Dash pepper**

MARINADE:

1 cup port wine	**2 cloves**
1/2 cup soy sauce	**1/4 teaspoon pepper**
1/2 cup salad oil	**2 teaspoons parsley, finely**
1/2 cup honey	**chopped**

Using Spit: Truss turkey and balance on spit or use rotary roast rack. Have slow coals at back, front and sides of fire box with a drip pan under revolving bird. Keep water in drip pan for moisture. Roast with hood down, basting every half hour with marinade. Toss damp hickory chips on coals. Each time you baste, check fire, hickory chips and water in pan. About 20 minutes before bird is done, "shake hands with the turkey." (Snip the cord that holds the drumsticks to the spit rod; grasp end of drumstick with paper towel; raise and lower leg to test. Leg should move easily or twist out of joint.) Takes 4 1/2 - 5 hours.

Using Smoker or Grill: Build fire in smoker or under one end of grill and place bird on grill away from fire and over pan of water. Baste in marinade and turn bird by hand every half hour or so. The time to smoke is about the same as on spit, but this depends on size of bird. Before carving, let bird rest 15 minutes. It will be easier to carve.

Seconds Please!

The Birmingham Zoo is a sprawling, 100-acre facility with over 1,000 animal species, including Siberian tigers, white rhinoceroses, gorillas, orangutans, rare birds, and reptiles.

Birdie Dressed Up
(Turkey or Chicken and Dressing Casserole)

1 1/2 cups herbed stuffing mix
2-3 cups crumbled cornbread
1 cup chopped onion
1 cup chopped celery
2 eggs
2 cups chicken broth
3 slices white sandwich bread,
  crusts removed
1/2 teaspoon salt

1/2 teaspoon black pepper
1/2 teaspoon poultry seasoning
3 cups cooked chicken or turkey
  meat
2 ounces butter
Flour
1/4 teaspoon black pepper
Pinch sage

In a well-greased 2-3-quart shallow baking dish, spread half of stuffing over bottom to cover. Combine cornbread, onion, celery, eggs, and broth. Add white bread, torn in pieces, to make a thick, moist consistency. Blend in seasonings and spread over crumbs in casserole.

Shred chicken into bite-size pieces and layer on top of dressing. Melt butter in a medium saucepan; blend in flour and cook about 3 minutes, stirring constantly. Add chicken broth and cook over medium heat, stirring constantly, until thickened. Add seasonings. Pour over chicken. Sprinkle remaining herb stuffing on top. Bake at 350° for 45 minutes. Serves 6-8.

This casserole may be prepared early in the day and reheated before serving or it may be frozen.

SAUCE: (optional)
3 hard-boiled eggs, sliced
Chicken giblets and liver, cooked
  and chopped

1 can cream of mushroom soup
1/2 cup milk
1 cup sour cream

In a small saucepan, combine soup, milk, and sour cream. Heat until bubbly. Add eggs and giblets; simmer to heat through. This does not freeze, but may be refrigerated and gently reheated.

Birdies in the Oven/Aces in the Kitchen

Bon Secour Oyster Dressing

1/2 cup butter
4 tablespoons chopped parsley
1/2 cup chopped celery
1/2 cup chopped onion
4 cups bread crumbs (may use
  cornbread)
1/8 teaspoon poultry seasoning
3/4 teaspoon salt

2 tablespoons parsley, minced
1/4 teaspoon pepper
1/2 teaspoon paprika
2 cup chicken stock (use oyster
  liquid as part of 2 cups)
3 eggs, well-beaten
1 pint oysters, drained and chopped

Melt butter and sauté chopped vegetables. Stir in bread crumbs and sea-sonings. Add stock and eggs. Cook all until heated through. Preheat oysters in butter, then add to mixture. Pour into casserole and bake at 400° for 15-20 minutes or use to stuff a 4-pound chicken. Triple for a 12-15 pound turkey.

Seconds Please!

Turkey Dressing

1 onion
1 bunch green onions
1 small green pepper
6 ribs celery
2 sticks margarine
1 pound bulk sausage
  (I use "Hot")

2 packages Pepperidge Farm
  Cornbread Stuffing mix
4 cups well seasoned chicken stock
2 eggs, slightly beaten
1 1/2 cups parsley, minced
Salt, pepper, Worcestershire sauce

Finely chop onions, green pepper and celery. Sauté these in butter and sausage. Be sure sausage is well done; you will have stirred it until it is in small bits. In a large bowl, combine dressing mix and chicken stock (you can make this from chicken bouillon cubes). Add sausage mixture, eggs, fresh parsley and seasonings. You may stuff the cavity of the tur-key or bake all of it in a shallow baking dish. Bake for 30 minutes at 350°. Serves 12.

One of a Kind

Wild Duck or Wild Goose

4 wild ducks or 2 wild geese,
 cleaned
Flour
Salt and pepper
Vegetable oil

Bacon drippings
1 (6-ounce) can frozen orange juice,
 thawed
1/2 juice can water

STUFFING:
1 apple, peeled and chopped
1/2 cup bread crumbs
2 celery stalks, chopped
1 onion, chopped

2 oranges, peeled and diced
1/4 teaspoon pepper
1 teaspoon salt

Wash birds in cold water and dry with paper towels. Refrigerate while stuffing is prepared. Combine all stuffing ingredients and set aside. Sprinkle outside of birds with salt and pepper and cover evenly with flour. Brown the birds one at a time in a deep fat fryer with enough hot vegetable oil to cover. Drain and cool birds. Stuff with prepared stuffing but do not truss. Place 2 tablespoons bacon drippings in a roasting pan and arrange the birds in it. Combine orange juice with 1/2 can water and pour over the birds. Cover with aluminum foil and bake at 275° for 2 hours for a medium-done bird or longer for a well-done or large bird. (The geese take a little longer than the ducks.) Baste with pan drippings every 20 minutes. Arrange on a platter with orange slices and parsley. Very good served with sweet potatoes, wild rice and green beans.

Bravo! Applaudable Recipes

Ducks Jubilee

4 duck breasts
4 teaspoons margarine
4 strips bacon

1 can mandarin oranges and juice
1/2 bottle orange extract

Cook ducks 1 hour in boiling salted water. Remove and dry. Salt ducks, rub with margarine and place in shallow pan. Top each with bacon strip in V-shape. Add orange juice; broil until bacon is crisp. Place in serving dish; garnish with orange sections. Before serving, pour extract over ducks; ignite. Serve with wild or brown rice.

Huntsville Heritage Cookbook

Doves

12 doves	1 teaspoon pepper
1 1/2 cups salad oil	1 teaspoon Beau Monde
1/2 cup vinegar	seasoning
1/2 red wine	1/2 stick butter
2-3 bay leaves	3 tablespoons flour
1 medium onion, sliced	1 medium onion, chopped
1 garlic clove, minced fine	2 bouillon cubes
1/2 teaspoon Worcestershire	2 cups boiling water
1 teaspoon salt	Salt and pepper to taste

Combine ingredients, salad oil through Beau Monde seasoning and marinate doves 7 to 8 hours. Brown doves in butter over very hot fire, remove when browned on all sides. To drippings in pan, add flour (more butter may be needed) and onion, stirring until flour is very brown. Dissolve bouillon cubes in boiling water, slowly add to roux stirring until smooth. Add salt and pepper. Put doves and gravy in electric skillet, set at 225° and cook 3 1/2 to 4 hours, basting frequently.

Recipe Jubilee!

Braised Quail or Doves
Excellent! Everyone will like this.

12 quail or doves	1/2 cup chopped onion
2 cups flour	1/2 cup chopped celery
Salt and pepper	2 tablespoons vinegar
1/2 cup butter	

1 (10 1/2-ounce) can beef bouillon or 2 cups water and 2 bouillon cubes Roll birds in flour seasoned with salt and pepper. Melt butter in frying pan; brown birds in butter. Add other ingredients. Cover and cook over low heat for 1 1/2 hours.

Note: Add sherry to make this even better.

Cookbook

Venison Roast I

2 (5 3/4-ounce) cans mushroom steak sauce	**Soy sauce**
2 (2 1/2-ounce) jars mushrooms	**Liquid smoke**
1/2 bottle Worcestershire	**Black pepper**
1 cup LaRosa Sherry or homemade wine	**Paprika**
1/2 cup cooking oil	**Meat tenderizer**
1 bell pepper	**Garlic salt**
	Seasoning salt

Debone meat and trim off fat. Add Worcestershire, sherry and cooking oil. Sprinkle on soy sauce, liquid smoke, tenderizer, garlic salt and seasoning salt. Add mushroom steak sauce and mushrooms. Chop bell pepper and add. Sprinkle on paprika and black pepper heavily. Cook at 325° for at least 4 hours or until tender, stirring every hour.

Anniversary Collection of Delectable Dishes

'Possum and Sweet Potatoes

1 opossum	**6-8 sweet potatoes**
Salt and pepper	**Water**

You secure 1 fat 'possum. Kill the possum and skin it. Boil it in water until tender. Be sure not to overcook. Take out and salt and pepper real good. Peel potatoes and boil until tender. Place 'possum in pan, place potatoes around 'possum and bake at 350° until brown. It should be done in about 20-30 minutes. This tastes like pork roast.

Dinner on the Ground

Martini Game Hens

4 Rock Cornish game hens
1/2 cup soy sauce
1 tablespoon honey
1 teaspoon ground ginger
3/4 cup olive oil
1/2 cup gin

2 cloves garlic, minced
2 onions, grated
1 tablespoon Worcestershire
 sauce
1/4 teaspoon black pepper
1/4 teaspoon red pepper

Cut hens in half. Make a marinade of remaining ingredients. Soak hens in marinade overnight. Roast, covered, (350°) for 50-60 minutes, basting frequently. Serve with rice. Serves 8. (Note: This is an especially good recipe which must be prepared ahead. If serving whole hens, roasting time will be longer. However, one-half of a bird is about all one person can eat.)

Seconds Please!

Meats

The USS Alabama earned nine battle stars during World War II and never received any damage or personnel casualties from enemy attacks. Mobile.

Earthen Roast

Step 1: Dig a hole 3 1/2 feet deep, 3 1/2 feet wide, and 3 1/2 feet long. Area may vary according to the amount of meat being cooked.

Step 2: Build a roaring fire in the hole with hardwood (hickory or oak). Add wood until hole is filled with hot coals to within 1 foot of top. This takes approximately 6-9 hours.

Step 3: Place a piece of tin on top of hot coals. Place roast(s), wrapped in heavy foil and secured tightly at the ends, on the tin. Place another piece of tin on top of meat. Cover with sand or dirt. Let cook for 10-12 hours. Add seasonings after opening the roast.

This size earthen hole has been used to cook 300 rib steaks. It has been used to cook a whole hog, head and all.

Dinner on the Ground

Eye of Round

(Roasted)

Have eye of the round roast at room temperature. Sprinkle with coarse black pepper or other seasoning. Preheat oven to 500° and bake 5 minutes per pound. Turn off and do not open oven for 2 hours. Roast will be pink.

What great news for the hostess! Imagine "do ahead" roast beef that will still be pink and juicy at serving time.

Cotton Country Cooking

Tasty One-Step Beef Brisket

1 (3-5-pound) fresh beef brisket	Worcestershire sauce
1 large oven cooking bag	Soy sauce
1 package dry onion soup mix	Garlic salt
Seasoned salt	
1 cup water	

Prepare cooking bag according to package instructions. Place brisket in bag and top with remaining ingredients. Close bag according to instructions. Bake at 325° for 2-3 hours. Yield: 6-10 servings.

Cooks and Company

Barbeque Roast Beef

5-pound eye of round roast

MARINADE:

1 medium onion, chopped	**2 teaspoon sugar**
3/4 cup catsup	**2 teaspoon dry mustard**
1/4 cup water	**1 teaspoon chili powder**
2 tablespoons vinegar	**1/2 teaspoon salt**
1 tablespoon prepared mustard	**1/2 teaspoon paprika**
2 tablespoons Lea and Perrins sauce	**Few drops Tabasco sauce**
2 tablespoons lemon juice	

Combine marinade ingredients in saucepan; heat to boiling and simmer 5 minutes. Pour over uncooked roast and let marinate for 48 hours, turning roast often. When ready to cook, wipe roast dry and brown on all sides in a large roasting pan with a small amount of oil or bacon grease. Pour on marinade, cover and start in cold oven at 325°. Cook for 2 1/2 hours. (For party purposes, make another recipe of marinade sauce to heat slices of roast in chafing dish. Serves 8-10 with thick, generous cuts. If the meat is sliced very thin, cocktail party style, it will go twice as far. Thick for family and thin for party.)

Bravo! Applaudable Recipes

Barbecued Spare Ribs

2 1/2-pounds spare ribs

(Have the butcher cut them in half and then cut each rib apart. Should be about 2-inch sections.)

MARINADE:

1/4 cup cocktail sherry
  (or 1 teaspoon sherry flavoring)
1/2 cup pineapple juice
1 cup soy sauce

2 tablespoons dark brown sugar
  (or brown sugar substitute)
1 clove garlic, crushed

Place the ribs in a plastic bag or bowl and cover with marinade mixture. Marinate for at least one day, turning frequently if the marinade does not cover all of the ribs. Remove ribs from the marinade and put in a broiler pan (not on a rack) and broil for 7 minutes on one side and then turn and broil on the other side for 5 minutes.

Auburn Entertains

Kabob Marinade and Basting Sauce

1/2 cup salad oil
1/2 cup soy sauce
2 tablespoons vinegar
2 small onions, chopped
1 clove garlic, minced

3 tablespoons chopped candied
  ginger
1/2 teaspoon pepper
1/2 teaspoon dry mustard

Mix together all ingredients. Marinade meat several hours or overnight in mixture. Brush meat with remaining marinade during cooking time.

Calling All Cooks

The First White House of the Confederacy, an Italianate-style house, was the home of President and Mrs. Jefferson Davis when Montgomery was the Confederate capital. It is now open to the public with no admission charge.

Corned Beef or Venison

Approximately 10 pounds venison or brisket of beef	**4 cloves garlic**
1 cup brown sugar	**1 teaspoon paprika**
1 cup salt	**1/2 teaspoon ground mustard seed**
Several shakes liquid smoke	**1/2 teaspoon salt peter**

Place meat in large crock or plastic container. Do not use metal. Mix together other ingredients in a boiler with a little water to make smooth. Bring to a boil. Pour over meat. Add enough water to cover meat. Cover and let stand in refrigerator for 10 days.

To cook, place corned meat in a pan of fresh water. Add bay leaves, peppercorns, carrot and onions. Simmer on top of the stove for several hours or until fork tender. Cool before slicing. Venison will taste just like corned beef.

Sumpthn' Yummy

Gertrude Style Sloppy Joes

2 tablespoons cooking oil	**1/4 teaspoon dry mustard**
1 can corned beef	**1 clove garlic, minced**
1 cup chopped celery	**1/4 cup Worcestershire sauce**
2 large or 3 small chopped onions	**1/2 cup catsup**
2 tablespoons brown sugar	**2 tablespoons water**
2 tablespoons vinegar	

Brown corned beef, celery and onion in oil. Add other ingredients and cook 15 minutes over low heat. Best if fixed early in the day and re-heated. Serve on buns.

Sumpthn' Yummy

Mushroom Stuffed Beef Birds

1 round steak, 1/2-inch thick
  (2 1/2-3 pounds)
1/2 pound fresh mushrooms
1/2 cup fresh parsley, chopped
1/2 cup onion, finely chopped
1 cup grated sharp Cheddar
  cheese

1/2 cup all-purpose flour
1 teaspoon salt
1 teaspoon pepper
3 tablespoons shortening
1 can (10 1/2-ounce) beef
  consommé
1/2 teaspoon dry mustard

Cut steak in 6 portions with knife; pound steak to 1/4-inch thickness. Remove mushroom caps from stems; add stems, parsley, onions and cheese to food processor and chop finely. Place approximately 3 tablespoons mushroom mixture in center of each piece of steak, reserving remainder of mixture. Roll steak around stuffing and fasten with toothpick. Tie with string if needed. Combine flour, salt, and pepper. Dredge meat rolls in seasoned flour. Heat oil, and brown rolls in large skillet. Pour off drippings. Combine consommé and dry mustard; add to beef rolls. Add mushroom caps; cover tightly and cook over low heat 45 minutes. Add remainder of mushroom mixture and continue cooking another 45 minutes or until meat is tender. Serve on a bed of rice. Yield: 6 servings.

Dining Under the Magnolia

Steak au Poivre

4 steaks
3 tablespoons crushed peppercorns
2 tablespoons butter
2 tablespoons oil
2 tablespoons finely chopped
  shallots

3 1/2 tablespoons heavy cream
3/4 cup rich brown stock
3/4 teaspoon cornstarch, dissolved
  in bit of stock
1/2 cup Cognac
1 1/2 tablespoons butter

Push crushed peppercorns in steak on both sides. Cover and refrigerate at least 1 hour. Pat steaks dry. Heat butter and oil; brown steaks about 3 minutes each side. Remove steaks from pan and keep warm in low oven. Sauté shallots 1 minute, stirring. Blot up excess oil from pan.

CONTINUED

CONTINUED

Add Cognac to pan immediately after blotting. Ignite. When flame dies, add remaining ingredients except cream and butter. Boil, stirring until sauce is reduced to desired thickness. Stir in cream. Add butter. Swirl pan to blend. Serve over steak. Serves 4.

DOWN HOME In High Style

Beef Stuffed Peppers

3 large green peppers
3 tablespoons minced onion
2 tablespoons butter
1 pound beef
1/2 cup instant rice, cooked
1/2 teaspoon salt

2 (8-ounce) cans tomato sauce
1/2 cup water
1/2 cup sherry
1 cup sour cream
1/4 pound sharp Cheddar cheese, grated

Split green peppers into halves lengthwise. Remove seeds and stems. Wash peppers; drop into a large pot of boiling salted water. Turn off heat; let stand 5 minutes. Drain; arrange peppers in baking dish. Sauté onion in butter for 5 minutes. Drain and mix onion with ground beef, rice, salt, and 1 can tomato sauce. Fill peppers with meat mixture. Combine 1 can tomato sauce, 1/2 cup water, sherry, and sour cream; pour over stuffed peppers. Bake at 350° for 40 minutes. Sprinkle with cheese and bake for 20 minutes longer. Yield: 6 servings.

Kitchen Sampler

Ivy Green, the birthplace of Helen Keller, is found in Tuscumbia. To commemorate her life, the facility presents *The Miracle Worker* each Friday and Saturday night from mid-June through July.

Veal Oscar

18 thin slices veal scalopine
  (1 1/2 ounces each)
Flour seasoned with salt and pepper
3 tablespoons olive oil
3 tablespoons butter

1/2 pound white lumb crabmeat
1/4 cup dry white wine
24-36 cooked asparagus spears
2 tablespoons chopped parsley
Bearnaise Sauce

Lightly pound veal slices until quite thin, being careful not to tear the meat. Dip slices in seasoned flour to coat both sides. Shake off excess. Heat olive oil and butter in a large heavy skillet and sauté veal over medium heat until golden brown on both sides. Remove from pan and keep warm, loosely covered in a 175° oven. Add wine to pan in which meat was cooked. Carefully add crabmeat and heat through, trying not to break up the lumps.

Arrange 3 slices of veal on each of six serving plates. Top with cooked asparagus and spoon Bearnaise Sauce over asparagus. Divide crabmeat evenly on top of each serving and sprinkle with chopped parsley.

BEARNAISE SAUCE:

6 tablespoons dry white wine
6 tablespoons tarragon vinegar
2 tablespoons finely chopped
  shallots
2 tablespoons butter

3 egg yolks
1/2 pound softened butter
Pinch cayenne pepper
Pinch salt

Combine wine, vinegar, shallots and two tablespoons of butter in small saucepan. Bring to a boil, then simmer for 3 minutes. Beat egg yolks well in glass bowl. Stir about 1/3 of the hot mixture, a little at a time, into the egg yolks. Return egg yolk mixture to the pot with the wine mixture, stirring constantly with a whisk. Place the saucepan over a larger pan of water that is barely simmering. Cut the butter into about 12 pieces and add to the sauce a piece at a time, beating constantly with the whisk. When all the butter has been incorporated into the sauce, continue to beat until the sauce is smooth and creamy. Season to taste with salt and cayenne pepper.

Try Me

Veal Bohemian

2 pounds veal steaks, cut in
  1/4-inch strips
2 tablespoons shortening
1 teaspoon salt
1/8 teaspoon garlic powder
1/8 teaspoon pepper

1/2 teaspoon paprika
1 teaspoon dry mustard
1/2 teaspoon Worcestershire
2 tablespoons catsup
1 cup hot water
1 cup sour cream

Roll veal in flour and brown in shortening. Combine remaining ingredients except sour cream and pour over veal. Cover and simmer 1 hour or until tender. Remove meat to platter and keep hot. Add sour cream to drippings and heat, but do not boil. Pour over meat and serve over noodles.

Huntsville Heritage Cookbook

Sukiyaki

(Beverly Sills is a star of the world's great opera houses, a prolific recording artist, a member of the Council of the National Endowment for the Arts, has been National Chairman of the March of Dimes' Mothers' March on Birth Defects. Miss Sills is an effective spokesman for the arts, believing "art is the signature of a civillization".)

2 tablespoons chopped beef suet	1 cup sliced fresh mushrooms
1 bunch green onions, finely chopped	3 pounds London Broil beef cut into serving pieces, 1/8-inch thick
3 cups thinly sliced onions	1/3 cup sugar
1 (8-ounce) can bamboo shoots	Soy sauce, to taste
1/3 cup blanched almonds	1/3 cup tomato juice
1 (1-pound) package fresh spinach, cut into 1-inch strips	1/3 cup Worcestershire sauce
1 (8-ounce) can water chestnuts	1 pound bean curd
1 (16-ounce) can bean sprouts	3/4 cup chicken stock (canned may be used)
1 bunch celery, chopped	

Over a hibachi (outdoors in summer; in an indoor fireplace in winter, or on a well-insulated card table), coat a Chinese wok with suet. Stir in onions, bamboo shoots, almonds, spinach, chestnuts, bean sprouts and celery. Cook 5 minutes. Add mushrooms, mix and stir for 5 minutes. Add meat, sugar, soy sauce, tomato juice, Worcestershire sauce and bean curd. Mix and cook 15 minutes, stirring frequently. Pour in chicken stock and cook another 8 or 10 minutes. Serve with rice. Serves 8.

Bravo! Applaudable Recipes

Beef Stroganoff

3 pounds round steak, cut into
  strips 1/4-inch thick and
  1-inch long
3 medium onions, chopped

1 pound mushrooms, sliced
1 cup butter
1 cup sour cream
Salt, pepper, Accent, paprika

Brown meat and onions in butter and season. Cook covered for about 30 minutes. Turn meat occasionally. Add mushrooms and cook for 10 minutes. Add sour cream and cook on low heat for 10 minutes. Serve over rice, noodles, or fluffy potatoes.

Eufaula's Favorite Recipes

Easy Chop Suey

2 pounds ground beef
1 cup chopped onion
1 cup chopped celery
1/2 cup chopped bell pepper
1 cup rice, uncooked
1 can cream of mushroom soup
1 can cream of chicken soup
1/4 cup soy sauce

1 tablespoon pepper
1 can bean sprouts (save liquid)
1 can mushrooms (save liquid)
1 can water chestnuts, drained
  and sliced
1 1/2 cups liquid (water plus
  saved juices)
1 can Chow Mein noodles

Brown beef in skillet. Add onion and bell pepper; sauté until tender. Drain off excess fat. Add rice, undiluted soups and other ingredients except noodles. Mix well. Place in 3-quart casserole (or 2 2-quart casseroles and freeze one). Bake at 350° for 45 minutes. Top with noodles and return to oven until noodles are toasted.

Sumpthn' Yummy

Mrs. Steve Clikas' Greek Meatballs

1 1/2 pounds ground beef
1 large, finely chopped onion
3 slices toasted brown bread,
  moistened with water & crumbled
2 whole eggs
2 cloves of garlic, mashed
4 sprigs of chopped, fresh parsley
  or 1 teaspoon dried parsley
1 teaspoon chopped, fresh mint or
  1/2 teaspoon dried mint

1/4 teaspoon leaf oregano
1/4 teaspoon sweet basil
Dash Italian seasoning
1/4 cup grated Romano cheese
Salt to taste
Pepper to taste
Flour
Salt
Oil

Place ground beef, onion, bread, eggs, garlic, parsley, mint, oregano, basil, Italian seasoning, cheese, salt and pepper in a large mixing bowl. Blend these ingredients lightly; cover bowl with plastic wrap. Refrigerate as long as possible; overnight is best. Roll mixture, a teaspoonful at a time, between the palms of your hands to form balls. Roll the balls in flour which has been lightly salted. Pour enough oil into a frying pan to cover the bottom of the pan (about 1/2 inch of oil). When hot, place the floured meatballs into the oil; fry until done. Turn meatballs to brown them evenly. Drain on layers of paper towels. Serve hot or cold. Excellent for picnics and parties. Makes 40-45 average meatballs or 60 tiny meatballs.

To this day, the smell of meatballs and cucumbers makes me think of those fantastic picnics on which our parents would take us. Singing in the car on the way--usually sleeping on the way back home, only Papa would remain awake--to drive, of course.

A Southern Lady Cooks with a Greek Accent

Sensitive Meat Balls

. . . yes, as opposed to leaden gray meatballs which are allowed, alas, to occur so often in home, restaurant and pavilion. A classic yellow-corn meal spoonbread is the ideal accompaniment to these delicious spicey globes.

1 pound ground chuck	1 cup sliced green onions
1/4 cup fine dry bread crumbs	1 1/2 cups thinly sliced celery (with
2/3 cup chopped onion	strings removed, naturally)
Salt to taste (go lightly, you	1/2 pound sliced fresh mushrooms
already have the soy) and I	1 beef bouillon cube
like a pinch of mace, too	1 tablespoon soy sauce
Freshly-ground black pepper	1/2 cup sauterne
2/3 cup unsweetened evaporated	1/2 teaspoon thyme
milk	1/2 teaspoon marjoram
1/4 cup unsalted butter	1/4 cup flour

Combine ground beef, crumbs, onion, salt, pepper, milk. Mix lightly but thoroughly. Shape in 12 nice even meat balls. Melt butter in big skillet. Brown balls on all sides, then push to one side. Add onion, celery, go on cooking until onion begins to look transparent. Remove from heat, add mushrooms, about 1 1/2 cups boiling water in which the cube has been dissolved, soy sauce, sauterne, seasonings. Mix lightly. Sprinkle flour over mixture, stirring constantly until it is well blended into liquid. Heat mixture to boiling, then at once reduce to simmer and cover and cook 25 minutes.

Delectable Dishes from Termite Hall

Pastissio

CREAM SAUCE:

5 cups milk   1/2 cup all-purpose flour
1 stick butter   4 eggs

Pastissio is made in three important separate steps then combined and baked in the oven. For this recipe use a 13 x 9 x 2 1/2-inch pan.

For sauce, melt butter and add flour, stirring constantly over low heat for 3-5 minutes. Remove from heat and add gradually scalded milk stirring constantly to blend smooth. Season to taste. Put back on slow heat for 1 minute blending well. Set aside covering with towel until used.

MACARONI MIXTURE:

12 ounces macaroni   1 cup cream sauce
2 tablespoons salt   1/2 cup grated Parmesan or
1/2 stick butter   Romano cheese

For macaroni mixture, boil macaroni in salt water stirring occasionally from 7-9 minutes. Drain well. Melt butter, when it begins to sizzle, pour over drained macaroni and mix well with 1/2 cup grated cheese and 1 cup cream sauce. Set aside.

MEAT MIXTURE:

2 medium onions, chopped   Salt and pepper
1/2 stick butter   Cinnamon (optional)
2 pounds ground meat   2 1/2 cups grated Parmesan or
8 ounces tomato sauce   Romano cheese

For meat mixture, sauté finely chopped onion in butter until onions are transparent. Add meat and simmer until lightly browned and separated. To this add tomato sauce. Season to taste with salt and pepper and a dash of cinnamon if desired. Cook until all liquid is absorbed. If too fat, skim off.

In pan spread 3/4 of macaroni mixture and sprinkle with 1 cup cheese patting down with hand to firm. Pour 1 cup of cream sauce over this. Spread meat mixture evenly over this. Then sprinkle with remaining cheese. Spread remaining macaroni mixture and pat down to firm. Pour remaining cream sauce and bake at 350° for 15 minutes. Lower heat to 325° for 30 minutes. Serve cut in squares. Yield: 12 servings.

Huntsville Entertains

Rings of Saturn

6 small onions
2 cloves
1 bay leaf
2 pounds ground beef
1/2 cup finely chopped onion
2 cups soft bread crumbs
1 cup chili sauce
1/2 cup finely-chopped green
   pepper

2 1/2 teaspoons salt
1/4 teaspoon freshly-ground
   black pepper
1 teaspoon mustard powder
Pinch of mace
2 tablespoons prepared horseradish
6 slices bacon

Cook 6 onions in boiling water with 2 cloves and 1 bay leaf for 15 minutes, drain. Combine meat, chopped onion, crumbs, 1/2 cup chili sauce, green pepper and seasonings. Using onion as Saturn, form a big ring of meat like a doughnut around it. Top each onion with strip of bacon. Bake at 350° for 45 minutes. Spread remaining chili sauce over meat, return to bake 5 minutes longer. If you disapprove of store-bought chili sauce, simmer some chopped tomatoes with a drop of cider vinegar, a teaspoon of brown sugar, a dash of mace, powdered mustard, few crushed corianders, powdered ginger, cayenne until thick and use as sauce for this dish.

Delectable Dishes from Termite Hall

Beef Turnovers

FILLING:

1 pound ground chuck
1 tablespoon flour
1 can celery soup (condensed)
  or mushroom
1/3 cup milk
1/4 cup finely chopped carrot

1/4 cup chopped green pepper
1/4 cup finely chopped onion
1/3 cup raisins
1 teaspoon salt
1/8 teaspoon pepper

Brown meat and drain off drippings. Sprinkle flour over meat. Mix well. Measure 1/3 cup condensed soup. Reserve remaining soup for sauce. Mix milk with soup and add to meat. Stir in green pepper, carrot, raisins, salt and pepper. Cover tightly and cook slowly for 20 minutes. Prepare dough.

DOUGH:

2 cups all-purpose flour
3 1/2 teaspoons baking powder
1/4 teaspoon soda

6 tablespoon shortening
1 cup buttermilk
3/4 teaspoon salt

Sift flour, baking powder, salt and soda together. Cut in shortening with pastry cutter until mixture is fine, even crumbs. Add milk and stir until well-mixed. Turn onto floured surface and knead gently gently 6 or 7 times. Roll out to 1/8-inch thickness circles or squares. Place a generous amount of meat mixture in the center of each. Moisten the edges. Fold over and seal with a fork. Place on baking sheet and bake in 400° oven until lightly browned.

SAUCE: Add a little milk to remaining soup and heat. Serve over turnovers.

Make these larger for buffet suppers and small for parties. Great for brunch, too.

Auburn Entertains

Football Casserole

"Keep one of these in the freezer for after the game."

1 pound ground beef
2 tablespoons shortening
1 medium onion, chopped
2 cups canned tomatoes
1 tablespoon catsup
1 tablespoon steak sauce

2 tablespoons parsley, chopped
1 (5-ounce) package elbow
  macaroni
Salt and pepper taste
1 can cream of mushroom soup
1 cup grated cheese

Brown beef in shortening. Add onions, tomatoes, catsup, steak sauce, green pepper, and parsley. Simmer 30 minutes. Cook macaroni according to directions on package. Drain. Combine macaroni and ground beef mixture in casserole. Season to taste. Gently spoon mushroom soup into mixture. Mix lightly. Sprinkle with grated cheese. Bake at 350° for 30 minutes or until bubbling and brown.

When Dinnerbells Ring

Cabbage Patch Stew

Delicious served over rice.

1 pound ground beef
1 medium onion, thinly sliced
4 cups chopped cabbage
1/2 cup diced celery
2 cups water
1 (16-ounce) can tomatoes, drained

1 (15-ounce) can light kidney beans
Salt
Pepper
Chili powder
Tabasco

Brown the beef. Add vegetables and sauté until clear. Add water and simmer for 15 minutes. Add beans, tomatoes and seasonings. Cook 20-30 minutes. Yield: 6 servings.

Cooks and Company

The Alabama June Jam in Fort Payne is a day-long concert hosted by the popular rock group "Alabama." Fort Payne is their home town.

Lasagna

SAUCE:

1/2 pound bulk sausage
1 1/2 pounds lean ground meat
1 clove garlic, minced
1 tablespoon whole basil
1 1/2 teaspoons salt

2 cups tomatoes
2 (6-ounce) cans tomato paste
2 (paste) cans water
1 pound pepperoni sausage,
   sliced (optional)

Brown sausage, ground meat, garlic, basil, and salt. Add tomatoes, tomato paste, and water; simmer 20-30 minutes.

CHEESE FILLING:

3 cups Ricotta or creamy cottage
   cheese
1/2 cup grated Parmesan or
   Romano cheese

2 tablespoons parsley flakes
2 eggs, beaten
2 teaspoons salt
1/2 teaspoon pepper

Mix ingredients together.

10 ounces lasagna or wide
   noodles, cooked and drained

1 pound mozzarella cheese,
   grated

Spoon a few tablespoons of Sauce on bottom of dish; layer noodles over Sauce. Spread with a layer of Cheese Filling, then sprinkle with mozzarella cheese. Repeat layers beginning again with more Sauce. Bake in 375° oven for 30 minutes. Let stand a few minutes before cutting into squares. Serves 12.

Treasured Tastes

Pizza by the Yard

1 loaf French bread
1 pound ground beef, cooked
    and drained
30 slices pepperoni
1 (6-ounce) can tomato paste
1/3 cup onion

1/4 cup ripe olives, chopped
1/2 teaspoon oregano
1/2 teaspoon salt
1 (8-ounce) package mozzarella
    cheese, halved diagonally
    and sliced

Cut bread in half lengthwise and set aside. Combine remaining ingredients except cheese. Stir well. Spread meat mixture evenly on bread halves and place bread on cookie sheet. Bake at 400° for 15 minutes. Place cheese over meat mixture and bake until cheese melts. Serve.

The Great Cookbook

Brunswick Stew
"A crowd pleaser - great for cookouts!"

3 (3-4-pound) Boston butts,
    cooked and chunked
4 whole chickens, cooked and
    chunked
8 (16-ounce) cans tomatoes,
    drained and mashed
12 (16-ounce) cans cream-style corn
6 (16-ounce) cans white corn
6 (16-ounce) cans green lima beans
4 pounds frozen okra, sliced
1 gallon chicken broth
3 (32-ounce) bottles catsup

5 pounds potatoes, finely diced
3 large onions, finely diced
1 tablespoon prepared mustard
4 teaspoons turmeric
4 teaspoons ground cumin
1 (10-ounce) bottle Worcestershire
    sauce
1 cup tomato juice
Tabasco to taste
Salt to taste
Pepper to taste

Cook and prepare meats, reserving chicken broth. Drain and mash tomatoes, reserving juice. In a very large cooking pan, combine all ingredients and mix well. Add reserved liquids to stew, as needed, during cooking. Cook over very low heat for 12-18 hours. Cooking time may vary according to taste. Serves 100.

When Dinnerbells Ring

Rose Davidson's Pork Chops

If you haven't eaten Rose Davidson's pork chops, then you have really missed something good. She was delighted to give me her recipe. I only wish it were possible to give you her recipe for the hospitality that always abounds in her kitchen!

Flour, salt, pepper
6 pork chops
1 can mushroom soup

1 soup can water
2 tablespoons Worcestershire sauce

Flour, salt and pepper pork chops. Fry in medium amount of grease until meat is golden brown. Remove from skillet and set aside. Add several teaspoons of flour to drippings with one can of mushroom soup and of water into skillet. Add Worcestershire sauce and simmer for a few minutes. Return pork chops to skillet. Place in preheated oven for about 30 minutes.

Hearthside at Christmas

Pork Tenderloin with Mustard Sauce

2 pounds whole pork tenderloin
  (1 - 1 1/2-inches diameter)
1 clove garlic, cut in half
1 1/2 teaspoons salt
MUSTARD SAUCE:
1 cup mayonnaise
1 tablespoon honey
1 tablespoon finely chopped fresh
  parsley

1 cup red wine
1/2 teaspoon onion salt
1/2 teaspoon Beau Monde

2 teaspoons prepared mustard
1 teaspoon curry powder
1/2 teaspoon paprika

Rub the tenderloin with the cut garlic thoroughly. Sprinkle with salt and bake in a shallow baking pan about 1 1/4 hours (until tender) at 325°. Combine the wine, onion salt and Beau Monde and simmer 1 minute. Combine all ingredients for the Mustard Sauce. Slice the tenderloin, pour hot wine sauce over the slices, and serve Mustard Sauce in a separate dish. Serves 4-6.

Bravo! Applaudable Recipes

Stuffed Boned Pork Loin or Pork Chops

6 pork chops (1-inch thick) or
    pork loin
1/2 cup corn bread, crumbled
1/2 cup white bread, crumbled
1/3 cup chopped celery
1/4 cup chopped onion
1/4 cup chopped green pepper,
    optional

1 cup boiling water
1 tablespoon dry parsley, optional
1 teaspoon salt
1/2 teaspoon pepper
1 egg
1/4 cup melted butter or pork stock

Have pocket cut in pork chops on bone side, or pork loin, boned. Beat egg and add other ingredients. Stuff each chop or boned loin, hold together with toothpicks. Bake in 400° oven for 20 minutes, add boiling water, reduce heat to 300°, and bake 1 hour or until tender.

Florence Cook Book

Pork Chop Casserole

4 large or 6 medium pork
    loin chops
1 large can sauerkraut

2 handful dried apples soaked
    for 5 minutes

Place layer of undrained kraut in botton of casserole, then a layer of 2 or 3 chops, layer of apple and then repeat. Pepper to taste, but little salt as kraut is salty. Cover, put in 250° oven and cook 2 to 2 1/2 hours - the longer the better as the flavors will all get together.

Old Mobile Recipes

Pork Chops Apricot

6 pork chops
Salt and pepper
Flour
Shortening

1 can apricot halves (No. 303)
1 medium onion, finely chopped

Flour, salt and pepper pork chops, brown in small amount of shortening. Add apricots and juice with onion. Simmer until juice thickens, about 45 minutes to an hour, covering the first 15 or 20 minutes. Can be prepared ahead of time, always a hit with guests.

Recipe Jubilee!

Marinated Pork Tenders on the Grill

1/2 cup soy sauce
1/2 cup dry Sherry
2 cloves garlic
1 tablespoon dry mustard

1 teaspoon thyme
1 teaspoon ginger
5 pounds pork tenders

About 24 hours ahead, mix together all marinade ingredients. Put tenders in a large plastic bag and pour marinade over them. Close bag and put in refrigerator overnight. Shift the meat in the marinade from time to time. When the fire is ready, remove meat from marinade. Cook on grill for about an hour, depending on size of tenders. Baste with marinade while cooking. Serves 12.

One of a Kind

Jeweled Buffet Ham

1 (8-ounce) can whole-berry
  cranberry sauce
1 (8-ounce) can jellied cranberry
  sauce
1 (8 1/4-ounce) can crushed
  pineapple, drained
1 (11-ounce) can Mandarin
  orange segments, drained

1/2 cup orange juice
1 teaspoon seasoned salt
1/2 teaspoon garlic powder
2-4 dashes Tabasco sauce
1 (5- to 6-pound) fully cooked ham

Combine all ingredients except ham in a medium saucepan. Cook over low heat 15-20 minutes, stirring occasionally. May be refrigerated several days and reheated.

Have butcher slice ham into 1/4-inch slices and tie in original shape. Preheat oven to 350°. Place ham in a shallow roasting pan. Bake 1 hour. Remove from oven. Pour off juices. Spoon enough fruit mixture over ham to coat well, mounding fruit generously on the top. Return ham to oven. Bake uncovered 30 minutes; baste occasionally with remaining fruit mixture. Place ham on serving platter. Cut and carefully remove strings. Serve any remaining fruit mixture with ham slices, if desired. Makes 10-12 servings.

Anniversary Collection of Delectable Dishes

Baked Ham

The longer baking time removes all the water from ham.

1 party ham
1 (3-ounce) can orange concentrate

1/4 cup A-1 Sauce
3/4 cup light brown sugar

Score ham. Mix concentrate, A-1 Sauce, and sugar together. Place ham in piece of foil larger than ham. Set into a baking pan. Pour half juice mixture over ham. Close very tightly with foil; cover baking pan. Cook at 325° for 1 hour per pound. Half hour before end of cooking, remove cover and open foil. Baste with remainder of juice mixture every 10 minutes at 350°. Let sit before slicing. It might crumble otherwise.

Try Me

Spaghetti Carbonara

1 (8-ounce) package spaghetti	1/2 cup sliced mushrooms
1/2 stick butter	Salt and pepper to taste
1 cup chopped ham or bacon	1 egg, beaten
1/3 cup sliced onion	1/2 cup half-and-half
1/3 cup chopped green pepper	1/2 cup Parmesan cheese

Boil spaghetti in large pot of salted water. Drain. Melt butter and sauté ham, onion, green pepper, and mushrooms until tender. Add drained spaghetti. Salt and pepper to taste. Add egg beaten with cream. Toss in Parmesan cheese and stir until heated through. Remove from heat and serve. Serves 4.

Magic

Sharp Hamburger

1 cup cooked ham, coarsely ground	1/2 teaspoon pepper
1/2 cup sour cream	2 tablespoons dill pickle,
1 teaspoon dill weed seed	chopped fine
1/2 teaspoon seasoned salt	Hamburger Buns

Mix first six ingredients, using a fork or mix with you hands. Spread thick layer onto hamburger buns or bread slices.

When You Can't Cook

Grilled Ham Steak

1 ham steak, cut 1 1/2-2 inches	Peach or apricot preserves or
thick, from a fully-cooked ham	orange marmalade

Have a butcher cut ham steak from center of whole ham. Freeze the ends to bake at another time or have as many as 5 steaks cut from the ham and save the ends to use for seasoning vegetables.

Place ham steak on grill over medium heat. Close the lid and cook for 40-60 minutes, turning from time to time, until meat is heated through. Open the lid, spread top of meat with thick coating of preserves. Continue to cook over low heat for 10-15 minutes or until meat is browned and top is glazed. To serve, cut in thin slices across the grain. Yield: 6-8 servings from the center cut; 20-24 servings using a whole ham.

Family Secrets

Tri-Color Pie

1 partially baked 8 or 9-inch pie shell	1 egg
1 1/2 cups finely chopped or ground ham, packed	1 package frozen chopped spinach
1 1/2 cups cottage cheese	1 tablespoon dried minced or 1/4 cup chopped onion
1/4 teaspoon salt	1/2 teaspoon salt
1/8 teaspoon pressed garlic or pinch dried	1/2 cup fine bread crumbs
	2 eggs
	Parmesan cheese

Press ham into partially baked pie shell. Mix cottage cheese, salt, garlic and first egg and spread on top of ham. Cook spinach in its own juices only until well defrosted and hot. Add onion, salt, bread crumbs and remaining eggs. Layer on top of cottage cheese. Sprinkle with Parmesan cheese and bake at 375° until knife in center comes out clean, about 25-30 minutes. Serves 6.

Loaves and Fishes

Pasta-Ham-Sugar Snap Peas

6 ounces sugar snap (or snow) peas	1 tablespoon dill
1 cucumber	1 teaspoon chives
1 tablespoon butter	1/3 of (9-ounce) package green angel's hair pasta
8 ounces ham, cut into bite-size squares	

String peas; cut into 1-inch pieces. Peel cucumber, quarter, scoop out seeds. Cut into thin slices. Stir fry vegetables in butter over moderately high heat, about 2 minutes. Add ham; toss. Add seasonings. Combine with pasta which has been cooked according to package directions.

A Samford Celebration Cookbook

Mysterious Indian burial grounds and treasures are found at DeSoto Caverns off Highway 76 about 36 miles from Birmingham. A visit to the park can bring such diverse activities as gold and gemstone panning, musical hayrides, hiking and nature trails, and sports.

Ham and Artichoke Rolls

4 tablespoons butter or margarine
4 tablespoon flour
2 cups milk, warm
1/4 teaspoon salt
Dash cayenne pepper
1/4 teaspoon ground nutmeg
Paprika
Pinch, white pepper

2/3 cup Swiss cheese, grated
2/3 cup Parmesan cheese
4 tablespoons dry sherry
2 (1-pound) cans artichoke hearts,
    drained
12 thin slices boiled or baked ham
2/3 cup buttered bread crumbs

Melt butter in saucepan over medium heat, blend in flour. When smooth, remove from heat and gradually stir in milk. Return to heat and continue to cook until sauce thickens. Add seasonings, 1/3 cup grated Swiss cheese and 1/3 cup grated Parmesan cheese. Stir constantly until cheese melts.

Remove from heat and stir in sherry. Wrap ham around artichoke heart. If artichokes are large, cut in half lengthwise. Arrange in buttered casserole, seam side down with sides touching. Pour sauce over ham rolls.

Make a topping of buttered breadcrumbs, 1/3 cup Swiss cheese and 1/3 cup Parmesan cheese and bake at 350° for 25-30 minutes. Serves 6 for dinner or 12 for luncheon.

Heavenly Hostess

 Hikers can explore over 100 miles of developed trails in Bankhead Conecuh, Talladega, and Tuskegee, Alabama's national forests. There are also five state forests: Baldwin, Choccolocco, Geneva, Little River, and Weogufka. Seafood booths and outdoor activities highlight the Annual National Shrimp Festival, held each October in Gulf Shores.

Hoppin' John
(Microwave)

4-6 slices bacon	1 teaspoon salt
1 onion, chopped	1/2 teaspoon black pepper
1 pound frozen black-eyed peas	1/2 teaspoon oregano
1 cup uncooked rice	1/4 teaspoon crushed red pepper
1 cup chopped ham	3 cups water

Cut each slice of bacon into several small pieces. Combine bacon and onion in microwave dish. Cook 7-10 minutes on HIGH. Drain grease. Add remaining ingredients. Cook for 10 minutes on HIGH; then cook 20-30 minutes at 50% power (simmer).

A Samford Celebration Cookbook

Sausage-Squash-Pecan Casserole

2 pounds yellow squash or zucchini sliced 1/2 inch thick
4 tablespoons butter
2 medium onions, sliced
1 finely chopped garlic clove
1 cup milk
1 cup bread crumbs

1 pound cooked crumbled sausage
4 eggs, lightly beaten
1 1/2 cups grated sharp cheese
1 cup chopped pecans
1 tablespoon salt
Freshly ground pepper

TOPPING:
4 tablespoons butter, melted
1/2 cup bread crumbs

1/2 cup chopped pecans

Preheat oven to 350°. Grease a 2-quart casserole and set aside. Put sliced squash in a heavy pan and add enough water to cover. Bring to a boil, uncovered; then reduce heat and simmer for 1/2 hour or until squash is soft enough to mash. Drain and mash. Melt butter in a separate pan; add onion and garlic and cook until soft. Add this to the squash. Heat milk in same pan; stir in bread crumbs and add this mixture to the onions and squash. Stir in sausage, eggs, cheese, pecans, salt, and pepper. Pour combined mixture into buttered casserole. For the topping, combine the butter, bread crumbs, and pecans and sprinkle over top of casserole. Bake for 30 minutes. Serves 4.

A Samford Celebration Cookbook

Sausage Wellington

2 pounds mild sausage
1 pound fresh mushrooms or
1 (12-ounce) can
1 large onion, chopped
2 (8-ounce) packages cream cheese

2 tablespoons chives
2 tablespoons Worcestershire sauce
2 boxes Pepperidge Farm patty
   shells or 2 packages crescent rolls

Cook sausage until done. Drain well. Brown mushrooms and onions in 2 tablespoons of sausage drippings and Worcestershire sauce. Mix in softened cream cheese and stir until cheese is melted. Stir in sausage. Using 1/2 cup of the sausage mixture at a time place on individual pastry that has been rolled out. Pull up sides and pinch top together. Place seam side down on cookie sheet and bake at 400° for 25 minutes. Serves 8-10.

Sumpthn' Yummy

Sausage, Red Beans and Rice Casserole

1/2 cup cooking oil
1 pound ground beef
2 teaspoons salt
1 tablespoon chili powder
1 large onion, chopped
1/4 bell pepper, chopped

1 can tomatoes
Dash black pepper
1 cup water
1 cup raw rice
1 can kidney beans
3/4 pound smoked sausage

Brown meat; add onion, and green pepper. Cook until transparent, stirring constantly. Add tomatoes, water, salt, chili powder and black pepper. Simmer 10 minutes. Remove from fire; add raw rice and beans. Pour into buttered dish. Slice half of sausage over top, cover with foil. Bake at 350° for 1 hour. Stir slightly, slice remainder of sausage, cover and bake 1/2 hour longer.

Treasured Taste

 Rich German dishes are featured at the Elberta German Sausage Festival, a German celebration with ethnic foods, music, arts and crafts, baked goods, and Elberta German Sausage.

Lamb Hash

1/2 cup canned mushrooms
4 tablespoons butter
3 tablespoons flour
1 1/2 cups milk, scalded
Salt and pepper to taste

2 cups diced cooked lamb
2 tablespoons chopped pimentos
1 bell pepper, chopped
1 egg yolk, well beaten

Brown mushrooms in 1 tablespoon butter. Combine remaining butter and flour in milk. Cook over hot water until thick and smooth. Season to taste. Add lamb, mushrooms, pimento and bell pepper, heat to a boil. Add egg yolk, heat to a boil. Serve over toast or rice. Yield: 4-6 servings.

Kitchen Sampler

Cakes

Vulcan, the great god of fire and the world's largest iron man, stands atop Red Mountain as a silent sentinel of safety. Birmingham.

Coconut-Black Walnut Pound Cake

2 cups sugar
1 cup salad oil
4 eggs, beaten
3 cups all-purpose flour
1/2 teaspoon salt

1/2 teaspoon soda
1 cup buttermilk
1 cup black walnuts, chopped
1 cup coconut, flaked
2 teaspoons coconut extract

Combine sugar, salad oil and eggs. Beat well. Combine dry ingredients and add to sugar mixture alternately with buttermilk, beating well after each addition. Stir in nuts, coconut and flavoring. Pour batter into a well greased and floured 10-inch tube pan. Bake at 325° for 1 hour and 5 minutes or until cake tests done. Pour hot Coconut Syrup over hot cake. Allow cake to remain in pan 4 hours to absorb syrup. Wrap well. Cake will be very moist.

COCONUT SYRUP:

1 cup sugar
1/2 cup water
2 tablespoons butter

1 teaspoon coconut extract

Combine sugar, water and butter in a saucepan. Bring to a boil and boil 5 minutes. Remove from heat and stir in flavoring. Yields 3/4 cups. Can be frozen.

The Great Cookbook

Butternut Pound Cake

2 cups sugar
1 cup Crisco
5 eggs
1 cup sweet milk

2 1/2 cups cake flour
1/2 cup self-rising flour
2 tablespoons butternut flavoring

Preheat oven to 325°. Cream Crisco and sugar. Add eggs, one at a time, then beat until well blended. Add 1/2 cup self-rising flour and beat well. Add milk and cake flour alternately, until all is used; then, beat on low speed about 3 minutes. Add flavoring and mix well. Pour into a greased and floured tube pan or two 9-inch cake pans and bake for 1 hour at 325°. Then set oven at 350° and bake an additional 15-20 minutes.

Treats For My Sweets

Pound Cake Squares

1 (16-ounce) box Dromedary
  (or other) pound cake mix
4 eggs
1 stick butter, softened
1 (8-ounce) package cream cheese
1 (16-ounce) package confectioners'
  sugar

1 teaspoon vanilla extract
1 cup chopped pecans
Whipped cream for topping
  (optional)

Combine cake mix, butter, and 2 eggs; mix until well blended. Spread in a greased (13x9x2-inch) pan. Reserve 3 tablespoons sugar and combine remainder with the softened cream cheese. Beat in 2 eggs and vanilla. Spread over cake mixture and sprinkle pecans over top. Cook at 350° for 45 minutes. While cake is warm, sift reserved sugar on top.

Serve like brownies or cut into larger squares and top with whipped cream for a luscious dessert! Yield: 2-3 dozen.

Family Secrets

Caramel Pound Cake

Vivian made this cake for a W. O. C. luncheon and we loved it!

1 cup butter or margarine	3 cups flour
1/2 cup shortening	1/2 teaspoon baking powder
1 (16-ounce) box dark brown sugar	1 cup milk
	1 teaspoon vanilla
1 cup granulated sugar	1 teaspoon butter flavoring
5 large eggs	1 cup chopped nuts (optional)

Cream margarine, shortening and sugars. Add eggs one at a time, beating well after each. Sift flour and baking powder together; add alternately with milk. Add flavorings and nuts. Spoon into greased, floured 10-inch tube pan. Bake 325ᵐ for 1 hour and 15-30 minutes. Do *not* use liquid brown sugar in this cake. Good plain or frosted.

CARAMEL FROSTING:

1 1/2 cups granulated sugar	3/4 cup evaporated milk
1 1/2 cups dark brown sugar	1 1/2 teaspoons vanilla
3/4 cup margarine	

Heat first 4 ingredients till sugar dissolves. Bring to rolling boil; cook 3 minutes. Set off heat; add vanilla. Beat to spreading consistency. If too thick, add milk in small amounts till spreads easily.

Cookbook

Old-Fashion Strawberry Shortcake
Just like Mom made...

2 1/2 cups Bisquick	2 pints fresh strawberries
3 tablespoons sugar	1/2 cup sugar
3 tablespoons butter, melted	2 pints whipping cream
1/2 cup milk	3-4 tablespoons powdered sugar

To make cake, mix Bisquick, sugar, butter, and milk into a dough and gently knead into a smooth ball. Pat into a disk about 8-inches in diameter and place on a baking sheet. Bake in a preheated 425° oven for about 15-20 minutes. Cool. Cut in half, horizontally.

Wash and cap strawberries. Reserve about 6 of the best for decoration and slice the remainder. Sprinkle with sugar and refrigerate overnight. Whip cream with the powdered sugar until stiff.

To assemble: Spoon some of the strawberry juice over the cut sides of the cake to moisten. Arrange 2/3 of the strawberry slices over the bottom half of the cake and spread with 1/3 of the whipped cream. Place the top on the cake and arrange the remaining 1/3 of berries on the top. Spread the remaining whipped cream over the berries and garnish with the reserved whole berries. This is best if allowed to sit in the refrigerator a couple of hours before serving. Serves 6-8.

Birdies in the Oven/Aces in the Kitchen

Burnt Sugar Cake

1/2 cup butter or shortening	2 teaspoons baking powder
1 1/2 cups sugar	1 teaspoon salt
3 eggs	2/3 cup cold water
2 1/4 cups sifted flour	4 tablespoons burnt sugar syrup

To burn sugar, place 1 cup of sugar in a skillet and heat over the fire. Stir until melted and brown. Remove from the fire and add 2/3 cup of boiling water. Stir and place back on the heat and boil until it begins to thicken. This makes enough for several cakes and will keep in jars in a cool place.

For the batter, cream the butter and sugar together. Break the eggs in one at a time, beating all the while. Sift together flour, baking powder and salt, and add alternately with the cold water. Add burnt sugar syrup last and beat well. Bake in a greased pan at 350° for 40 minutes.

Heirlooms From the Kitchen

Pineapple Love Dove Cake

1 (18 1/4-ounce) yellow cake mix
1 (20-ounce) can crushed
   pineapple (not drained)
1/2 cup sugar
1/3 cup cornstarch

1/8 teaspoon salt
2 tablespoons margarine or butter
1 tablespoon lemon juice
1 teaspoon vanilla
1 1/2 (8-ounce) cartons sour cream

Prepare and bake 2 (9-inch) layers of yellow cake according to package directions. Cool. Slice each layer in half with a long bread knife. Combine undrained pineapple, sugar, cornstarch, and salt in saucepan. Cook, stirring constantly, until clear and thickened. Remove from heat and stir in butter, lemon juice, and vanilla. Cool. Whip sour cream until thick and fluffy. Spread each layer of cake with sour cream, then pineapple filling, including top. Stack 4 layers together and frost sides with whipped sour cream. Chill. Store cake in refrigerator.

Anniversary Collection of Delectable Dishes

Coca Cola Cake

2 cups unsifted flour
2 cups sugar
2 sticks margarine
2 tablespoons cocoa
1 cup Coca Cola

1/2 cup buttermilk
2 unbeaten eggs
1 teaspoon baking soda
1 teaspoon vanilla
1 1/2 cups miniature marshmallows

Combine sugar and flour in a bowl. Heat margarine, cocoa, and Coca Cola to boiling; pour over sugar and flour mixture. Mix well, then add buttermilk, eggs, soda, and vanilla. Mix well; add marshmallows floating on top. Bake in 9x13x2-inch pan for 35 minutes at 350°.

ICING:

1 stick margarine
2 tablespoons cocoa
6 tablespoons Coca Cola

1 pound powdered sugar
1 cup chopped nuts

Combine butter, cocoa, and Coca Cola, and bring to a boil. Pour over powdered sugar. After beating well, add pecans and pour over hot cake.

More Fiddling with Food

Harvey Wallbanger Cake

1 box yellow cake mix	4 eggs
1 (3 3/4-ounce) package vanilla	1/4 cup vodka
instant pudding	1/4 cup galliano
1/2 cup cooking oil	3/4 cup orange juice

GLAZE:

1 stick butter	1/4 cup orange juice
1 cup sugar	1/4 cup galliano

Mix first 7 ingredients and beat on medium speed for 2 minutes or follow instructions on cake mix box. Pour into well-greased and lightly floured bundt pan. Bake at 350° for 45-50 minutes. Remove from pan after 20 minutes cooling time. Invert on platter and dust with confectioners' sugar or glaze. Combine the glaze ingredients and boil for 4 minutes. Pour over cake. Yield: 15 servings.

Huntsville Entertains

Black Magic Cake

1 3/4 cups flour	1 teaspoon salt
2 eggs	1 cup strong black coffee
2 cups sugar	1 cup buttermilk
3/4 cup cocoa	1/2 cup vegetable oil
2 teaspoons baking soda	1 teaspoon vanilla
1 teaspoon baking powder	

Preheat oven to 350°. Grease and flour bundt pan, combine dry ingredients, add eggs, coffee, milk, oil and vanilla. Beat at medium speed 2 minutes. Batter will be thin. Bake 30-40 minutes. Serve each slice with dollop of Caramel Fluff.

CARAMEL FLUFF:

2 cups chilled whipping cream	1 teaspoon vanilla
3/4 cup brown sugar	Shaved chocolate

In a chilled bowl, beat whipping cream, brown sugar and vanilla until stiff. Can sprinkle with shaved chocolate for additional decoration.

Auburn Entertains

Prune Cake

1 1/2 cups sugar	1 teaspoon cinnamon
3 eggs	1/2 cup buttermilk
1 cup Wesson oil	1 teaspoon soda
2 cups sifted flour	1 teaspoon vanilla
1 teaspoon salt	1 cup chopped nuts
1 teaspoon nutmeg	1 cup cooked mashed prunes
1 teaspoon allspice	

Mix sugar, eggs and oil. Sift flour with spices. Add to first mixture. Add remaining ingredients and mix well. Cook in greased and floured tube pan 45 minutes to one hour at 350°. Pour topping over the cool cake while in the pan.

TOPPING:

1 stick oleo	1 teaspoon soda
1 1/4 cups sugar	1/4 teaspoon cinnamon
1/2 cup buttermilk	

Bring to a boil and cook for 1 to 1 1/2 minutes.

Old Mobile Recipes

Applesauce Cake

3/4 cup butter	1 package mixed fruitcake fruit
2 1/4 cups sugar	3 cups flour
5 eggs	2 1/2 teaspoons soda
2 1/4 cups applesauce	1 1/2 teaspoons cinnamon
1 cup chopped nuts	3/4 teaspoon cloves
1 1/2 cups chopped dates	3/4 teaspoon nutmeg
1 cup chopped figs	3/4 teaspoon salt
1 cup raisins	

Cream butter and sugar until light and fluffy. Add eggs, mixing well. Combine nuts, dates, figs, raisins, fruit, flour, soda, cinnamon, cloves, nutmeg, and salt. Add alternately with applesauce to creamed mixture. Bake in a greased and floured tube pan at 325° for about 1 1/2 hours or until cake tests done. This cake is best when make a couple of days before serving.

Birdies in the Oven/Aces in the Kitchen

Hummingbird Cake

3 cups all-purpose flour (plain)
2 cups sugar
1 teaspoon salt
1 teaspoon soda
1 teaspoon cinnamon
3 eggs, beaten

1 1/2 cups salad oil
1 1/2 teaspoons vanilla
1 (8-ounce) can crushed
    pineapple, drained
2 cups chopped bananas
1 cup chopped nuts

Mix by hand. Combine dry ingredients; add eggs and salad oil; stir until well mixed. Add vanilla, pineapple, bananas and nuts. Spoon batter into large greased and floured sheet pan. Bake at 350° for 40-45 minutes.

ICING:
1 box confectioners' sugar
1/2 cup margarine
1 (8-ounce) package cream cheese

1 teaspoon vanilla
1 cup chopped nuts

Combine first 4 ingredients. Sprinkle chopped nuts on top of icing.

Calling All Cooks

Holiday Cake

FROSTING:

2 cups dairy sour cream	2 cups coconut
2 cups granulated sugar	1 teaspoon vanilla extract

Combine ingredients for frosting and refrigerate for 24 hours before baking cake.

CAKE:

2 1/2 cups sifted cake flour	1 cup buttermilk
1 teaspoon baking soda	1/4 teaspoon salt
5 eggs	2 cups granulated sugar
1 cup butter or shortening	2 teaspoons vanilla extract

Sift flour once; measure baking soda and salt; sift with flour 3 times. Cream butter; add sugar gradually and cream until fluffy. Add eggs, one at a time, beating well after each addition. Add flour alternately with milk, beating until smooth. Add vanilla. Grease and flour 3 (9-inch) cake pans. Pour batter into pans and bake at 350° for 25 minutes or until done.

When cake is cool, split layers and frost. Refrigerate cake for 4 days before cutting.

Family Secrets

Japanese Fruit Cake

1 cup butter	1/2 pound raisins
2 cups sugar	1/4 cup sherry or wine
3 cups flour	1 teaspoon allspice
4 eggs	1 teaspoon powdered cloves
1 cup milk	1 teaspoon powdered cinnamon
1 teaspoon vanilla	1 teaspoon powdered nutmeg
3 teaspoons baking powder	

Cream butter and sugar, add eggs. Add flour and baking powder sifted together alternately with milk and vanilla. To one-half of this batter add raisins, sherry and spices. Bake two layers of plain and 2 layers of fruited batter in well greased and floured pans at 375° for 30-40 minutes.

FILLING:

3 eggs	1 cup water thickened with
1 cup sugar	flour to consistency of cream.
2 lemons, juice and grated rind	

Boil these 4 ingredients together stirring constantly. When cool, spread between alternating layers and sprinkle with grated coconut. Cover top and sides with Boiled White Icing.

BOILED WHITE ICING:

2 cups sugar	2 egg whites beaten stiff
3/4 cup water	1 teaspoon vanilla
1/4 teaspoon salt	
1 tablespoon Karo syrup or	
1/4 teaspoon cream of tartar	

Cook first 4 ingredients to soft ball. Pour over stiff egg whites and beat until cold. Add vanilla. Spread on sides and top of cake.

Eufaula's Favorite Recipes

 On Memorial Day weekend, the Alabama Jubilee, held at Point Mallard in Decatur, features among other events, thirty hot-air balloons in three competitive races.

Upside-Down Apple Cake

4 or 5 tart cooking apples	1 cup sugar
Lemon juice	1 cup whipping cream
2 tablespoons butter	1 teaspoon vanilla extract
1 cup (packed) light brown sugar, sifted	2 cups all-purpose flour
1 egg	2 teaspoons baking powder
	Confectioners' sugar

Peel the apples and remove the cores. Slice the apples paper-thin, then sprinkle lightly with the lemon juice to keep from discoloring. Place the butter in a 9-inch round, shallow baking dish. Place in a pre-heated 325° oven until melted then remove from oven. Do not turn off heat. Sprinkle the brown sugar over the butter. Overlap the apple slices in the baking dish, working from the center to the edges, until the bottom is covered.

Place the egg in a medium-size mixing bowl and beat well with an electric mixer. Add the sugar gradually and beat until mixed. Mix the cream and vanilla. Sift the flour with baking powder, then add to the egg mixture alternately with the cream mixture, beating well after each addition. Pour over the apples. Bake for about 35 minutes or until a cake tester inserted comes out clean. Let cool 10 minutes, then turn onto a rack and cool. Place on a cake plate and cut into servings. Sprinkle with confectioners' sugar. Yield: 8 servings.

Dining Under the Magnolia

Cherry Torte Eleganté

FEATHER SPONGE CAKE:

6 egg yolks	1 1/2 cups sifted cake flour
1/2 cup cold water	1/4 teaspoon salt
1 1/2 cups sugar	6 egg whites
1/2 teaspoon vanilla	1/4 teaspoon cream of tartar
1/2 teaspoon almond extract	

Beat egg yolks until thick and lemon colored; add water and continue beating until very thick. Gradually beat in sugar, then extracts.

Sift flour with salt 3 times; fold into egg yolk mixture a little at a time.

CONTINUED

CONTINUED

Beat egg whites until foamy; add cream of tartar and beat until they form moist, glossy peaks. Fold into the first mixture, turning bowl gradually.

Bake in 2 greased and floured 8x3-inch round cake pans in a 325° oven for 30-40 minutes. Cake will shrink and fall slightly as it cools. Cook in pan for 5 minutes. Turn out on wire rack and cool.

FILLING FOR CHERRY TORTE:

1 (1-pound) can pitted dark sweet cherries	1 1/2 tablespoons cornstarch
1/3 cup kirsch	1 tablespoon port
	1/4 teaspoon almond extract

Drain cherries and cut in half reserving several whole cherries for garnish. Pour kirsch and port over them and let stand for 2 hours.

In saucepan, gradually blend reserved syrup into cornstarch. Add cherries, liqueurs, and almond extract and heat, stirring constantly, until the mixture thickens and boils. Cook and stir 1 minute. Cool and chill.

BUTTERCREAM ICING FOR CHERRY TORTE:

1 box confectioners' sugar	1/2 teaspoon almond extract
1 cup (1/2-pound) softened butter	1/2 teaspoon vanilla
3 eggs yolks	Chocolate shot (sprinkles)

Cream butter. Add confectioners' sugar and beat until smooth. Beat inegg yolks until light and fluffy. Add vanilla and almond extract.

To assemble cake: Split layers in half horizontally. Place bottom layer on a cake plate. Pipe a 1-inch buttercream border around top edge of cake. Fill center with cherry filling. Top with another cake layer and repeat layers of buttercream and cherry with chocolate shot. Do not fill top layer. Ice top with buttercream, piping a decorative edge around top and bottom layer of cake. One half of the buttercream icing may be flavored additionally by adding two squares of melted chocolate to the icing.

Garnish with the reserved cherries which have been soaked in kirsch.

The Alabama Heritage Cookbook

Luscious Chocolate Cake

3 (1-ounce) squares unsweetened
  chocolate
1 stick butter (no substitute)
1 1/2 cups firmly packed brown
  sugar
3 eggs

1/2 teaspoon salt
2 teaspoons baking soda
2 1/4 cups cake flour, sifted
1/2 cup buttermilk
2 teaspoons vanilla
1 cup boiling water

Preheat oven to 375°. Grease 2 round cake pans and line with wax paper. Melt chocolate. Cream butter and sugar, then add eggs and melted chocolate. Stir in salt and baking soda. Alternately add flour and buttermilk, vanilla, and then boiling water. Bake for 45 minutes or until cake tester comes out clean. Check after 30 minutes.

FROSTING:
2 cups whipping cream
3 tablespoons cocoa

1/2 teaspoon vanilla
Chocolate shavings for garnish

Mix ingredients together and chill for at least 2 hours. Whip cream mixture and frost cool cake. Top with chocolate shavings and store in refrigerator.

Magic

Devil's Food Cake, Caramel Icing

2 1/2 cups sugar
1 cup butter
4 tablespoons cocoa
2 1/2 cups flour
1 cup buttermilk

1 teaspoon soda (dissolved in
  the buttermilk)
5 eggs
2 teaspoons vanilla

Cream butter, sugar and cocoa. Add eggs 1 at a time, beating well. Add vanilla. Add sifted flour alternately with buttermilk. Bake in greased layer pans at 350° for 30 minutes.

ICING:
3 cups sugar
1 cup milk
1/2 cup sugar, caramelized

1 stick butter
2 teaspoons vanilla

Bring sugar and milk to boil. Caramelize sugar in large skillet. Pour boiling milk and sugar mixture into caramelized sugar. Cook until it forms a soft ball in water. Remove from heat; add butter and vanilla. Beat to spreading consistency.

Sumpthn' Yummy

Chocolate Cookie Sheet Cake

2 cups flour	3 tablespoons cocoa
2 cups sugar	2 eggs
1/2 teaspoon salt	1 teaspoon soda
1 teaspoon cinnamon	1/2 cup buttermilk
1 cup margarine	1 teaspoon vanilla
1 cup water	

Sift flour, measure, and resift with sugar, salt and cinnamon. Bring to boil the margarine, water and cocoa. Pour over the flour and sugar mixture. Mix eggs, soda, buttermilk and vanilla together. Add to above mixture. Bake in a greased and floured 15 1/2x10 1/2x1-inch pan for 20 minutes at 350°. May use 9x13-inch pan. Cook about 40 minutes.

ICING:

1/2 cup margarine	1 box confectioners' sugar
2 tablespoons cocoa	1/2 cup chopped pecans
6 tablespoons milk	1 teaspoon vanilla

Start cooking icing the last five minutes cake is baking. Mix margarine, cocoa and milk in saucepan over low heat. Remove and add sugar, nuts and vanilla. Frost cake while hot. Makes 36 squares.

The cinnamon makes the difference!

Cotton Country Cooking

Mound Cake

1 box devil food cake mix	3/4 cup sugar
1 pound coconut	1/2 cup water
1 (1-pound) bag marshmallows	

Cook cake mix by directions on low. Use two layers. Let cool and slice into 4 layers. Combine marshmallows, sugar and water in a double boiler and stir until completely melted. Add coconut and spread between layers of sliced cake.

ICING:

2 cups sugar	2 tablespoons cocoa
1/4 cup white Karo syrup	1/2 stick margarine
1/2 cup sweet milk	

Mix all ingredients together. Boil for 4 minutes and beat for 2 minutes with an electric mixer. Pour over cake. Can be frozen.

The Great Cookbook

Cheesecake Supreme

1 1/4 cup graham cracker crumbs	3 tablespoons flour
1/4 cup sugar	2 teaspoons grated lemon peel
1/4 cup melted butter or margarine	1 tablespoon grated orange peel
5 (8-ounce) packages cream cheese,	5 whole eggs
at room temperature	2 egg yolks
1 3/4 cups sugar	1/4 cup heavy cream

Heat oven to 500°. Work graham cracker crumbs, sugar and butter together until well blended. Butter a 9-inch spring-form pan and press crumb mixture over the bottom and about 2 1/4 inches up the sides of the pan.

In the large bowl of an electric mixer, combine cheese, sugar, flour, lemon peel and orange peel on low speed. Add whole eggs and egg yolks, one at a time, beating well after each addition. Add cream and beat at medium speed just until mixture is smooth.

Pour cheese mixture into prepared pan; bake for 10 minutes. Reduce oven temperature to 200° and continue baking for 1 hour. Remove from oven and cool on wire rack away from drafts. Refrigerate until cold.

When cold, remove rim of pan and place cake on a serving plate. Top with Pineapple Glaze.

PINEAPPLE GLAZE:

1 tablespoon cornstarch	1 (8 1/2-ounce) can crushed
2 tablespoons sugar	pineapple

Combine cornstarch and sugar in a small saucepan; gradually stir in undrained pineapple. Cook on moderately low heat, stirring constantly until thickened. Add a few drops of yellow food coloring, if desired. Remove from heat; stir occasionally. Cool before using. Serves 12-14.

Calling All Cooks

Roulage

1 (6-ounce) package Nestle
  semisweet chocolate chips
3 tablespoons extra strong coffee
  (liquid)
5 eggs, separated

1 cup + 1 tablespoon sugar
Cocoa
1/2 pint whipping cream
1 teaspoon vanilla flavoring

Preheat oven to 350°. In top of double boiler slowly melt the chocolate chips. After chocolate is melted, add coffee; mix well and set aside. Keep it melted.

Butter a jelly roll pan; line with wax paper and butter it heavily. Put yolks in large mixing bowl and beat exactly 5 minutes until light and fluffy. Gradually add 1 cup of sugar; mix well. Beat chocolate mixture into the egg mixture. Beat egg whites until stiff and fold into the chocolate mixture. Pour batter into the jelly roll pan and spread evenly. Bake for exactly 15 minutes. Remove from oven; leave in pan; place on a cooling rack and sprinkle cocoa over it with a sifter; then spread a dish towel over the pan. Leave like this for 30 minutes. Run knife around edges to loosen from pan. Put another piece of wax paper over the top. Put a large cookie sheet on top of the wax paper and flip over. Take the jelly roll pan off and carefully remove the wax paper left on top of the cake.

Whip whipping cream with 1 tablespoon sugar and vanilla flavoring until stiff. Spread evenly on cake. Keep 1 inch from outside edge. Lift wax paper on bottom which should cause it to start rolling. After it is completely rolled, remove wax paper and cover with aluminum foil and shape to keep the cake round. Put in freezer. When ready to use, slice across roll. This is really easy to make and can be made a day or two ahead of time. Yield: 8 servings.

Once Upon a Stove

Northeast Alabama's Sequoyah Caverns are an underground showcase of natural wonders, featuring mirrored lakes, geological formations and fossils, and beautiful wildlife.

Lemon Roulage

4 eggs, separated	1 tablespoon vegetable oil
1/2 cup sugar	1/4 cup sugar
1 teaspoon lemon extract	2/3 cup sifted cake flour
1/4 teaspoon almond extract	1 teaspoon baking powder
1/4 teaspoon coconut extract	1/4 teaspoon salt
1/4 teaspoon orange extract	Confectioners' sugar

Whisk egg yolks until light and lemon colored; gradually add 1/2 cup sugar while beating. Stir in lemon, almond, coconut, and orange extracts along with the vegetable oil. Beat egg whites until foamy; gradually add 1/4 cup sugar. Beat until stiff but not dry. Fold egg whites into yolk mixture.

Combine flour, baking powder, and salt. Fold into batter. Grease a 15x10x1-inch jelly roll pan and line with waxed paper. Grease and flour waxed paper. Spread batter evenly in pan. Bake at 375° for 10-15 minutes.

Sift confectioners' sugar in a 15x10-inch rectangle on a linen towel. When the cake is done, turn out onto sugar, peel off waxed paper, and roll up the cake and towel together starting at the narrow end. Cool on a wire rack with seam side down.

Unroll the cake. Spread with Lemon Filling, reserving half for sides and top of cake.

LEMON FILLING:

1 (14-ounce) can sweetened condensed milk	Several drops yellow food coloring
1/3 cup fresh lemon juice	1 (4-ounce) carton frozen whipped topping, thawed
1 teaspoon grated lemon rind	

Combine first four ingredients. Fold in whipped topping. Reroll cake. Place on serving platter, seam side down. Spread with Lemon Filling on top and sides of cake.

COCONUT TOPPING:

1/2 cup coconut	1-2 drops yellow food coloring
1/2 teaspoon water	

Place coconut, water and food coloring in a plastic bag or covered jar. Shake to color evenly. Sprinkle over cake. Refrigerate for 1-2 hours before serving.

Decorate with candied African violets and candied or crystalized mint leaves.

The Alabama Heritage Cookbook

Dump Cake

1 box butter cake mix
3/4 cup melted margarine
1 large can crushed pineapple

1 can cherry pie filling
1 cup chopped nuts

Combine cake mix and butter until crumbly. Stir in pineapple and pie filling. Pour into oblong pan. Bake in 350° oven for 35 minutes. Sprinkle with nuts; bake 15 minutes longer.

Treasured Taste

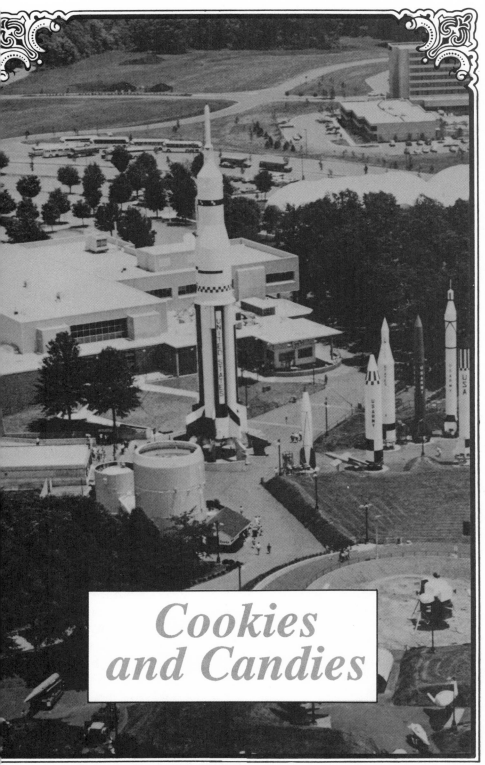

Cookies
and Candies

Earth's largest rocket and missile collection is on display at The Space and Rocket Center, home of the U.S. Space Camp programs. Huntsville.

Chocolate Puffs

1/2 cup Crisco oil	4 eggs
4 squares of unsweetened chocolate (melted)	2 teaspoons vanilla
	2 cups self-rising flour
2 cups sugar	1 cup confectioners' sugar

Mix oil, chocolate and granulated sugar. Blend in eggs, one at a time, until well mixed. Add vanilla. Stir sifted flour into mixture. Chill for 2 hours. Preheat oven to 350°. Drop dough, by teaspoon, into bowl of confectioners' sugar. Roll in sugar, making balls. Place 2 inches apart on greased cookie sheet. Bake 10-12 minutes. Watch them puff.

Treats For My Sweets

Sugar Cookies

During my teen age years Christmas Eve was always spent carolling with friends around the neighborhood. We would always stop at the same homes. After singing for Marguerite Freeman she would serve us her wonderful sugar cookies.

2 sticks margarine	3 tablespoons milk
1 1/2 cups sugar	3 cups flour
3 eggs	2 1/2 tablespoons baking powder
1 teaspoon vanilla	1/4 teaspoon salt

You will need to set the oven to 375°. Put the margarine into the mixer bowl. Turn the mixer to slow and cream the margarine, slowly add the sugar, then break the eggs, one at a time in a cup, and add to the mixer. Add the vanilla and the milk. Put the flour, baking powder and salt into the sifter and sift it into a bowl. Using a spatula, add the flour slowly, and keep the spatula out of the way of the beaters. When it is mixed, turn off the mixer. Sprinkle some flour onto a flat surface and dip out some of the cookie batter. Sprinkle flour over the top and work the dough a little bit. Be gentle and do not treat it rough. Get a rolling pin and roll the dough out to about 1/4-inch thick. Dip a glass or cookie cutter into flour, and cut out the cookies. Lay them on a cookie sheet. Sprinkle sugar over the tops and bake until just barely brown.

Hearthside at Christmas

Avoine Biscuits
(Oatmeal Flake Cookies)

8 ounces butter, softened	1/2 teaspoon soda
1 cup brown sugar	1 cup coconut
1 cup white sugar	1 cup nuts
2 eggs	3 cups corn flakes
2 cups flour	1 cup oatmeal
1 teaspoon baking powder	1 teaspoon vanilla
Dash salt	

Cream butter, sugars, and eggs. Sift together flour, baking powder, salt, and soda; add to creamed mixture. Stir in the remaining ingredients. Drop by spoonfuls onto greased baking sheets. Bake at 350° until just golden (about 10-12 minutes).

Birdies in the Oven/Aces in the Kitchen

Ritz Delights

Ritz crackers	1/2 stick paraffin wax
Peanut butter	Pecans, chopped
1 pound white chocolate or	
12-ounces chocolate chips	

Spread peanut butter between 2 Ritz crackers to form cookie. In a double boiler, melt chocolate with paraffin wax. Dip cookie into chocolate. I find that the chocolate stays on the cookies better if I let the chocolate cool some. Immediately place the dipped cookies in chopped pecans; place on waxed paper. Yield: 50 cookies.

Note: This cookie is perfect for bridal teas and fancy parties!

Once Upon a Stove

Free blacks who came to this country on the schooner *Clothilde,* the last American slaveship, founded Africatown USA State Park near Mobile. A museum on the grounds features the highly successful experiments of George Washington Carver.

Cherry Surprises

1 cup margarine
1/2 cup powdered sugar
2 egg yolks
2 cups sifted flour

1/8 teaspoon salt
2 teaspoons almond flavoring
1 (9 1/4-ounce) bottle maraschino
   cherries, drained

Cream margarine and sugar. Add egg yolks. Blend in flour and salt. Add flavoring. Chill until firm enough to handle, about 2 hours. Pinch off pieces of dough with floured hands, insert cherry and cover with the dough. Bake in 325° oven about 25 minutes, until lightly browned. When cool, ice with the following:

ICING:
1 tablespoon melted shortening
1 tablespoon cherry juice
1 tablespoon water

1/8 teaspoon salt
1 1/3 cups powdered sugar

Melt shortening, add juice and water, beat in salt and powdered sugar. Beat until spreading consistency. Spread on tops of cookies. Makes 36.

Florence Cook Book

Melting Moments

1 cup butter or margarine, softened
2 cups confectioners' sugar
1 1/4 cups unsifted all-purpose
   flour

3/4 cup cornstarch
3 tablespoons orange juice

Cream butter and 1/2 cup confectioners' sugar until light and fluffy. Beat in flour and cornstarch until well mixed. Wrap and refrigerate dough at least 2 hours. Roll dough into 1-inch balls. Bake on ungreased cookie sheet 8-10 minutes at 325°. Cool slightly in pans, then remove to wire racks and cool completely. Mix remaining ingredients (1 1/2 cups confectioners' sugar and orange juice). Glaze cookies.

Anniversary Collection of Delectable Dishes

Jerome Cookies

1 box graham crackers	1/2 cup milk
1 1/2 sticks butter	1 cup nuts
1 cup sugar	1 can coconut
1 egg	

Line a 9x13-inch pan with whole graham crackers. Melt 1 1/2 sticks butter in saucepan. Add sugar. Beat egg and milk together, add to butter and sugar. Bring to a boil, stirring constantly. Remove from heat. Add chopped nuts, coconut and 1 cup of graham cracker crumbs. Pour this over graham crackers in pan. Cover with another layer of graham crackers. Top with the following icing.

ICING:

2 cups powdered sugar	3 tablespoons milk
1/2 stick margarine	1 teaspoon vanilla

Mix all together and spread over cookies. Chill and cut in small squares.

Anniversary Collection of Delectable Dishes

Cream Cheese Cookies

1/2 (8-ounce) package cream cheese
1/2 cup solid shortening
1/2 cup butter
1 cup sugar

1/2 teaspoon salt
1 teaspoon vanilla
2 cups flour

Mix all ingredients together. Make into rolls. Chill. Slice when ready to bake, and bake at 325° for 15-20 minutes.

DOWN HOME In High Style

Red and Green Coconut Bars

Bread slices, trimmed, and cut
  into fingers
Sweetened condensed milk

Coconut
Red and green food coloring

Dip bread into milk, coating all sides; immediately roll into coconut which has been tinted with a little red or green food coloring. Bake at 350° until very lightly browned. This is a delicious macaroon-like cookie.

Gazebo I Christmas Cookbook

Tea Dainties

White bread
Salad oil

Peanut butter

Stack up slices of white bread. Trim. Cut down through the stack into all five (5) strips. Place strips on baking sheet (spread out) and toast at 200° until completely crisp all through (1-2 hours.) At same time, toast the crusts same way. When all are crisp, set strips aside. Crush the crusts into fine crumbs with rolling pie. Now mix together enough salad oil and peanut butter to make a thick liquid. Dip each strip in this and then roll in crumbs. Drain on paper. Keeps well in foil or tight container.

Kum' Ona' Granny's Table

Cinnamon Logs
Spicy and "short," easy to make..

1 cup butter or margarine	**2 teaspoons cinnamon**
1 cup sugar	**1 egg, separated**
2 cups flour	**1 cup ground pecans**

Cream butter and sugar. Sift flour and cinnamon together and add to butter-sugar mixture. Add egg yolk. Mix well and spread mixture on greased cookie sheet, 15x10 inches. Brush top with beaten egg white. Sprinkle nuts on top. Bake in 350° oven until slightly brown, about 15 minutes. Remove from oven and cut into bars. Makes 4 dozen 1x3-inch logs.

Cotton Country Cooking

Amaretta Bars

1 package yellow (butter recipe)
  cake mix
3 eggs
1/3 cup butter
1/2 cup granulated sugar
1/2 teaspoon baking powder

1/4 teaspoon salt
1/4 cup Amaretta liqueur
1/2 teaspoon almond flavoring
Sliced almonds
Confectioners' sugar

Combine 1 egg, butter and cake mix until crumbly. Reserve 1 cup, and put aside. Pat remaining mixture lightly into ungreased 13x9x2-inch pan. Bake at 350° for 15 minutes.

Beat remaining eggs, sugar, baking powder, salt, Amaretto and flavoring with a beater until light and foamy *(do not overbeat)*. Pour over hot crust. Sprinkle with reserved cup of mixture and sliced almonds. Bake at 350° an additional 15-20 minutes until lightly browned. Cut into bars and sprinkle with confectioners' sugar. Makes 32-40 bars.

Heavenly Hostess

Fudgy Iced Brownies

1 stick margarine	1 cup flour
1 cup sugar	1 (16-ounce) can chocolate syrup
4 eggs	1 cup pecans, chopped

Cream margarine until fluffy. Gradually add sugar and beat. Add eggs, one at a time, beating after each addition. Stir in flour and beat until smooth. Add syrup and nuts and mix. Pour into greased 9x13x2-inch pan and bake at 350° for 25 minutes. *Do not overbake.*

ICING:

1 stick margarine	1/2 cup chocolate morsels
1 1/2 cups sugar	1 cup pecans, chopped
1/3 cup evaporated milk	

In saucepan, combine margarine, sugar, and milk and cook over low heat to boiling, stirring constantly. Let boil for one minute without stirring. Remove from heat and add morsels. Stir until melted. Add nuts and mix. Pour icing over brownies while both are hot. Cool. Cut into squares.

When Dinnerbells Ring

Chocolate-Caramel Brownies

1 (14-ounce) bag caramels	1 cup chopped nuts
2/3 cup evaporated milk, divided	1 (6-ounce) package semi-sweet
1 (18 1/2-ounce) package German	chocolate chips
chocolate cake mix	
3/4 cup softened butter	
or margarine	

Preheat oven to 350°. Combine caramels and one-third cup evaporated milk in top of double boiler. Heat, stirring constantly, until caramels are melted completely. Remove from heat and set aside. Combine cake mix, one-third cup evaporated milk, and butter. Beat with an electric mixer until mixture holds together. Stir in nuts. Press half of cake mixture into a well-greased 9x13-inch pan. Bake six minutes. Sprinkle chocolate chips over crust and cover evenly with caramel mixture. Crumble remaining cake mixture on top. Bake 15-18 minutes. Cool and then chill 30 minutes before cutting into small squares.

Try Me

Lemon Meringue Squares

1/2 cup shortening	1 cup sifted all-purpose flour
1/2 cup sifted confectioners' sugar	1/2 cup granulated sugar
2 tablespoons grated lemon rind	1 tablespoon lemon juice
2 eggs, separated	1/2 cup finely chopped nut meats

Cream shortening and confectioners' sugar together until light and fluffy. Blend in lemon rind. Beat egg yolks until thick and light. Add to first mixture. Add flour slowly and mix until smooth. Spread and pat this stiff mixture in a thin, even layer in a greased 9x13x2-inch pan. Bake in 350° oven for 10 minutes. Meanwhile beat egg whites until fluffy. Add sugar gradually while beating. Beat until stiff, but not dry. Fold in lemon juice, a little at a time. Fold in nuts. Spread over baked layer. Return to oven and bake 25 minutes longer. Cool about 3 minutes and cut into about 48 squares.

Recipe Jubilee!

Pecan Nuggets

5 cups sugar	1 (13-ounce) jar marshmallow
1 stick butter or margarine	cream
1 large can evaporated milk	1 quart pecans
1/2 teaspoon salt	
1 1/2 pounds chocolate kisses (unwrapped)	

Combine sugar, butter, milk and salt in a heavy saucepan. Bring to a boil; boil for 6 minutes. Combine chocolate kisses and marshmallow cream in a large bowl; pour boiling syrup over. Stir until chocolate kisses are dissolved; add pecans. Drop by teaspoon onto waxed paper.

Hallmark's Collection of Home Tested Recipes

 A recipe contest and tasting party attracts food-lovers to Monroeville for the Annual Pecan Harvest Festival. The festival also provides entertainment, a children's dog show, petting zoo, and arts and crafts.

Peanut Butter Turtles

1 pound semi-sweet chocolate morsels	1 pound light caramels
1/2 pound peanut butter morsels	1 pound package pecans (halves)

Melt chocolate morsels, in separate pan slowly melt caramels, when partially melted, add peanut butter morsels. Mix thoroughly. Add 3/4 of the pecans to caramel/peanut butter mixture. Alternate drops-- chocolate then caramel then chocolate, top with pecan. This process works best if dripped on waxed paper.

Hearthside at Christmas

Peanut Butter Secrets

3 boxes confectioners' sugar	Toothpicks
1 pound margarine, melted	1 block paraffin
2 cups peanut butter	1 (12-ounce) bag semi-sweet
3 tablespoons vanilla extract	chocolate chips

Mix sugar, margarine, peanut butter, and vanilla together. Roll into one-half inch balls. Place a toothpick in each ball. Chill until firm.

Melt paraffin in double boiler. Mix in the chocolate chips. Stir until melted. Dip the balls in the chocolate (keep the chocolate on low heat while you dip the balls). Place on wax paper. Refrigerate. Yields 15 dozen.

The Great Cookbook

English Toffee
(Shhh - secret recipe)

1 cup water
2 cups white sugar
3/4 pound butter

1 pound chopped pecans
2 cups milk chocolate
(giant Hershey bars)

Soften chocolate in double boiler. Do not stir. Boil water, sugar and butter on medium heat until it reaches 280°. Add 1/2-pound chopped nuts at 280° and stir constantly until it reaches 310°. Pour real thin on marble slab (ungreased) and spread with spatula. Spread half of chocolate on one side; immediately sprinkle 1/4-pound pecans and lightly pat. Run spatula under slab of candy and turn over. Spread this side with remaining chocolate and pecans. Put in cool room, preferably overnight. When cool, loosen from marble and break into desired size pieces. (Cook on medium entire time.) Chop pecans and soften chocolate before beginning. This recipe is easy and foolproof.

Auburn Entertains

Old Fashioned Butter Crunch

1 cup slivered almonds
1 cup butter or margarine
1 1/4 cups sugar
2 tablespoons light corn syrup

2 tablespoon water
1 (12-ounce) package semi-sweet
chocolate pieces, melted

Spread almonds in shallow pan, toast in moderate oven, (350°) until golden. Melt butter or margarine in large heavy saucepan; add sugar, corn syrup and water. Cook, stirring often, to hard crack stage. Pour quickly into 13x9x2-inch pan. Cool completely. When set, turn out in one piece on wax paper. Spread half the melted chocolate over top; sprinkle with 1/2 cup almonds; let set. Turn candy over; spread with remaining chocolate, sprinkle with remaining almonds.

Let stand until chocolate sets. Break into pieces. This candy is a favorite at my house. It's delicious. We always make it a Christmas time.

Kum' Ona' Granny's Table

Petite BonBons

1/2 cup margarine	1 1/2 teaspoons butter flavoring
3/4 cup confectioners' sugar	1 1/2 cups plain flour
1 1/2 teaspoons vanilla flavoring	A few drops of chosen food coloring

FILLING:

Nuts	Butterscotch pieces
Cherries	Reese's peanut butter pieces
Chocolate pieces	Miniature marshmallows

Preheat oven to 350°. Mix butter, sugar, vanilla and butter flavoring and coloring. Blend sifted flour in thoroughly by hand. If mixture is dry, add 3-4 teaspoons cream or milk. For each BonBon, wrap 1 tablespoon of dough around chosen filling. Bake 1 inch apart on ungreased cookie sheet 12-15 minutes. Do not brown. Cool and dip in confectioners' icing.

CONFECTIONERS' SUGAR ICING:

1 cup confectioners' sugar	1 teaspoon vanilla
3 tablespoons milk	Food coloring of choice

Mix sugar, milk, vanilla and food coloring until smooth. Dip BonBons into this icing.

Treats For My Sweets

Forever Ambers

2 cans Eagle Brand condensed
  milk
1 pound bag orange slice candy,
  chopped
1 cup chopped pecans

2 cans Angel Flake coconut
1 teaspoon vanilla
1 teaspoon orange extract
Confectioners' sugar

Mix above ingredients except confectioners' sugar. Pour into an 11x14-inch pan. Bake at 300° for 30 minutes. Cool. Roll into balls the size of a walnut, then roll in the sugar.

Hallmark's Collection of Home Tested Recipes

Reese's Pieces

1 cup butter
1 1/4 pound powdered sugar
2 cups peanut butter, smooth
  or crunchy

2 1/2 cups graham cracker crumbs
1 (12-ounce) package semi-sweet
  chocolate chips
1/4 of 1 block of paraffin

Melt butter and mix with sugar, peanut butter and graham cracker crumbs. Batter is so stiff you must mix it with a wooden spoon and press by hand into a greased cookie sheet with sides. Top with chocolate chips and paraffin that have been melted together in a double boiler. Allow to harden and cut into 1-inch squares. Yield: 10 dozen.

So good you will think it's a Reese Cup. Makes a great snack to munch on.

Cooks and Company

Microwave Chocolate Fudge

1 stick butter
3 tablespoons cocoa
1 pound powdered sugar
4 tablespoons milk

1 teaspoon vanilla
1/2 cup pecans, chopped
1 cup miniature marshmallows

Melt butter and cocoa in a Microwave for 2 minutes. Stir in the powdered sugar and milk. Cook in a Microwave for 30 seconds. Stir in the vanilla and pecans and cook in a Microwave for 30 seconds. Stir in the marshmallows until dissolved. Pour in a buttered 8x8x2-inch pan and place in the refrigerator for 30 minutes. Cut into 1-inch squares. Yield: 64 1-inch pieces.

One of a Kind

Amaretto Fudge

4 cups sugar
2/3 cup Amaretto Liqueur

2 cups half-and-half
or light cream

In a large saucepan combine all ingredients and brush sides of pan with butter or margarine. Stir over moderate heat until sugar is dissolved, then bring to a boil and cook without stirring until 238° is reached on the candy thermometer, or until a soft ball is formed when dropped in water. Remove from heat and let stand until 140° is reached. Beat with spoon until mixture begins to thicken slightly, pour quickly into a foil lined 8-inch pan. (I pour into buttered Pyrex container). Let stand until hard and cool.

Hearthside at Christmas

Orange-Coconut Balls

1 (6-ounce) can frozen orange juice
1 (16-ounce) box vanilla wafers,
   crushed
1 stick margarine, melted

1 (16-ounce) box confectioners'
   sugar
1/2-1 cup nuts, chopped
1 (7-ounce) can coconut, shredded

Mix first five ingredients thoroughly. Form into small balls and roll in coconut. More flavorful when made at least one day before serving. Makes 100.

When Dinnerbells Ring

No Bake Pink Lemonade Balls

1/2 cup margarine (melted)
2 cups Graham Cracker crumbs
1 (6-ounce) can pink lemonade
4 cups confectioners' sugar

1 cup chopped nuts
Confectioners' sugar
1/2 cup coconut (flaked)

Melt margarine and pour into graham cracker crumbs. Add pink lemonade and confectioners' sugar gradually. Mix well. Add chopped pecans. Roll into small balls, then into pink-tinted coconut or confectioners' sugar. Refrigerate until candy is firm.

Treats For My Sweets

Pies
and
Desserts

"The Charm of the Deep South," Bellingrath Gardens and Home offers year-round strolls of sensual delight on its many natural pathways. South of Mobile.

Mrs. Coons' Sherry Cream Pie

Absolutely marvelous! Undoubtedly a big favorite of our ladies. A very special dessert that is well worth the effort to make.

1 1/2 cups crisp chocolate cookie crumbs	1/2 cup sugar
	1 cup milk
1/2 cup butter, melted	1/8 teaspoon salt
1 tablespoon plain gelatin	1/4 teaspoon nutmeg
1/4 cup cold milk	1/2 cup sherry wine
3 eggs, separated	1 cup heavy cream

Mix cookie crumbs and butter. Press into 10-inch glass pie plate and chill 1 hour. Soften gelatin in cold milk. Put egg yolks in top of double boiler and beat slightly, adding sugar and 1 cup milk. Cook and stir 10 minutes or until custard coats spoon. Remove from heat; add gelatin, salt and nutmeg. Stir till gelatin dissolves. Add wine very slowly, stirring constantly. Refrigerate mixture to thicken. When thick beat egg whites until stiff; fold in gently. Whip cream until firm and fold in. Pour into chilled pie shell and sprinkle top with grated semi-sweet chocolate. Refrigerate at least 8 hours.

Cookbook

Mobile Apple Cream Pie

You'll want a 9-inch cooked pie shell; it must be cool before you put in the filling.

FILLING:

3/4 cup sugar
2 tablespoons flour
1 cup sour cream
1 egg, beaten

1/2 teaspoon vanilla extract
Good pinch salt
2 cups finely-chopped apples

Combine sugar with flour, then add sour cream, beaten egg, vanilla, salt and beat all this together until smooth. Stir in apples and pour mixture into pie shell. Bake at 450° for about 30 minutes or until filling is almost set. Meanwhile prepare the following topping.

TOPPING:

1/2 cup sugar
6 tablespoons flour
1 teaspoon cinnamon

Dash of mace
1/4 cup unsalted butter

Blend all above ingredients until you have a crumbly mix. Spread this over pie, bake 10 minutes longer. You can include a few raisins, or if you're Baroque you can put in some chopped candied ginger.

Delectable Dishes from Termite Hall

Surprise Pie

1 (9-inch) pie shell, baked
3 egg yolks
1 cup sugar
Juice of 1 large lemon
4 tablespoons self-rising flour

1 stick margarine, cut up
2 cups buttermilk
3 egg whites
1 cup sugar

Beat egg yolks at medium speed. Continue mixing while adding next 5 ingredients in order. Pour into top of double boiler over boiling water. Cook, stirring until thickened. Set aside to cool. Beat egg whites until stiff. Mix in 1 cup sugar. Pour slightly cooled filling into pie crust. Top with meringue. Run under broiler to brown when ready to serve. Serves 6-8.

Magic

Frozen Mincemeat Holiday Pie

CRUST:

1 1/2 cups pecans, finely chopped   2 tablespoons butter, melted
3 tablespoons sugar

Combine pecans, sugar, and melted butter and mix well. Press into a well-greased 9-inch pie plate. Bake at 350° for 10 minutes. Cool thoroughly.

FILLING:

1 cup prepared bottled mincemeat	1 quart vanilla ice cream
1/2 teaspoon ground cinnamon	1/2 pint heavy cream, whipped
1/2 teaspoon ground ginger	Candied red cherries
1/4 teaspoon ground allspice	Pecan halves or other garnish
1 tablespoon grated orange rind	

When crust is thoroughly cooled, spread it evenly with mincemeat straight out of the bottle. Add cinnamon, ginger, allspice, and grated orange rind to softened ice cream. Spread this mixture evenly over the mincemeat layer. Put in freezer and freeze until firm. Wrap for longer freezing if pie is not to be used now. It can be frozen for several weeks.

When pie is to be served, it should be taken from the freezer 10-15 minutes before time. Garnish with sweetened whipped cream piped through a decorator bag or use one of the good cans available now on the market. Garnish with cherry, pecans, twist of orange peel, or something festive.

Gazebo I Cookbook

Peanut-Butter Pie

1 package (4-ounce) cream cheese, softened	1 tub (8-ounce) non-dairy whipped topping
1/2 cup confectioners' sugar	1 chocolate cookie pie crust (9-inch)
1 cup peanut-butter	
1/2 cup milk	

In a mixing bowl beat cream cheese and sugar until creamy smooth, scraping sides often. Add peanut butter and milk; beat slowly until smooth, about 3 minutes. Blend in topping until no streaks appear. Pour into pie shell and freeze. May be topped with whipped cream and chocolate syrup. Yield: 8 servings.

Dining Under the Magnolia

"Our" Pumpkin Pie

1 package pie crust mix	1/2 teaspoon salt
1 (#1) can of pumpkin	3/4 teaspoon cinnamon
1 can Eagle Brand sweetened	1/2 teaspoon nutmeg
condensed milk	1/2 teaspoon ginger
1 egg	Pecan Topping Crumble

PECAN TOPPING CRUMBLE:

1/2 package pie crust mix	1/2 cup brown sugar
(from above)	1/3 cup chopped pecans

Mix together. Heat oven to 375°. Prepare pastry for one crust as directed (or you can use a frozen one and save the rest of the pie crust mix package).

With rotary beater, blend remaining ingredients except topping. Pour into pie shell. Sprinkle topping evenly over pie. Cover edges with 1 1/2-inch aluminum strips to prevent excessive browning. Bake for 50-55 minutes. If top is browning too quickly, you may place a sheet of aluminum foil lightly over the top.

This pie is great; it is a tradition at our house on Christmas, Thanksgiving, and any other family gathering time.

Gazebo I Cookbook

Mystery Pecan Pie

1 (8-ounce) package cream	9-inch baked pie shell
cheese, softened	1 1/4 cups chopped pecans
1/3 cup sugar	3 eggs
1/4 teaspoon salt	1/4 cup sugar
1 teaspoon vanilla	1 teaspoon vanilla
1 egg	1 cup light corn syrup (Karo)

In medium bowl, combine cream cheese, first amount of sugar, salt, vanilla and egg. Pour into pie shell. Sprinkle with pecans.

Combine remaining eggs, sugar, vanilla and syrup. Pour over pecans. Bake at 375° for 35-40 minutes or until center is firm. Pie will be a golden brown. Layers will change in baking, with pecans floating to top, cream cheese layer next and egg-syrup mixture sinking to the bottom. May serve with vanilla ice cream or whipped topping. Serves 6-8.

Loaves and Fishes

Pineapple-Coconut Pie

1 stick butter, melted
1 1/2 cups sugar
4 eggs
1 (8 1/4-ounce) can crushed
   pineapple

1 cup shredded coconut
1 tablespoon vanilla
2 (8-inch) unbaked pie shells

Melt butter. Cool. Mix sugar and eggs together and blend with butter.
Mix in pineapple, coconut and vanilla. Pour into two 8-inch unbaked
pie shells. Bake in 350° oven for 35 mintues or until done. Yield: 2
(8-inch) pies.

Huntsville Entertains

Lemon Cobbler
Delightfully different!

2 lemons, sliced thin, remove seeds
1 tablespoon flour
2 cups sugar
1 stick butter

1 1/2 cups hot water
Dash salt
1 recipe favorite pie dough

Place sliced lemons in 11x8x2-inch (or similar size) pan. Sprinkle with flour and sugar. Cut butter in small pieces and dot tops of lemons. Pour hot water and dash salt over all. Place strips of favorite pie dough over top of lemons. Bake at 375° for 45 minutes. Serve warm to 6 people.

Twickenham Tables

Best Ever Apple Cobbler

1/2 cup (1-stick) butter
2 cups sugar
2 cups water
1 1/2 cups sifted Martha White
  self-rising flour

1/2 cup shortening
1/3 cup milk
2 cups apples, finely chopped
1 teaspoon cinnamon

Heat oven to 350°. Melt butter in 13x9x2-inch baking pan. In a sauce-pan, heat sugar and water until sugar melts. Meanwhile, cut shortening into flour until particles are like fine crumbs. Add milk and stir with fork only until dough leaves the side of the bowl. Turn out on floured board, knead until smooth. Roll dough into a large rectangle about 1/4-inch thick. Sprinkle cinnamon over apples, then sprinkle apples evenly over dough. Roll up dough like a jelly roll. Dampen the edge with a little water to seal. Slice dough into about 1/2-inch thick slices. Place in pan of melted butter. Pour sugar syrup carefully around rolls. (This looks like too much liquid, but the crust will absorb it.) Bake 55-60 minutes.

Variation: This cobbler may be make with other fresh, frozen or canned fruits, such as blackberries, blueberries, cherries or peaches. If packed in liquid, drain and substitute for part of sugar syrup. Always use 2 cups of liquid. An all time favorite, this swirled cobbler is moist and juicy yet flaky on top.

Auburn Entertains

Fresh Strawberry Pie

1 cup sugar
1/4 cup cornstarch
1/4 cup white Karo
1 1/2 cups hot water

1 package strawberry Jello
2 pastry shells, baked
1 quart strawberries

Mix sugar and cornstarch. Add Karo and water. Cook, stirring constantly until clear. Remove from heat. Add strawberry Jello. Cool. Line bottom of pastry shells with whole fresh strawberries and pour mixture over them. Chill. When ready to serve, add whipping cream as topping. Yield: 2 (8-inch) pies.

Anniversary Collection of Delectable Dishes

Creme de Menthe Pie

1/2 gallon vanilla ice cream   8 tablespoons creme de menthe

Let ice cream soften until soft enough to mix. Add creme de menthe, stir well. Pour into chocolate crust. Freeze. Serve with chocolate syrup.

CHOCOLATE CRUST:

2 cups crumbled chocolate Oreo
   cookies

1/3 cup melted margarine
Chocolate syrup

Mix cookies and margarine together. Press onto bottom and sides of a 9-inch pie pan. Freeze.

Hallmark's Collection of Home Tested Recipes

Apple Tarts

1 package dried apples   **1 cup sugar**

Cook apples in water until tender. Drain. Add sugar.

DOUGH:
2 cups plain flour   **1 cup ice water**
1 cup shortening

Mix flour, ice water and shortening. Roll real thin. Cut in circles. Spoon in the apple mixture; fold over; press around edge with fork. Fry in deep fat.

Kum' Ona' Granny's Table

Creole Bread Pudding

6 slices bread, cubed	Pinch of salt
3 1/2 cups milk, divided	1/4 cup butter or margarine,
4 eggs, separated	melted
1/2 cup sugar, divided	1/2 cup raisins
1 tablespoon vanilla extract	Rum sauce (recipe follows)

Combine bread cubes and 1 cup milk; set aside. Beat egg yolks, 6 table-spoons sugar and remaining 2 1/2 cups milk. Stir in vanilla, salt, butter and raisins. Pour mixture over bread and mix well. Pour into shallow 2-quart baking dish. Place dish in a pan of hot water. Bake at 300° about 50 minutes or until knife inserted in center comes out clean. Beat egg whites until stiff; gradually beat in remaining 2 tablespoons sugar. Spread meringue over pudding; bake at 350° about 10 minutes or until golden. Serve with Rum Sauce. Yield: 6-8 servings.

RUM SAUCE:

1/2 cup sugar	2 tablespoons butter or margarine
1/4 cup water	1 tablespoon rum

Combine sugar, water and butter in a small saucepan; bring to a boil and boil 1 minute. Remove from heat; stir in rum. Serve warm. Yield: about 1/2 cup.

Auburn Entertains

Pistachio Pudding

1 small box Instant Pistachio	1 large carton Cool Whip
pudding and pie filling	
1 (20-ounce) can crushed pineapple	
(well drained)	

Use juice of pineapple and mix with pudding; beat well. Blend in 1 large-size carton Cool Whip. Ready to eat!

Optional: Add a few miniature marshmallows and maraschino cherries (drained well) for decorations.

Treats For My Sweets

Alabama Banana Pudding

3/4 cup sugar	1/2 teaspoon vanilla
Dash of salt	2 cups milk
1/4 cup flour	15 vanilla wafers
3 egg yolks, beaten	2-4 bananas, sliced

Combine sugar, salt and flour; add to egg yolks and vanilla. Heat milk in saucepan; slowly add egg mixture. Cook until thick. Arrange wafers and bananas in shallow 1 1/2-quart baking dish. Add pudding.

MERINGUE:

3 egg whites	1/2 teaspoon vanilla
6 tablespoons sugar	

To make meringue, beat egg whites, sugar and vanilla until very stiff. Spread over pudding and bake at 400° until golden brown. Serve warm or cold. Serves 8.

Huntsville Heritage Cookbook

Santa's Christmas Trifle

We aren't sure just why this is named Santa's Christmas Trifle, but it may be because making this is like a gift. Keep these ingredients on hand and you can whip up a great trifle in a very few minutes. Looks impressive, too!

1 frozen pound cake	2 cups prepared vanilla pudding
1/4 cup orange juice	1 (8-ounce) container Cool Whip
1 (20-ounce) can apple pie filling	Toasted coconut for garnish
4 tablespoons raspberry jelly	

The bowl you choose for trifle is very important because the effect is gained by seeing the layers of the trifle through glass. You could make an individual serving by using a clear parfait or sherbet glass, but it is a lot more trouble. Arrange in layers. Cut half of cake into cubes. Sprinkle on orange juice, then half of pie filling; dot with all the jelly, then top with half of pudding. Repeat all these layers except jelly which has all been used; top with Cool Whip and garnish with toasted coconut.

Gazebo I Christmas Cookbook

Jeff Davis Custard

1 quart milk, scalded (do not scorch!)	6 whole eggs
1/2 cup sugar	1/2 cup cold milk
Pinch of salt	1/4 teaspoon vanilla or almond extract

Scald 1 quart milk; add sugar and a pinch of salt. Beat eggs and add the cold milk to them. Stir and add gradually to the hot milk mixture. Cook in top of a double boiler until custard coats the spoon. When cold, add the flavoring. Serve in dessert dishes. Top with a heaping tablespoon of whipped cream, peaked at the top, and add a red cherry to the side of the dish. This was a favorite dessert at Christmas time at my Aunt Rosa Middleton's home. She lived to be 103 years old.

Kum' Ona' Granny's Table

Lemon Torte

1 tablespoon sugar	Juice and rind of 3 lemons
1 cup margarine	8 egg whites
2 cups flour	1 cup sugar
1 envelope gelatin	Pinch of salt
2/3 cup water	2 cups heavy cream, whipped
1 cup sugar	1 cup coconut, toasted
8 egg yolks, beaten	Grated rind of 1 orange

Mix sugar, margarine and flour as for pie crust and press into 10x14-inch pan. Bake 30 minutes at 325°.

Soften gelatin in water. Mix sugar, egg yolks, lemon juice and rind in top of double boiler and cook over boiling water until thick. Add gelatin and stir to dissolve. Let cool. Beat egg whites to soft peaks, gradually add sugar and salt, and beat to form stiff peaks. Fold into lemon custard. Spread over baked crust and refrigerate. Spread whipped cream over top and sprinkle with coconut mixed with orange rind. Serves 18-20.

Loaves and Fishes

Coffee Tortoni

2 egg whites
1 1/2 tablespoons instant coffee
1/4 teaspoon salt
4 tablespoons sugar
2 cups heavy cream

1/2 cup sugar
2 teaspoons vanilla
1/4 teaspoon almond extract
3/4 cup toasted almonds,
   finely chopped

Add coffee and salt to egg whites; beat until stiff. Gradually beat in 4 tablespoons sugar. Whip cream; add 1/2 cup sugar, vanilla and almond extract. Continue to beat until stiff. Fold cream and 1/2 cup almonds into egg-white mixture. Spoon into 12 paper muffin liners inserted in muffin tins. Sprinkle remaining almonds on top. Freeze. Dream Whip or Cool Whip may be used for whipped cream. Serves 12.

Seconds Please!

Rich Ice Box Cake

3 dozen lady fingers
1 cup butter
2 cups 4-x sugar
1/4 pound Baker's unsweetened
   chocolate (4 squares)

5 eggs
1/4 cup milk
1 1/4 cups granulated sugar
2 teaspoons vanilla
1 pint whipping cream

Line the bottom and sides of a spring pan with the lady fingers, placing flat side to pan. Put chocolate, granulated sugar and milk in double boiler and when melted and smooth, add beaten egg yolks. Cook until thick, then cool and add vanilla. Cream the butter and 4-x sugar and add to chocolate mixture. Stir well, and then fold in stiffly-beaten egg whites. Pour into form pan over the lady fingers and place in refrigerator overnight to become firm. Before serving, whip the cream and sweeten slightly. Spread on top. Chopped pecans may be used in the filling and dusted on top of the whipped cream.

Old Mobile Recipes

Charlotte Russe with Raspberry Sauce

Every year Marie takes this charlotte to the Willing Workers' Christmas party. The ladies love it!

1 tablespoon plain gelatin	5 tablespoons sugar
1/3 cup cold water	3 tablespoons rum
1 cup heavy cream	1 (3-ounce) package lady fingers,
3 large eggs, separated	halved and split
Pinch of salt	

Dissolve gelatin in cold water placed over boiling water; cool. Whip cream until nearly stiff; put in refrigerator. Beat egg whites with salt. Gradually add 3 tablespoons sugar; beat until very stiff and refrigerate. Beat egg yolks, add 2 tablespoons sugar and beat until light and fluffy. Add cooled gelatin to egg yolks, then add rum. Fold in egg whites, then fold in whipped cream. Put 3 lady finger pieces in each sherbet glass (work fast); fill each glass with charlotte. Refrigerate 3-4 hours or overnight. Top with Raspberry Sauce just before serving. Serves about 8.

RASPBERRY SAUCE:

1 (10-ounce) box frozen	1 heaping teaspoon cornstarch
raspberries, thawed	1/2 cup sugar

Add a little water to berries and bring to boil. Press through a strainer to remove seeds and return to stove. Mix sugar and cornstarch; add a little water to make a paste. Stir into boiling berries and cook a few minutes. Cool and refrigerate till serving time.

Cookbook

Butter Pecan Delight

60 Ritz crackers
1/4 cup butter
1 quart butter pecan ice cream
2 boxes instant coconut pudding

1/4 cup angel flake coconut
1 3/4 cups milk
1 carton Cool Whip (9 ounces)

Melt butter and combine with crushed crackers. Put all except 1 cupful in a 9x13-inch pan. Pat down. Don't bake. Mix pudding, coconut and milk together. Add ice cream (allow to soften). Place mixture over the cracker crumbs. Spread the Cool Whip over the mixture. Sprinkle the remaining crumbs over the topping. Make 10-12 hours before serving and store in refrigerator.

Optional: Use vanilla pudding in place of coconut pudding and add 1/3 cup angel flake coconut in place of 1/4 cup.

Treats For My Sweets

Chocolate Nut Tart

4 sticks butter
4 cups all-purpose flour

2 (8-ounce) packages cream
    cheese

Soften butter to room temperature. Add cream cheese and flour; mix together. Roll into balls, with thumb against sides and bottom of mini-muffin pans. Press dough to form shell.

FILLING:

2 cups sugar
1 cup all-purpose flour
1 cup melted butter
4 eggs, beaten

1 teaspoon vanilla
2 cups pecans, chopped
12 ounces semi-sweet chocolate
    morsels

Combine sugar and flour, mixing well. Stir in melted butter, beaten eggs and vanilla. Fold in chopped pecans and chocolate morsels. Pour into mini-muffin pans. Bake for 15-20 minutes.

Huntsville Entertains

Chocolate Torte Royal

2 egg whites
1/4 teaspoon salt
1/2 teaspoon vinegar
1/2 cup sugar

1/4 teaspoon cinnamon
1/4 teaspoon instant coffee
1/2 cup ground nuts

Beat egg whites with salt and vinegar to soft peaks. Blend in sugar, cinnamon, coffee and nuts, gradually. Beat until stiff peaks form. Put on brown paper on a cookie sheet. Shape like a pie shell with high sides. Bake in 275° oven for 1 hour. Turn off heat and dry shell in oven for 2 hours.

FILLING:
1 (6-ounce) package chocolate bits
2 egg yolks, beaten
1/4 cup water
1 cup heavy cream

1/4 teaspoon cinnamon
1/4 cup sugar
1/4 teaspoon instant coffee

Melt chocolate over hot water, cool slightly and spread 2 tablespoonfuls over bottom of cooled shell. Add egg yolks and water to rest of chocolate, blend well. Chill until thick. Whip cream with cinnamon, sugar and coffee. Beat until stiff. Spread half over chocolate in shell. Fold remaining whip cream mixture into remaining chocolate mixture. Spread over top of torte. Decorate with pecan halves or cut up pecans. Chill several hours or overnight.

Recipe Jubilee!

Rainbow Frozen Cake

1 angel food cake
1 (10-ounce) package frozen blueberries (can use canned) (drain well)
1 (10-ounce) package frozen strawberries, partially thawed

1 can mandarin oranges, drained
1 (3-ounce) package each strawberry, lime, and orange Jello
1 gallon ice cream, softened (I use
   1/2 gallon)

Divide cake into three sections in three bowls. Pinch pieces. Sprinkle dry Jello into each and mix well.

In tube pan layer as follows: strawberry cake pieces, thawed straw-berries, layer of ice cream, lime cake pieces, blueberries (drained), layer of ice cream, orange cake pieces, mandarin oranges (drained), layer of ice cream. Freeze. Thaw with hot cloth around pan.

More Fiddling With Food

Tipsy Cake

4 egg yolks
1/4 cup sugar
Dash salt
2 cups scalded milk
1/2 teaspoon vanilla

1 package lady fingers
Apricot jam
1/2 cup whiskey
Toasted almonds
Whipped cream

Prepare custard. Beat egg yolks; lightly stir in sugar and salt. Stir milk in gradually and cook over hot water, stirring constantly until mixture coats spoon. Chill and flavor with vanilla.

Split lady fingers and spread with apricot jam. Put layer in glass bowl and pour whiskey over it and let cake soak up liquor. Cover with half of custard. Repeat layer of lady fingers sprinkled with whiskey and pour over remaining custard sauce. Garnish with toasted almonds and whipped cream.

Old Mobile Recipes

 Oktoberfest is a 112-year old tradition for the German colony of Cullman.

Strawberry Pizza

CRUST:
2 sticks margarine
2 cups flour

1 cup nuts

FIRST LAYER:
1 (8-ounce) package cream cheese
3 cups confectioners' sugar

1 (12-ounce) Cool Whip

TOP LAYER:
1 cup sugar
1 cup water
3 tablespoons cornstarch

1 (3-ounce) box strawberry Jello
2 pints strawberries

CRUST: Melt margarine with flour; press into 9x13-inch pan and add chopped nuts on top; press in. Bake 350° until brown; cool completely.
FIRST LAYER: Blend cream cheese and sugar until smooth; fold in Cool Whip. Peak up on sides so top layer won't run off.
TOP LAYER: Mix first 3 ingredients in pan and bring to boil; cook till clear. Cool a little. Add 1 box strawberry Jello; cool completely. Add strawberries and spread on top.

Calling All Cooks

Strawberry Kahlua Sauce

1 1/2 pints heavy cream
1/4 cup Kahlua

4 drops red food coloring
7 ounces marshmallow cream

Add Kahlua and food coloring to cream and beat until stiff. Add marshmallow cream and blend well. This sauce can be used as a dip for fresh strawberries or folded into the strawberries. It should be made the day you plan to serve it as the sauce loses some of its flavor overnight. Yield: 4 cups.

The Alabama Heritage Cookbook

Sliced Strawberries in Lingonberry Caramel Cream

1/2 cup sugar
3 tablespoons water
1/2 cup lingonberry preserves
2 egg yolks
1/2 cup powdered sugar

1 teaspoon vanilla
1 cup whipping cream
2 pints fresh strawberries,
  hulled and sliced

Oil a baking sheet with sides. Combine 1/2 cup sugar and water in a small heavy saucepan. Cook over low heat, stirring occasionally until sugar dissolves. Increase heat to medium, cover and cook 1 minute. Uncover and cook until syrup is a rich medium brown. Immediately pour into prepared sheet. Cool and break caramel into chunks. Put caramel into food processor with steel blade and process until finely ground.

Mix preserves, yolks, sugar, and vanilla until smooth. Gently fold in whipped cream. Just before serving, fold caramel into lingonberry cream mixture. Serves 6.

Serving Suggestion: Put in stemmed goblets and top with sliced strawberries. This is wonderful.

Twickenham Tables

Chocolate Mint Frozen Dessert

DESSERT:

25 chocolate Oreos, crushed
1/2 stick margarine, melted

1/2 gallon Peppermint ice cream

Mix together the crushed Oreos and the melted margarine. Press into a 9x13-inch pan. Spread the softened (slightly) ice cream onto the chocolate crust and freeze. Mean while, prepare the following sauce.

SAUCE:

3 ounces unsweetened chocolate
1/4 cup margarine

3/4 cup sugar
Small can Pet milk

Combine all the sauce ingredients in a medium saucepan. Cook over medium heat, stirring constantly, until chocolate is melted. Takes 4 minutes. Remove from heat and cool completely. Spread over the frozen ice cream and return to freezer. Cut into squares to serve.

Note: You may substitute a sauce made from 4 melted Goldbricks, if you prefer. Serves 12-16.

One of a Kind

Chocolate Mint Ice Cream

A rich thick ice cream that is a favorite at the church ice cream suppers. It's gone before you can turn around.

2 eggs
3 cups heavy cream
1 cup milk
1/2 cup sugar
1/4 cup light corn syrup
1 teaspoon vanilla

1/4 teaspoon salt
1/3 cup green creme de menthe
Few drops green food coloring
2 ounces semi-sweet chocolate, shaved

In mixer beat eggs on high speed until light (about 4 minutes). Add cream, milk, sugar, corn syrup, vanilla and salt; stir till sugar is dissolved. Add creme de menthe and coloring. Pour into 1 gallon ice cream container and freeze according to directions. Remove dasher and fold in shavings. Pack and let season. Makes 5 cups and serves 8.

Cookbook

Strawberry Spring Thaw

1/2 cup butter or margarine, melted	1 cup sugar
1/4 cup brown sugar	1 pint sliced strawberries
1 cup flour	1 teaspoon lemon juice
1/2 cup chopped nuts	1 teaspoon vanilla extract
2 egg whites	1 cup whipping cream, whipped

In jelly roll or 9x13-inch pan, stir melted butter with brown sugar. With a fork, mix in flour and nuts. Distribute evenly over bottom of pan. Bake at 350° for 15-20 minutes, stirring occasionally. Remove from oven to cool.

In a large mixing bowl beat egg whites to soft peaks. Gradually add one cup of sugar. Add strawberries, lemon juice and vanilla. Beat at high speed of mixer until triple in volume and stiff peaks form. Fold in whipped cream.

Spread crumbs in bottom of 9-inch spring form pan, reserving 1/2 cup. Top with berry mixture, then add remaining crumbs. Freeze. Yield: 12 servings.

Cooks and Company

Watermelon Sorbet

2 cups watermelon, puréed	2 cups simple syrup , (2 cups water,
Juice of 2 lemons	1 cup sugar boiled for 5 minutes)

Mix all together. Freeze overnight. Whip in food processor. Form into balls with ice cream server. Garnish with mint. Serves 12.

Twickenham Tables

Butter Pecan Ice Cream

4 eggs
2 cups sugar
2 cups evaporated milk
1 (3-ounce) box instant butter
  pecan pudding mix

1 teaspoon vanilla extract
1 cup pecans, finely chopped
1/8 teaspoon salt

Beat eggs. Add sugar, milk, pudding mix, vanilla, nuts and salt. Mix thoroughly. Freeze in electric or hand cranked ice cream freezer until firm. Yields 1 gallon. Can be frozen.

The Great Cookbook

Peach de Menthe

1 (#2 1/2) can cling peach halves
1 quart vanilla ice cream

Fresh or canned flaked coconut
Green creme de menthe liqueur

Chill and drain peach halves. Place 1 half in each serving dish. Roll balls of ice cream in coconut and place on peach half. Drizzle with cream de menthe and serve.

Florence Cook Book

Pralines and Cream

1/2 cup oatmeal	2 cups flour
1/2 cup brown sugar	2 (12-ounce) jars caramel topping
2 sticks butter	1/2 gallon vanilla ice cream
1 cup chopped pecans	

Combine first five ingredients. Bake for 20 minutes at 350°. Stir every 5 minutes. Cool. Divide mixture in half. Place half of crumbs in a 9x15-inch pan. Pour one jar of topping over crumbs. Soften ice cream and spread on top of caramel. Pour another jar of topping over ice cream. Top with remainder of crumbs. Cover and freeze. Cut in squares to serve. Serves 20.

Anniversary Collection of Delectable Dishes

Shirley's Praline Sauce
(Microwave)

1 1/4 cup coarsely broken pecans	3 tablespoons all-purpose flour
3 tablespoons butter or margarine	3/4 cup light corn syrup
1/4 cup butter or margarine	1 (5-ounce) can evaporated milk
1 1/4 cups firmly packed brown sugar	

Spread pecans evenly in a 12x8x2-inch glass baking dish. Add 3 tablespoons butter. Microwave at HIGH for 8-10 minutes, stirring every 4 minutes until toasted; set aside.

Place 1/4 cup butter in a large glass bowl. Microwave at HIGH for 55 seconds or until butter melts. Add brown sugar and flour, stirring well. Microwave at HIGH 3-4 minutes, stirring every 2 minutes until mixture comes to a boil. Stir well, and microwave an additional 3-4 minutes. Let cool to lukewarm, gradually stir in milk and pecans. Serve warm or cold over cheesecake wedges or vanilla ice cream. Yield: 3 cups.

Sauce can be refrigerated overnight and reheated the next day. To reheat, microwave at HIGH for 1 minute intervals until sauce reaches desired consistency and temperature.

Twickenham Tables

Frosty Melon Mold

1 medium-sized honeydew or
  cantaloupe
1 (3-ounce) package raspberry Jello
1 cup hot water

1 (10-ounce) package frozen
  raspberries
(8-ounce) package cream cheese
2 tablespoons milk

Peel the melon, cut a slice from one end. Remove seeds and drain. Dissolve Jello in hot water. Chill until it begins to congeal. Fold fruit into Jello mixture and fill the melon. Chill until Jello is firm. Blend milk with softened cream cheese until it is smooth, and frost the melon. Slice to serve. The Jello and fruit may be varied to suit your taste. Mint leaves make a nice garnish.

Auburn Entertains

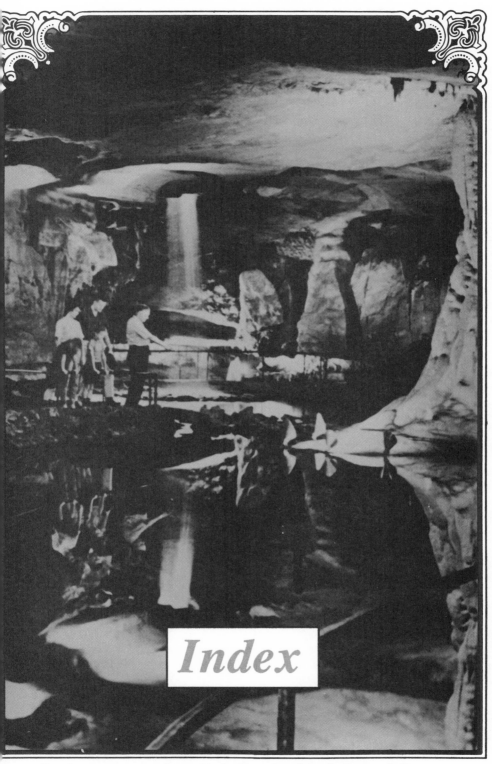

Index

*Soaring caverns are mirrored in looking-glass lakes in Sequoyah Caverns.
Northeast (off I-59) near Valley Head..*

INDEX

INDEX

Catalog of
Contributing
Cookbooks

Noccalula Falls. A statue of the legendary Princess Noccalula looks over the edge of the bluff near the Falls. Gadsden.

CATALOG OF CONTRIBUTING COOKBOOKS

All recipes in this book have been selected from the Alabama cookbooks shown on the following pages. Individuals who wish to obtain a copy of any particular book may do so by sending a check or money order to the address listed. Prices are subject to change. Please note the postage and handling charges that may be required. Alabama residents add tax only when requested. Retailers are invited to call or write to same address for discount information. Some of these books may have gone out of print since the original printing of this book. Quail Ridge Press is proud to preserve America's food heritage by keeping some of their recipes in print.

THE ALABAMA HERITAGE COOKBOOK

Heritage Publications
Birmingham, AL

Filled with the rich variety of Southern Cuisine, the book includes 164 pages and 84 color photographs of antebellum homes and table settings. Twenty-four menus offer a selection of 168 recipes ranging from Angelic Chocolate Torte to Lobster with Curry Sauce Divine, to old Southern favorites such as Jambalaya and Peach Cordial. Currently out of print.

ANNIVERSARY COLLECTION OF DELECTABLE DISHES

The Woman's Club of Jackson
P. O. Box 621
Jackson, AL 36545-0621   334/246-2377

Recipes from the private collections of some of Alabama's most gracious hostesses—recipes passed down from mothers to daughters or shared between friends—were collected, tested and edited. A broad range of favorites from downhome Southern cooking, wild game and seafood, to menus and recipes for entertaining. 297 pages, 818 recipes.

$10.00 Retail price
$ 2.00 Postage and handling
Make check payable to Woman's Club

AUBURN ENTERTAINS

by Helen Baggett, Jeanne Blackwell, and Lucy Littleton

Auburn Entertains is a charming cookbook containing more than 900 recipes that reflect the special social atmosphere created by the presence of a large university in a small southern town. Currently out of print.

BIRDIES IN THE OVEN/ ACES IN THE KITCHEN

by Trish Leverett
479 Heatherwood Drive
Birmingham, AL 35244   205/991-5295

A dual cookbook with a sporty flair, the *Birdies* half of the book has recipes, menus, and art related to a golf theme. Flip the book over and the *Aces* half is created around a tennis theme. More than 50 full menus make entertaining comfortable and easy. The 253 recipes are fast and simple to allow more time at play and less in the kitchen.

$10.00 Retail price
$ .60 Tax for Alabama residents
$ 1.50 Postage and handling
Make check payable to Miss Annie's Publications
ISBN 0-9617878-0-5

BRAVO! APPLAUDABLE RECIPES

Mobile Opera Guild
Mobile, AL

Bravo! Applaudable Recipes is a collection of excellent and creative recipes from guest artists and patrons of the Mobile Opera. Proceeds from the sales benefit the Mobile Opera and scholarship programs of the Mobile Opera Guild. Excellent choices of wines accompany many of the recipes. Currently out of print.

CALLING ALL COOKS

Telephone Pioneers of America, Alabama Chapter 34
3196 Highway 280 South Room 301N
Birmingham, AL 35243   205/972-2724

The Telephone Pioneers currently have three books available, all called *Calling All Cooks* and distinguished by color. The "yellow" book featured here contains 713 pages and 2,000 recipes, some of which have been handed down from generation to generation. No fancy recipes, just good old southern cooking. The "red" and "blue" books are also available for the same price each.

$10.00 Retail price
$ 2.00 Postage and handling
Make check payable to Telephone Pioneers of America

COOKBOOK

First Presbyterian Church
307 Gates Avenue
Huntsville, AL 35801   205/536-3354

Within these pages are 870 delicious recipes from the oldest Presbyterian church in Alabama. The women of this church use every occasion to share their good food with family and friends. Now their favorite, thoroughly tested recipes are in a durable hardbound book of 400 pages, laced with the rich historical heritage of this congregation.

$10.00 Retail price
$ 1.25 Postage and handling
Make check payable to W.O.C. First Presbyterian Church

COOKS AND COMPANY

Muscle Shoals District Service League
Sheffield, AL

A collection of our favorite recipes to tease and appease your taste buds. 286 pages of recipes which include sections on: Appetizer and Beverages, Soups and Sandwiches, Salads and Dressings, Eggs and Cheese, Vegetables, Entrees, Breads, Desserts, and Gifts from the Kitchen. Currently out of print.

COTTON COUNTRY COOKING

Junior League of Morgan County, Inc.
P. O. Box 486
Decatur, AL 35602   205/350-1917

Cotton Country Cooking is an authentic guide to southern food, a reliable everyday reference, and a gourmet's challenge. The "Southern Hospitality Section" encourages the art of entertaining "southern stule," the most casual to the most elegant. The Junior League's new cookbook, *Beyond Cotton Country*, became available Fall 1998.

$16.95   Retail price
$ 1.36   Tax for Alabama residents
$ 3.50   Postage and handling
Make check payable to Junior League of Morgan County
ISBN 0-9614406-0-0

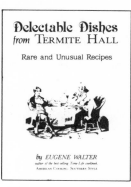

Delectable Dishes
from TERMITE HALL

Rare and Unusual Recipes

by EUGENE WALTER
author of the best selling Time-Life cookbook,
AMERICAN COOKING: SOUTHERN STYLE

DELECTABLE DISHES FROM TERMITE HALL

by Eugene Walter
The Willoughby Institute, Inc.
Mobile, AL

Rare and unusual recipes from Old Mobile—and across the world. Clever copy around delectable dishes are found throughout the book (including witty captions beneath old woodcuts from the Willoughby Institute). Currently out of print. Reissued under the title *Delectable Dishes from Old Mobile* by the University of Alabama Press.

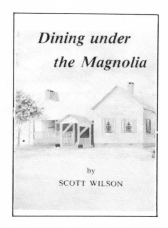

Dining under

the Magnolia

by
SCOTT WILSON

DINING UNDER THE MAGNOLIA

by Scott Wilson, CEC
Grove Hill, AL

Author/chef Scott Wilson shares his wonderful culinary secrets in these outstanding recipes from the Magnolia Inn in Grove Hill. There are line drawings by Jeff Kilpatrick throughout the book of the lovely interior of the inn with a full-color illustration of the inn and grounds on the cover. Currently out of print.

DINNER ON THE GROUND

Joy Sunday School Class
Town Creek, AL

Dinner on the Ground—the name titles the span and area of time in which a lot of these recipes were used and passed on from generation to generation. In 159 pages, these 204 recipes are original and have been tested through the years, but are just as useful in modern kitchens. Currently out of print.

DOWN HOME IN HIGH STYLE

Dothan, AL

Down Home in High Style reflects the delightful diversity of Dothan's culture and cuisine. Receipts date from four generations back to the latest dishes for the microwave. The graciousness and charm associated with a small southern town thoroughly flavors this cookbook. Destined to be a classic of beauty and good taste. 396 pages. Over 800 recipes. Currently out of print.

EUFALA'S FAVORITE RECIPES

The Eufala Tribune
P. O. Drawer 628
Eufaula, AL 36072-0628   205/687-3506

Eufaula's Favorite Recipes was published by The Eufaula Tribune in 1976 as a Bicentennial project. Reprinted several times, the attractive, softback book contains 460 recipes in 225 pages, contributed by some of the aristocratic old town's best cooks. Section dividers are architectural drawings of some of the town's most famous antebellum homes.

$12.95 Retail price
$ .90 Tax for Alabama residents
$ 3.00 Postage and handling
Make check payable to The Eufaula Tribune

FAMILY SECRETS: FAMOUS RECIPES FROM THE HOMEPLACE

Thomas Family Memorial Association
c/o Mrs. Catherine Eason
62 Carter Road SW
Cartersville, GA 30120   770/386-0410

This Lexotone-covered book is composed of 416 spiral-bound pages containing 750 recipes (from old-fashioned to the most modern), tips and cooking secrets from a large southern family noted for its fine food. A family history and anecdotes familiarize the reader with the 1897 home in Bib County, Alabama, that is being preserved through the proceeds from the cookbooks.

$12.95 Retail price
$ 2.50 Postage and handling
Make check payable to The Thomas Family Memorial Association
ISBN 0-9614787-0-5

FLORENCE COOK BOOK

Trinity Episcopal Churchwomen
P. O. Box M
Florence, AL 35631   205/764-6149

Florence Cook Book, compiled and edited by the Trinity Churchwomen, contains favorite recipes of members and other Florence residents. It has a green cover with plastic binding and contains a total of 173 pages with an index and herb chart.

$ 3.00 Retail price
$ 2.00 Postage and handling
Make check payable to Trinity ECW

GAZEBO I CHRISTMAS COOKBOOK

by Rex Barrington
607 Green Street
Auburn, AL 36830   334/826-6090

A holiday collection of eats, sweets and neats. A treasure chest of Christmas recipes and helpful ideas for a wonderful Christmas. Twelve different sections: Brunch, Breads, Cranberries, Desserts, Eggnog, After-the-Fact, Salads, Vegetables, Meats, Nuts, Special Stuff, and New Year's. 275 recipes, 191 pages.

$ 6.95 Retail price
$ .52 Tax for Alabama residents
$ 2.00 Postage and handling
Make check payable to Gazebo I
ISBN 0-933095-02-3

GAZEBO I COOKBOOK

by Rex Barrington
Auburn, AL

A collection of eats, sweets and neats. An excellent cookbook containing over 200 absolutely delicious recipes that are very simple to make. Special sections on Tea and Brunch. 128 pages. Currently out of print.

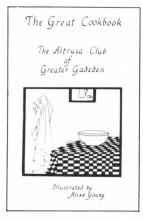

THE GREAT COOKBOOK

The Altrusa Club of Greater Gadsden
P. O. Box 2188
Gadsden, AL 35903   205/546-1661

The Altrusa Club of Greater Gadsden was organized in June of 1980. The club selected a community project of helping the deaf. The club voted in 1980 to publish a cookbook and collected and tested recipes from members. Only recipes that rated "good" or higher were used. There are 499 recipes in the book.

$10.00   Retail price
$ 1.50   Postage and handling
Make check payable to Altrusa Club of Greater Gadsden

HALLMARK'S COLLECTION OF HOME TESTED RECIPES

by Freeda Rogers Hallmark
Tuscaloosa, AL

This book is the result of many years of collecting and preparing new recipes. My book has 323 pages and contains 1,059 recipes that I have personally prepared and served to family and friends. The compliments have been fantastic. Currently out of print.

HEARTHSIDE AT CHRISTMAS

by Patricia G. Edington
Mobile, AL

These recipes were collected from family and close personal friends, with comments about childhood memories. Proceeds from the sale of the book are going to Penelope House, Mobile's battered women's shelter. 117 pages of recipes and cooking aids. Cover picture is of the fireplace in my restored 19th century cabin in my back yard. Currently out of print.

HEAVENLY HOSTESS

St. John's Episcopal Church Women
305 Sunset
Monroeville, AL 36460   334/743-3395 or 4808

Heavenly Hostess is a project of the women of St. John's Episcopal Church. It contains 249 pages of proven recipes (454 recipes) plus the history of the church and index. The ladies are known for their Chicken Salad Sandwiches dating back to the seven original ladies who sold them to start the church.

$10.00   Retail price
$ 2.50   Postage and handling
Make check payable to Episcopal Church Women

HEIRLOOMS FROM THE KITCHEN

Joan Hutson
1117 Chesterfield Road
Huntsville, AL 35801   205/881-5034

A treasure trove of outstanding family recipes passed down from generation to generation. Fried Apples, Hoppin John, Potato Candy, Burnt Sugar Cake—300 recipes, 220 pages. A special section on care of heirlooms, plus grandmother's favorite household hints makes this a favorite of everyone.

$ 8.95   Retail price
$ 5.00   Postage and handling
Make check payable to Joan Hutson
ISBN 0-9615542-0-7

279

HUNTSVILLE ENTERTAINS

Historic Huntsville Foundation
P. O. Box 786
Huntsville, AL 35804   256/536-3631

Features tested recipes, Flower Section, History of Food, Historic Houses, Art, History of the Past, and Tips. The book has a beautiful hardcover with spiral binding. 935 recipes in 478 pages.

$18.95 Retail price
$ 1.28 Tax for Alabama residents
$ 3.50 Postage and handling
Make check payable to Historic Huntsville Foundation
ISBN 0-9610830

HUNTSVILLE HERITAGE COOKBOOK

The Junior League of Huntsville, Inc.
P. O. Box 816
Huntsville, AL 35804   256/533-3554

Southern hospitality with a historical flair is found in the *Huntsville Heritage Cookbook*. Try Alabama's Watercress-Cheese Soup, Copper Pennies, Grits and Cheese Souffle, or Flower Garden Cake. Over 1,000 recipes in a classic hardbound cover enhanced with original drawings by Betty Monroe. Over 20 years of success—a basic kitchen necessity!

$14.95 Retail price
$ 1.20 Tax for Alabama residents
$ 3.00 Postage and handling
Make check payable to Junior League Publications
ISBN 0-9618113-0-7

KITCHEN SAMPLER

Bessemer Junior Service League
Bessemer, AL

Great addition for your cookbook collection. Wonderful recipes from some of Bessemer's finest chefs. Proceeds from our cookbook will be used for community and service projects sponsored by the Bessemer Junior Service League such as a pediatric playroom for our local hospital, founding the Bessemer Girls Club, the Bessemer Hall of History and the West Jefferson Historical Society. Currently out of print.

KUM' ONA' GRANNY'S TABLE

Senior Citizens Retirement Facility
Montgomery, AL

One of the many enthusiasts of our book says, "It is one of the most interesting cookbooks I have ever seen . . . it is great that you have captured some of the 'old time' recipes for dishes that we recall, but do not know how to prepare." The book includes personal anecdotes about the recipes. Currently out of print.

LOAVES AND FISHES
FROM THE EASTERN SHORE

St. Paul's Episcopal Church
Daphne, AL

The Birmingham Post-Herald says "Great catch!" A big haul—over 800 recipes in 300 pages—of enticing recipes. Emphasis is on seafood and breads, but *Loaves and Fishes* is a superb general cookbook with the best of area classics, local ethnic specialties, and fine restaurants. 3rd printing. Currently out of print.

MAGIC

Junior League of Birmingham
2212 - 20th Avenue South
Birmingham, AL 35223-1000   205/879-9861

Magic, by Junior League of Birmingham of Alabama, is a collection of good taste that spans from traditional down-home classics to exotic international cuisine. There are 365 pages filled with more than 600 recipes; researched over three years; each recipe tested three times for taste and accuracy; color-coded sections for quick, easy reference.

$14.95   Retail price
$ 1.20   Tax for Alabama residents
$ 3.50   Postage and handling
Make check payable to Junior League of Birmingham.
ISBN 0-9607810-0-5

MORE FIDDLING WITH FOOD

First Baptist Church of Mobile
Mobile, AL

The book is compiled of recipes submitted by members and friends. Many were brought to tasting parties given to raise money for Youth Mission Trips. All were tried by Committee and served at a Tasting Party. There is also a brief history of the Admiral Semmes Home which was given to admiral Raphael Semmes by the City of Mobile and is now owned by the church. 193 pages. Currently out of print.

OLD MOBILE RECIPES—TRIED AND PROVEN

St. Paul's Episcopal Church
Cookbook Chairman
4051 Old Shell Road
Mobile, AL 36608-1337   334/342-8521

Old Mobile Recipes—Tried and Proven has been a Mobile favorite since it was first published in 1956. This spiral-bound book of 129 pages and over 400 recipes is in its 11th printing. Old recipes worth reviving— well worth the price.

$ 8.50   Retail price
$ 3.00   Postage and handling
Make check payable to St. Paul's Cookbook Fund

ONCE UPON A STOVE

Birmingham Children's Theatre
P. O. Box 1362
Birmingham, AL 35201-1362   205/458-8181

Over two years in the making, *Once Upon A Stove* is a collection of 650 recipes in a 400-page volume. Some 2,500 recipes were submitted by friends of Birmingham Children's Theatre (a non-profit organization); 1,200 were chosen to be tested; and 650 were selected from 10 categories. Artwork was submitted by area school children.

$10.00 Includes postage and handling
Make check payable to Birmingham Children's Theatre
ISBN 0-9617659-0-9

ONE OF A KIND

Junior League of Mobile
P. O. Box 7091
Mobile, AL 36607   334/471-3348

One of a Kind greatly compliments the League's original cookbook, *Recipe Jubilee!* A collection of innovative new recipes make it a guaranteed success. By including sections on menus, microwave cooking, and "Things your Mother Never Told You," it makes a wonderful and much used addition to a cookbook collector's bookshelf.

$14.95 Retail price
$ 1.35 Tax for Alabama residents
$ 3.50 Postage and handling
Make check payable to Mobile Junior League Publications
ISBN 0-9603054-2-4

RECIPE JUBILEE!

Junior League of Mobile
P. O. Box 7091
Mobile, AL 36607   334/471-3348

Recipe Jubilee!, the Junior League of Mobile's original cookbook, has proven a best seller since 1964. Beloved recipes from our area make this cookbook a favorite throughout the southeast and across the nation. Gourmet cooks as well as those just starting down the culinary path will appreciate the variety of recipes within.

$14.95 Retail price
$ 1.35 Tax for Alabama residents
$ 3.50 Postage and handling
Make check payable to Mobile Junior League Publications
ISBN 0-9603054-1-6

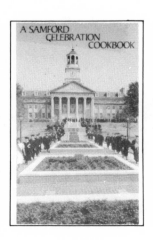

A SAMFORD CELEBRATION COOKBOOK

Samford University Auxiliary
Samford University Dept. of Home Economics
Birmingham, AL

Over 700 family-favorite recipes collected from two Samford University Auxiliary tasting parties and from faculty, alumni, and friends of the University. The 353 pages feature 13 sections with pictures of the present campus and insets of the former Howard College. (A joint project of Samford University Auxiliary and Samford University Department of Home Economics.) Currently out of print.

SECOND PLEASE!

Nan Dessert, Sara Engelhardt and Betsy Plummer
Montgomery, AL

First printed in 1978, the book has had four subsequent printings, the last in August 1981. By may 1982 the stock was completely exhausted. Due to repeated interest, the book was brought back in February of 1988. The book has 416 pages including Helpful Hints, Menus, Garnishes, Measuring Tables, and a complete chapter on nutrition. Currently out of print.

A SOUTHERN LADY COOKS WITH A GREEK ACCENT

Sophia Clikas
250 North Jackson Street
Mobile, AL 36603   334/438-1884

Subtitled "A Love Story Cookbook," Sophia Clikas says that whether you are preparing a meal, making a sandwich, or serving a cup of coffee, you are saying, "I care. I love you." Her "Southern Greek" recipes are interwoven with heartwarming stories of shared recipes and shared love. Revised in 1998 to include more love stories.

$14.00 Includes postage and handling
Make check payable to Sophia Clikas
ISBN 0-918544-64-5

SUMPTHN' YUMMY

Monroe Academy Band Boosters
P. O. Box 927
Monroeville, AL 36460   334/743-3932

Sumpthn' Yummy was compiled as a fund-raising project for the Monroe Academy Band. It is fabulous because of the generous people who shared their most treasured recipes. *Sumpthn' Yummy* contains 251 pages which include 578 proven recipes. We invite you to cook up *Sumpthn' Yummy!*

$10.00 Retail price
$ 2.00 Postage and handling
Make check payable to Monroe Academy Band

TREASURED ALABAMA RECIPES

Kathryn Tucker Windham
2004 Royal Street
Selma, AL 36701   334/872-3398

Treasured Alabama Recipes is divided into sections of the state with the traditional favorite recipes of each geographic area featured in its section: the Coast, Piney Woods, Wiregrass, Black Belt, Tennessee Valley, Appalachians, and Cities. Stories accompany some recipes. 115 pages; 347 recipes.

$10.00 Retail price
$ 2.25 Postage and handling
Make check payable to Kathryn T. Windham

TREASURED TASTES

Mobile College Auxiliary
Daphne, AL

A collection of 500 recipes, many of which have been used over the past 20 years in the annual "Tasting parties." People or groups of people from around the Mobile area bring samples and recipes of their favorite foods to sell. The proceeds are used for a college-related project each year. Currently out of print.

TREATS FOR MY SWEETS

Gail C. Jaye
Bay Minette, AL

Easy directions with photographs and diagrams for making all sorts of adorable characters, animals and party theme "things" from ice cream cones, cup cakes, petit fours, etc. Includes "regular" recipes for cakes, cookies, candies, and pies. This book can show you how to make party favors too cute to eat and too delicious not to! Currently out of print.

285

TRY ME

Arthritis Foundation
Mobile, AL

Pure feasting delight from the Arthritis Volunteer Actions Committee (AVAC), *Try Me* is a collection of 320 of Mobile's best kept culinary secrets. The proceeds will assist the South Alabama Chapter of the Arthritis Foundation in providing existing and new programs for arthritis patients. Currently out of print.

Twickenham
Tables

TWICKENHAM TABLES

Weeden House Museum
300 Gates Avenue
Huntsville, AL 35801   256/539-8926

A 245-page treasure of 36 menus with lovely sketches of the houses and dining rooms in which they were served. Over 300 recipes, amusing stories, plus information about the Twickenham Historic District. Recipes so good they are featured at the Huntsville Hilton. Proceeds benefit the Weeden House Museum.

$10.00   Retail price
$ 2.00   Postage and handling
Make check payable to Weeden House Museum

WHEN DINNERBELLS RING

Talladega Junior Welfare League
P. O. Box 144
Talladega, AL 35160

Known for its antebellum mansions, Talladega, nestled in the foothills of the Appalachians, is the epitome of gracious southern hospitality. Its 237 pages contain over 900 superb southern recipes. It features "Special Menus" and beautiful artwork of historical sites.

$15.95   Retail price
$ 1.28   Tax for Alabama residents
$ 2.50   Postage and handling
Make check payable to *When Dinnerbells Ring*
ISBN 0-918544-95-5

A No-Cook Cookbook

WHEN YOU CAN'T COOK . . .
OR DON'T WANT TO

by Rex Barrington
607 Green Street
Auburn, AL 36830   334/826-6090

A no-cook cookbook—you don't even have to turn your stove on. Over 500 recipes for all kinds of foods. A wonderful gift for yourself or anyone. 350 pages.

$ 8.95   Retail price
$ .67   Tax for Alabama residents
$ 3.00   Postage and handling
Make check payable to Gazebo I
ISBN 0-933095-07-4

Special Discount Offers!

The Best of the Month Club

Experience the taste of our nation, one state at a time!

Individuals may purchase BEST OF THE BEST STATE COOKBOOKS on a monthly (or bi-monthly) basis by joining the **Best of the Month Club**. Best of the Month Club members enjoy a 20% discount off the list price of each book. Individuals who already own certain state cookbooks may specify which new states they wish to receive. No minimum purchase is required; individuals may cancel at any time. For more information on this purchasing option, call 1-800-343-1583.

Special Discount

The entire 41-volume BEST OF THE BEST STATE COOKBOOK SERIES can be purchased for $521.21, a 25% discount off the total individual price of $694.95.

Individual BEST cookbooks can be purchased for $16.95 per copy plus $4.00 shipping for any number of cookbooks ordered. See order form on next page.

Join today! 1-800-343-1583

Speak directly to one of our friendly customer service representatives, or visit our website at **www.quailridge.com** to order online.

Recipe Hall of Fame Collection

The extensive recipe database of Quail Ridge Press' acclaimed BEST OF THE BEST STATE COOKBOOK SERIES is the inspiration behind the RECIPE HALL OF FAME COLLECTION. These HALL OF FAME recipes have achieved extra distinction for consistently producing superb dishes. *The Recipe Hall of Fame Cookbook* features over 400 choice dishes for a variety of meals. The *Recipe Hall of Fame Dessert Cookbook* consists entirely of extraordinary desserts. The *Recipe Hall of Fame Quick & Easy Cookbook* contains over 500 recipes that require minimum effort but produce maximum enjoyment. *The Recipe Hall of Fame Cookbook II* brings you more of the family favorites you've come to expect with over 400 all-new, easy-to-follow recipes. Appetizers to desserts, quick dishes to masterpiece presentations, the RECIPE HALL OF FAME COLLECTION has it all.

All books: Paperbound • 7x10 • Illustrations • Index
The Recipe Hall of Fame Cookbook • 304 pages • $19.95
Recipe Hall of Fame Dessert Cookbook • 240 pages • $16.95
Recipe Hall of Fame Quick & Easy Cookbook • 304 pages • $19.95
The Recipe Hall of Fame Cookbook II • 304 pages • $19.95

NOTE: The four HALL OF FAME cookbooks can be ordered individually at the price noted above or can be purchased as a four-cookbook set for $40.00, almost a 50% discount off the total list price of $76.80. Over 1,600 incredible HALL OF FAME recipes for about three cents each—an amazing value!